WITH
JESUS
DAILY

Jordan Nassie

Table of Contents

With Jesus Daily 1

January: A Fresh Start with God 5

February: God's Love and Our Identity 37

March: Walking by Faith, Not by Sight 66

April: Trusting God's Plan 98

May: The Power of Prayer 129

June: Finding Peace in God's Presence 161

July: Living in Freedom through Christ 191

August: Growing in Spiritual Maturity 223

September: Serving Others with Joy 255

October: God is With You in Your Trials 286

November: Living with Gratitude and Grace 318

December: The Gift of Christ 349

Final Word 381

With Jesus Daily

I am really praying that God would speak to you in a powerful and life-changing way! Have you ever wanted to spend an entire year getting closer to Jesus? Imagine hearing God's voice with greater clarity, knowing His will for your life, and stepping into the dreams He has for you. Wouldn't that be incredible? If you're ready for Jesus to transform everything for His purpose in your life, then this book is your next step!

Throughout the Bible, we see countless examples of people who spent time with God and accomplished extraordinary things. Whether walking beside Jesus in the New Testament or following God's presence in the Old Testament, these individuals show us the power of living *With Jesus Daily*.

Remember the disciples in the New Testament who walked with Jesus daily. Ordinary fishermen like Peter, James, and John were transformed into leaders of the early church, bringing the Gospel to the world. Their lives were forever changed because they spent time with Jesus. As Acts 4:13 (NIV) says, "When they saw the courage of Peter and John and realized that they were unschooled, ordinary men, they were astonished and took note that these men had been with Jesus."

Even in the Old Testament, we see powerful examples of people who spent time with God and achieved incredible things. Moses, who spoke with God face to face, led an entire nation to freedom. David, known as a man after God's own heart, found strength and victory in battle because of his close relationship with the Lord. And Joshua, who succeeded Moses, conquered the Promised Land because God assured him, "As I was with Moses, so I will be with you; I will never leave you nor forsake you" (Joshua 1:5, NIV).

These stories show us that walking *With Jesus Daily* or seeking God's presence transforms not just our hearts, but also the impact we can have in the world. Jesus tells us in John 15:5 (NIV), "I am the vine; you are the branches. If you remain in me and I in you, you will bear much fruit; apart from me you can do nothing." The same is true for us today—when we live our lives in daily connection with Jesus, we are empowered to fulfill God's purpose for us.

God promises that *"He who began a good work in you will carry it on to completion until the day of Christ Jesus"* (Philippians 1:6, NIV). Let's walk together, trusting that through these daily reflections, God will do a mighty work in and through you.

In *With Jesus Daily*, each entry is thoughtfully crafted to guide you closer to God through four powerful elements:

1. **An Inspiring Title** – Setting the tone for the day, each title invites you into a focused moment with Jesus.

2. **A Bible Verse** – Grounding your experience in God's Word, this verse offers wisdom, encouragement, or insight for your journey.

3. **A Call to Action** – Moving beyond reflection, this step encourages you to live out your faith in practical, meaningful ways.

4. **A Simple Prayer** – Closing each entry, this prayer helps you connect personally with God, seeking His guidance and presence.

Together, these four elements create a transformative daily experience that deepens your relationship with Jesus one step at a time.

Here's what you can expect each month:

- **January:** A Fresh Start with God – Begin the year with renewed hope. Each day will remind you that God's mercies are new every morning, inviting you to embrace the fresh start He offers.

- **February:** God's Love and Our Identity – Explore the depth of God's love for you. Daily, you'll discover how living in His love shapes your identity and gives you the confidence to walk in His purpose for your life.

- **March:** Walking by Faith, Not by Sight – Strengthen your faith as you learn to trust God, even when the future seems unclear. Each day will encourage you to step out in faith, trusting in God's promises, regardless of what you see.

- **April:** Trusting God's Plan – Surrender your worries to God's perfect timing. Through this month, you'll learn to rest in the assurance that God works all things together for good.

- **May:** The Power of Prayer – Develop a deeper, more consistent prayer life. You'll be reminded each day of the power of connecting with God through prayer and trusting Him for answers.

- **June:** Finding Peace in God's Presence – In the chaos of life, this month will teach you to find true peace by resting in God's presence, surrendering your anxieties, and letting His peace fill your heart.

- **July:** Living in Freedom through Christ – Experience the freedom that comes from knowing Christ. Each day, you'll reflect on what it means to walk free from guilt and shame and live boldly in the grace Christ offers.

- **August:** Growing in Spiritual Maturity – Dive deeper in your relationship with God by developing habits that will mature your faith. Daily devotion will help you grow in Christlikeness and spiritual discipline.

- **September:** Serving Others with Joy – Learn the joy of serving others as Jesus did. This month, you'll discover the fulfillment that comes from loving and serving others with a heart like God's.

- **October:** God is With You in Your Trials – Life is not without hardship, but you'll find daily encouragement to lean on God's presence through every trial, knowing that He is working for your good.

- **November:** Living with Gratitude and Grace – Cultivate a heart of gratitude in all circumstances. This month, you'll learn to see God's blessings and live with an open heart, full of grace.
- **December:** The Gift of Christ – Celebrate the greatest gift—Jesus. As you reflect on His birth, you'll be filled with the hope and joy that comes from knowing Christ as your Savior.

Every day, as you read, reflect, and pray, you'll not only grow closer to God but also experience how His Word is alive and active in your daily life. You'll find that your spiritual journey doesn't have to be walked alone. We encourage you to connect with friends, family, or a group of believers to discuss what you're learning. If you prefer, take this devotional time as a personal, quiet moment with God. Either way, you'll find support, community, and encouragement as you grow in your faith.

Are you ready to experience God? Let's begin this journey together, discovering the beauty and power of a life lived in close relationship with Jesus.

God bless you,

Jordan Nassie

January

A Fresh Start with God

January 1
A New Creation in Christ

Verse: *"Therefore, if anyone is in Christ, the new creation has come: The old has gone, the new is here!"*

(2 Corinthians 5:17, NIV)

Message: When we come to Christ, we are made new. The old life—our past mistakes, sins, and failures—no longer defines us. God transforms us from the inside out, giving us a fresh start. We are not who we used to be, and we don't have to live in the shadow of our past. In Christ, we have a new identity as children of God, forgiven and loved.

Think of the apostle Paul. Before his encounter with Christ, Paul (then Saul) persecuted Christians. But after meeting Jesus on the road to Damascus (Acts 9), everything changed. He became one of the most influential apostles, spreading the Gospel across the world. Paul's transformation reminds us that no one is too far gone for God's grace. If God could change Paul, He can change anyone.

This means you don't have to be trapped by guilt or shame from your past. God offers you a new beginning. Whether you've struggled with mistakes, addictions, or regret, God's transforming power can renew your heart and give you purpose. Just as Paul found new life in Christ, so can you. Each day is a chance to walk in your new identity, knowing that you are loved, forgiven, and empowered by God.

Call to Action: Write down one thing from your past that you need to leave behind. Pray for God to help you release it.

Prayer: Lord, thank You for making me a new creation. Help me let go of the past and walk confidently in my new identity. Amen.

January 2
New Mercies Every Morning

Verse: "Because of the Lord's great love we are not consumed, for His compassions never fail. They are new every morning; great is Your faithfulness."

(Lamentations 3:22-23, NIV)

Message: God's mercies are new every morning. No matter what mistakes we made yesterday, today is a new day filled with fresh grace. We don't have to carry the weight of our failures because God's love is greater than our shortcomings. His faithfulness never runs out, and He offers us the chance to start each day renewed and refreshed.

The story of Peter's denial of Jesus illustrates the power of God's mercy. Peter, one of Jesus' closest disciples, denied knowing Him three times on the night of His arrest (Luke 22:54-62). Yet after His resurrection, Jesus restored Peter, forgiving him and reaffirming his calling (John 21:15-17). Peter went on to become a key leader in the early church, showing us that failure isn't the end when we turn to God.

We often fall short of our own expectations or God's standards, but His mercy allows us to get back up and keep moving forward. Whether it's a small mistake or a major failure, God's love meets us with grace and forgiveness. Just as Peter found restoration in Christ, we can wake up each morning knowing that God's mercies are new and His faithfulness is constant.

Call to Action: Start your day by thanking God for His new mercies. Release any guilt or regret from yesterday and walk in His grace.

Prayer: Father, thank You for Your mercy that is new every morning. Help me receive Your forgiveness and live in Your grace today. Amen.

January 3
God is Doing a New Thing

Verse*: "Forget the former things; do not dwell on the past. See, I am doing a new thing! Now it springs up; do you not perceive it? I am making a way in the wilderness and streams in the wasteland."*

(Isaiah 43:18-19, NIV)

Message: God is constantly at work, creating new opportunities and opening new doors in our lives. He asks us not to dwell on the past—whether good or bad—but to focus on the new things He is doing. Sometimes, holding onto the past can prevent us from seeing the new direction God wants to take us. Trusting Him means being open to change and willing to follow where He leads.

The Israelites experienced this when they were delivered from Egypt and headed toward the Promised Land. As they wandered in the wilderness, many of them longed to return to Egypt because it was familiar, even though it represented slavery (Numbers 14:1-4). God, however, was calling them into a new future, one filled with freedom and blessing. By looking back, they risked missing out on the new things God had for them.

It's easy to get stuck in past disappointments, successes, or comfort zones. But God is always inviting you to step into something new—whether it's a new relationship, job, dream, or spiritual growth. Just like the Israelites, you may be tempted to cling to what's familiar, but God's best lies ahead. Trust Him to lead you into new beginnings and be willing to let go of the old to embrace the new.

Call to Action: Identify an area where God may be leading you into something new. Pray for the courage to step forward in faith.

Prayer: Lord, help me release the past and trust in the new things You are doing in my life. Give me the courage to follow Your lead. Amen.

January 4
Trusting God with the Unknown

Verse: *"Trust in the Lord with all your heart and lean not on your own understanding."*

(Proverbs 3:5, NIV)

Message: Life is full of uncertainties, but God calls us to trust Him wholeheartedly, even when we don't understand the way ahead. Our limited perspective can make the future feel scary, but God's wisdom far exceeds ours. He asks us to trust His plan and lean on His understanding, not our own. When we do, He promises to direct our paths and guide us toward His perfect will.

The story of Abraham is a powerful example of trusting God with the unknown. In Genesis 12, God called Abraham to leave his home and go to a land He would show him. Abraham didn't have all the details—he didn't know where the land was or what challenges lay ahead. But he trusted God and stepped out in faith. As a result, Abraham became the father of many nations, and his faithfulness changed the course of history.

We often face situations where the future is unclear—whether it's a career decision, a relationship, or a personal challenge. Like Abraham, we don't need to know every detail to trust God's plan. We can take the next step in faith, knowing that God is leading us. His plans are good, and even though we can't always see what's ahead, we can trust the One who holds the future.

Call to Action: Think about an area where you're unsure of the future. Pray for faith to trust God's plan, even when it's unclear.

Prayer: Lord, I place my trust in You, even when I don't understand the path ahead. Help me lean on Your wisdom and follow Your guidance. Amen.

January 5
God is Your Shepherd

Verse: *"The Lord is my shepherd, I lack nothing."*

(Psalm 23:1, NIV)

Message: As our Shepherd, God provides for every need, guiding and protecting us through every season of life. Just as a shepherd cares for his sheep, God cares for you with love and attention. When you trust Him to lead you, you lack nothing because He knows exactly what you need. Whether you're walking through green pastures or dark valleys, God is with you, watching over you every step of the way.

David, the author of Psalm 23, understood the role of a shepherd firsthand. As a young boy, he tended his father's sheep, protecting them from predators and leading them to safe pastures (1 Samuel 17:34-35). David recognized that just as he cared for his sheep, God was caring for him. No matter what challenges he faced—whether fighting giants or fleeing from enemies—David knew that God was his Shepherd.

Trusting God as your Shepherd means believing that He is actively involved in your day-to-day needs. You don't have to worry about provision or protection because God is watching over you. Whether you're facing uncertainty, fear, or lack, God is leading you to green pastures and still waters, offering you rest and refreshment in His presence.

Call to Action: Reflect on how God has provided for you in the past and thank Him for His faithfulness.

Prayer: Lord, thank You for being my Shepherd. Help me trust You to meet my needs and guide me each day. Amen.

January 6
God's Strength in Our Weakness

Verse: *"But He said to me, 'My grace is sufficient for you, for My power is made perfect in weakness.'"*

(2 Corinthians 12:9, NIV)

Message: God's strength is most evident in our moments of weakness. When we feel like we've reached the end of our rope, God's grace steps in to carry us. His power doesn't depend on our abilities, but on our reliance on Him. In our weakness, His strength is made perfect, reminding us that we are never alone in our struggles.

Paul, the author of 2 Corinthians, struggled with a "thorn in the flesh" that he asked God to remove. But instead of taking away the problem, God told Paul that His grace was enough. Paul learned that through his weakness, God's strength was magnified (2 Corinthians 12:7-10). Rather than removing the obstacle, God provided the strength to endure it, showing that His grace is always sufficient.

In our lives, we all face moments where we feel weak—whether physically, emotionally, or spiritually. But God uses these moments to draw us closer to Him. When we admit our need for Him, we open the door for His power to work through us. Just as Paul learned to boast in his weakness, we too can trust that God's strength will carry us through every trial.

Call to Action: Think about an area in your life where you feel weak. Ask God to give you His strength and grace to endure it.

Prayer: Lord, I am weak, but Your strength is perfect. Help me rely on Your grace to carry me through this day. Amen.

January 7
God's Plans Are Good

Verse: "'For I know the plans I have for you,' declares the Lord, 'plans to prosper you and not to harm you, plans to give you hope and a future.'"

(Jeremiah 29:11, NIV)

Message: God's plans for your life are filled with hope and a bright future. Even when circumstances seem uncertain or difficult, you can trust that God is in control and that His purpose for you is good. He sees the bigger picture and is always working for your good, even in the midst of challenges.

Jeremiah 29:11 was spoken to the Israelites while they were in exile, a time of hardship and confusion. Though they were far from home, God reassured them that His plans for their future were full of hope. This promise wasn't just for their immediate situation but for the ultimate redemption and restoration that God had in store for them.

When life feels uncertain or when you face setbacks, it's easy to doubt the goodness of God's plans. But just like the Israelites, you can trust that God's hand is at work, guiding you toward a future filled with hope. His plans are bigger and better than anything we can imagine, and He invites us to trust Him through every step of the journey.

Call to Action: Reflect on an area where you've been doubting God's plans. Surrender it to Him in prayer, trusting that His purpose is good.

Prayer: Father, thank You for the plans You have for me. Help me trust in Your goodness and hold onto hope, even in difficult times. Amen.

January 8
God is Faithful

Verse: *"Let us hold unswervingly to the hope we profess, for He who promised is faithful."*

(Hebrews 10:23, NIV)

Message: God is faithful, and His promises never fail. When we hold onto the hope of His Word, we can trust that He will bring His promises to pass. God's faithfulness is not dependent on our circumstances—it's rooted in His unchanging character. Because He is faithful, we can have confidence in His promises, no matter what life looks like.

Abraham's life is a testament to God's faithfulness. Even though he was old and childless, God promised him that he would be the father of many nations. Though it took years for that promise to come to fruition, God was faithful to His Word, and Abraham's descendants became as numerous as the stars (Genesis 15:5). Abraham's story shows us that God's timing may not always align with our expectations, but His faithfulness is certain.

Whether you're waiting on a promise or going through a challenging season, remember that God is faithful. His promises are sure, and His timing is perfect. Trust that He is working behind the scenes, and continue to hold onto the hope that He is who He says He is.

Call to Action: Write down a promise from God's Word that you are holding onto. Spend time in prayer, thanking God for His faithfulness.

Prayer: Lord, thank You for Your faithfulness. Help me to trust in Your promises and hold onto the hope I have in You. Amen.

January 9
Peace in the Storm

Verse: *"You will keep in perfect peace those whose minds are steadfast, because they trust in You."*

(Isaiah 26:3, NIV)

Message: Peace isn't found in the absence of trouble but in the presence of God. When we fix our minds on Him and trust in His promises, He gives us a peace that surpasses understanding. This peace guards our hearts and minds, even when life's storms are raging around us.

One of the most powerful examples of peace in the storm is when Jesus calmed the sea in Mark 4:35-41. As His disciples panicked in the midst of the storm, Jesus remained at peace. He rebuked the wind and waves, and everything became calm. Jesus demonstrated that when we trust in God's power and presence, peace is always available, no matter how chaotic life may seem.

In your own life, you may face storms that feel overwhelming—financial struggles, health challenges, or relational conflicts. But God promises to keep you in perfect peace when your mind is steadfast, trusting in Him. Instead of focusing on the size of the storm, focus on the greatness of the One who controls the wind and the waves.

Call to Action: Identify a situation that's causing you stress or anxiety. Bring it to God in prayer and ask for His peace to fill your heart.

Prayer: Lord, thank You for the peace You offer. Help me trust You in the middle of my storms and rest in Your perfect peace. Amen.

January 10
The Lord is My Strength

Verse: *"The Lord is my strength and my shield; my heart trusts in Him, and He helps me."*

(Psalm 28:7, NIV)

Message: God is your strength when you feel weak, and He is your shield when you need protection. Trusting in Him gives you the strength to keep going, even when life feels overwhelming. His presence empowers you to face challenges with courage, knowing that He is fighting for you and helping you every step of the way.

David, who wrote this psalm, often faced enemies and difficult situations, yet he continually relied on God as his source of strength and protection. Whether facing Goliath as a young shepherd or fleeing from King Saul, David knew that God was his shield. He didn't depend on his own abilities but on the strength that came from the Lord (1 Samuel 17:45-47).

When you're feeling weak or under attack, remember that God is your strength. You don't have to face life's battles alone. He is your helper and your shield, always ready to protect and empower you. Lean on Him for the strength you need today, and trust that He is fighting for you.

Call to Action: Reflect on a challenge you're facing, and ask God to be your strength and shield in that situation.

Prayer: Lord, You are my strength and my shield. Help me trust in You and rely on Your power to carry me through today's challenges. Amen.

January 11
God's Love is Unfailing

Verse: *"Give thanks to the Lord, for He is good. His love endures forever."*

(Psalm 136:1, NIV)

Message: God's love is eternal and unchanging. No matter what you're going through, you can rest in the fact that His love will never fail. He loves you deeply, and His goodness surrounds you every day. His enduring love means that you are never alone, never abandoned, and never outside of His care.

Throughout Scripture, we see God's unfailing love for His people. Even when the Israelites turned away from Him, God remained faithful. His love never gave up on them, and He continually offered them grace and restoration. Psalm 136 repeats the phrase "His love endures forever" as a reminder that no matter what, God's love never runs out.

Just as God's love was steadfast toward the Israelites, it is steadfast toward you. You may face difficulties or seasons of doubt, but God's love is constant through it all. You can give thanks every day for His goodness, knowing that His love will never leave you. It's a love that covers your past, sustains you in the present, and secures your future.

Call to Action: Reflect on how you've experienced God's love in your life. Take time today to thank Him for His unfailing love.

Prayer: Lord, thank You for Your love that endures forever. Help me rest in Your love today and give thanks for Your goodness. Amen.

January 12
God Will Never Leave You

Verse: "The Lord Himself goes before you and will be with you; He will never leave you nor forsake you. Do not be afraid; do not be discouraged."

(Deuteronomy 31:8, NIV)

Message: One of God's most reassuring promises is that He will never leave us. No matter what we face, we can trust that God is right by our side, guiding and protecting us. He goes before us, preparing the way, and He stands with us, giving us strength and courage. When we trust in His presence, fear and discouragement lose their power.

Moses shared this promise with Joshua as he prepared to lead the Israelites into the Promised Land. Joshua faced uncertainty, but God's presence was a constant source of comfort. Joshua didn't have to rely on his own strength or wisdom—he simply needed to trust that God was with him, just as He had been with Moses.

God's promise to never leave you applies today just as it did to Joshua. Whether you're stepping into a new season or facing a difficult challenge, you can be confident that God goes before you and walks with you. His presence is your source of strength, so you don't have to fear what lies ahead.

Call to Action: Think about a situation where you've been feeling fearful or discouraged. Pray for God's presence to fill you with courage and peace.

Prayer: Lord, thank You for never leaving me. Help me trust in Your presence and not be afraid of what lies ahead. Amen.

January 13
God Hears Your Prayers

Verse: *"This is the confidence we have in approaching God: that if we ask anything according to His will, He hears us."*

(1 John 5:14, NIV)

Message: Prayer is powerful because God hears us when we pray. We can approach Him with confidence, knowing that He listens and responds to our needs. When we pray according to His will, we align our hearts with His purposes, and we can trust that He is working on our behalf, even when we don't see immediate answers.

In 1 Samuel 1, we see the story of Hannah, who prayed earnestly for a child. She poured out her heart before the Lord, and He heard her prayer. In time, God answered by giving her a son, Samuel, who went on to become a great prophet. Hannah's story shows us that God hears the cries of His children and answers in His perfect timing.

You can be confident that God hears your prayers today. Whether you're praying for guidance, healing, or provision, know that your prayers are reaching the heart of a loving Father who desires good for you. Trust in His timing and His will, knowing that He is always listening.

Call to Action: Bring a specific request before God today, trusting that He hears you and will answer in His time.

Prayer: Father, thank You for hearing my prayers. Help me trust in Your will and Your timing as I wait for Your answers. Amen.

January 14
God is Your Refuge

Verse: "*God is our refuge and strength, an ever-present help in trouble.*"

(Psalm 46:1, NIV)

Message: God is your refuge, your safe place in times of trouble. When life feels overwhelming or you face challenges, you can run to Him and find shelter. He is a constant source of strength and protection, offering peace in the midst of the storm. Trusting in God as your refuge gives you the assurance that no matter what comes your way, He is with you.

David experienced God as his refuge many times throughout his life. Whether he was fleeing from Saul or facing enemies in battle, David continually turned to God for protection. Psalm 46 reminds us that God is not distant in times of trouble—He is ever-present, ready to help and defend His people.

When you feel stressed or under attack, remember that God is your refuge. You don't have to fight your battles alone. He is a strong fortress, surrounding you with His love and grace. Run to Him for strength and let Him be your shield in every circumstance.

Call to Action: When you feel overwhelmed today, pause and remind yourself that God is your refuge. Spend a few moments in prayer, seeking His peace and protection.

Prayer: Lord, thank You for being my refuge and strength. Help me trust You to protect and guide me through every challenge. Amen.

January 15
God's Word Lights Your Path

Verse: *"Your word is a lamp for my feet, a light on my path."*

(Psalm 119:105, NIV)

Message: God's Word is a light that guides us through life's journey. It illuminates the path before us, giving us wisdom and direction. When we seek God through His Word, He shows us the next steps to take and provides clarity in moments of confusion. Trusting in God's Word means allowing it to shape our decisions and lead us toward His will.

The Israelites depended on God's guidance during their time in the wilderness. As they journeyed toward the Promised Land, God led them with a pillar of cloud by day and a pillar of fire by night (Exodus 13:21-22). Just as He guided the Israelites through the wilderness, He guides us through the light of His Word, showing us where to go.

God's Word is just as relevant today as it was in ancient times. It offers guidance, comfort, and wisdom for every situation you face. When you rely on Scripture, you allow God to light your path and lead you in the right direction. Let His Word be your guide as you navigate life's challenges and decisions.

Call to Action: Spend time in God's Word today, asking Him to show you the next step He wants you to take in a specific area of your life.

Prayer: Lord, thank You for the light of Your Word. Help me trust in it and follow the path You've laid out for me. Amen.

January 16
God Will Fight for You

Verse: *"The Lord will fight for you; you need only to be still."*

(Exodus 14:14, NIV)

Message: There are moments in life when we feel overwhelmed, like we are fighting battles we cannot win on our own. God's promise is that He will fight for us. Instead of striving in our own strength, we are called to be still and trust in Him. His power is more than enough to handle whatever we are facing, and He invites us to rest in His ability to bring victory.

The Israelites faced an impossible situation at the Red Sea, trapped between the water and the approaching Egyptian army. Panic set in, but God reminded them through Moses that He would fight for them. They only needed to trust and be still. God parted the waters, delivering them from their enemies and leading them to safety (Exodus 14:21-22).

Like the Israelites, you may be facing a situation that seems overwhelming, where you don't know how to move forward. God is asking you to trust that He is fighting for you. When you place your battles in His hands, He can work in ways you never imagined. You don't need to exhaust yourself trying to fix everything—be still, and let God be your defender.

Call to Action: Think of a battle you're facing right now and commit it to God in prayer. Be still and trust that He is fighting for you.

Prayer: Lord, thank You for fighting on my behalf. Help me to be still and trust in Your power and victory. Amen.

January 17
God's Grace is Sufficient

Verse: "But He said to me, 'My grace is sufficient for you, for My power is made perfect in weakness.'"

(2 Corinthians 12:9, NIV)

Message: God's grace is enough for every situation we face. When we feel weak or incapable, His grace fills the gap. His power shines brightest when we acknowledge our need for Him. We don't have to be perfect or have everything together for God to work through us—He delights in showing His strength through our weakness.

Paul experienced this firsthand with the "thorn in his flesh," a challenge he asked God to remove. But instead of taking it away, God reminded Paul that His grace was sufficient. This thorn kept Paul dependent on God's strength, and it was through that reliance that God's power was fully displayed (2 Corinthians 12:7-10).

In your own life, you may be facing difficulties that feel overwhelming or situations where you feel inadequate. God is reminding you that His grace is sufficient. You don't have to rely on your own strength—lean on Him and let His grace carry you through. His power is made perfect in your weakness, and He will sustain you through every challenge.

Call to Action: Reflect on a weakness or challenge you're currently facing, and ask God to give you His grace and strength.

Prayer: Lord, thank You that Your grace is more than enough for me. Help me rely on Your strength in my weakness. Amen.

January 18
God Will Direct Your Steps

Verse: "In their hearts humans plan their course, but the Lord establishes their steps."

(Proverbs 16:9, NIV)

Message: We may make our plans and set our goals, but ultimately, it is God who directs our steps. His wisdom far exceeds ours, and He sees the path we cannot yet see. When we surrender our plans to Him, He leads us in the way we should go. Trusting God with our future means allowing Him to guide us one step at a time.

Throughout the Bible, we see God directing the steps of His people. In Genesis 24, Abraham's servant was tasked with finding a wife for Isaac. He set out with a plan, but he prayed for God's guidance. God led him directly to Rebekah, who became Isaac's wife. This story shows us that when we seek God's direction, He is faithful to lead us to the right place at the right time.

As you plan for the future, remember that God is the one who directs your steps. You may have dreams and ideas about where you want to go, but trust that God will establish your path in His perfect wisdom. He knows what's best, and He is guiding you every step of the way.

Call to Action: Surrender your plans to God today, and ask Him to direct your steps in the path He has for you.

Prayer: Father, I trust You to guide my steps. Help me surrender my plans to You and follow the path You've prepared for me. Amen.

January 19
God is Your Provider

Verse: "And my God will meet all your needs according to the riches of His glory in Christ Jesus."
(Philippians 4:19, NIV)

Message: God promises to provide for all of our needs—not just some, but all. He is not limited by our resources or circumstances. His provision flows from the riches of His glory, and He delights in taking care of His children. When we trust in God as our provider, we can let go of anxiety and rest in the assurance that He will meet every need.

In the Old Testament, we see God's provision in the story of Elijah and the widow at Zarephath (1 Kings 17:8-16). During a time of drought and famine, God provided for Elijah through the widow's limited resources. Even though she only had a small amount of flour and oil, God multiplied it so that it didn't run out. Both Elijah and the widow experienced God's miraculous provision, demonstrating that He can meet our needs in unexpected ways.

If you're worried about provision—whether financial, emotional, or spiritual—trust that God is your provider. He knows your needs and will meet them in His perfect timing and way. Rest in the knowledge that He cares for you and will provide abundantly, just as He promised.

Call to Action: Take a need you have to God in prayer today, trusting Him to provide for you.

Prayer: Lord, thank You for being my provider. Help me trust in Your abundant provision for all my needs. Amen.

January 20
The Lord is Close to the Brokenhearted

Verse: "The Lord is close to the brokenhearted and saves those who are crushed in spirit."

(Psalm 34:18, NIV)

Message: God is especially near to those who are hurting. When your heart is broken or your spirit is crushed, God draws close, offering comfort and healing. His presence is a balm to the wounded soul, and He understands the depth of your pain. Trusting in God during times of sorrow brings hope, knowing that He is with you and will carry you through.

In John 11, we see Jesus' deep compassion as He wept with Mary and Martha over the death of their brother Lazarus (John 11:33-35). Even though Jesus knew He was about to raise Lazarus from the dead, He took the time to grieve with His friends. This shows us that God is not distant from our pain—He is present in it, offering comfort and love.

If you are feeling brokenhearted today, know that God is near. He understands your pain and offers you His comfort. You don't have to go through this alone—God is walking with you every step of the way, bringing healing and restoration to your heart.

Call to Action: Bring your pain to God in prayer, asking Him to comfort and heal your heart.

Prayer: Father, thank You for being close to me when I'm hurting. Bring healing to my broken heart and help me trust in Your loving presence. Amen.

January 21
God is With You Always

Verse: *"And surely I am with you always, to the very end of the age."*

(Matthew 28:20, NIV)

Message: Jesus promised that He would be with us always. This is a comforting reminder that no matter where we go or what we face, we are never alone. His presence is constant, and He walks with us through every season of life. Whether we are on the mountaintop or in the valley, His promise remains the same: He is with us.

In Matthew 28, just before Jesus ascended to heaven, He gave the Great Commission to His disciples, instructing them to go and make disciples of all nations. With this huge task, He also gave them a promise: He would be with them always, even to the end of the age. Jesus' assurance of His presence wasn't just for the disciples then, but for all of His followers—including you.

As you go through your day-to-day life, remember that Jesus is with you. Whether you're facing challenges at work, home, or in relationships, His presence gives you strength, peace, and courage. You don't walk alone—He is with you always, guiding and comforting you.

Call to Action: Take a moment today to acknowledge God's presence in your life. Thank Him for walking with you, no matter what you face.

Prayer: Lord, thank You for being with me always. Help me remember that I am never alone, and give me the strength to trust in Your presence. Amen.

January 22
Cast Your Cares on Him

Verse*: "Cast all your anxiety on Him because He cares for you."*

(1 Peter 5:7, NIV)

Message: Life is full of worries and stresses, but God invites us to cast all our anxiety on Him. He doesn't want us to carry the weight of our burdens alone. When we give our cares to God, we are trusting Him to handle what we cannot. He cares for us deeply, and He is more than capable of providing the peace and solutions we need.

Peter understood this truth well. As one of Jesus' closest disciples, he experienced the highs and lows of following Christ. He faced fears, doubts, and uncertainties, yet he learned to trust Jesus in all things. In 1 Peter 5:7, he encourages believers to cast their anxieties on God, reminding them that God truly cares for them.

Whatever worries are weighing you down today, give them to God. You don't have to figure everything out on your own—God is ready and willing to carry your burdens. His love for you is so great that He wants to lift the weight of anxiety off your shoulders. Trust Him with your cares, and let His peace fill your heart.

Call to Action: Take a few moments to pray and give God any anxieties or worries you're holding onto.

Prayer: Lord, thank You for caring for me. Help me trust You with my anxieties and cast all my worries onto You. Amen.

January 23
The Power of Prayer

Verse: *"The prayer of a righteous person is powerful and effective."*

(James 5:16, NIV)

Message: Prayer has the power to change situations, hearts, and lives. When we pray, we are partnering with God to bring His will to earth. It's not about our own power, but about aligning with God's purposes and trusting in His ability to move. Prayer invites God to work in ways beyond what we can imagine, and He responds to the prayers of His people.

In the book of James, we are reminded of the power of prayer, particularly when it comes to healing and restoration. James encourages believers to pray for one another, assuring them that the prayer of a righteous person is effective. He uses Elijah as an example—Elijah was a human just like us, but through his fervent prayers, God stopped and started the rain (James 5:17-18).

Prayer is just as powerful today as it was in Elijah's time. When you pray, you are tapping into the same power that created the universe. Whether you're praying for healing, wisdom, or provision, trust that God hears and answers. Your prayers are effective, and God is at work through them.

Call to Action: Spend time in focused prayer today, bringing your needs and the needs of others before God, trusting in His power to answer.

Prayer: Lord, thank You for the power of prayer. Help me pray with faith, knowing that You hear and respond. Amen.

January 24
God's Faithfulness Never Fails

> **Verse:** *"Know therefore that the Lord your God is God; He is the faithful God, keeping His covenant of love to a thousand generations of those who love Him and keep His commandments."*
>
> *(Deuteronomy 7:9, NIV)*

Message: God is faithful to keep His promises, no matter how long it takes. His covenant of love extends through all generations, and His faithfulness never wavers. While people may fail us and circumstances may change, God's faithfulness remains steadfast. When we trust in His faithfulness, we can have confidence that He will fulfill His promises to us.

Throughout the Bible, we see examples of God's faithfulness. One such example is His promise to Abraham that he would become the father of many nations (Genesis 12:1-3). Even though Abraham and Sarah were well past childbearing age, God remained faithful to His word. Isaac was born, and through Abraham's descendants, God's promise was fulfilled.

God's faithfulness is just as real in your life. Whatever promises you are holding onto, trust that God is faithful to bring them to pass. It may not happen in the way or timing you expect, but His faithfulness is sure. Rest in the knowledge that God's love and faithfulness extend to you, just as they did to Abraham and all those who came before you.

Call to Action: Reflect on God's faithfulness in your life. Spend time thanking Him for keeping His promises and ask for renewed trust in His faithfulness.

Prayer: Father, thank You for Your unfailing faithfulness. Help me trust in Your promises and rest in Your covenant of love. Amen.

January 25
God's Word Never Fails

Verse: *"The grass withers and the flowers fall, but the word of our God endures forever."*

(Isaiah 40:8, NIV)

Message: In a world that is constantly changing, God's Word remains the same. Everything around us may fade or fail, but His Word endures forever. His promises are eternal, and we can trust that what He has spoken will always stand. God's Word is the firm foundation on which we build our lives, and it is an anchor in the midst of life's uncertainties.

In Isaiah 40, the prophet contrasts the temporary nature of creation with the enduring nature of God's Word. While grass withers and flowers fade, God's Word remains unshakable. It is reliable, steadfast, and true. From the beginning of time to the end of the age, God's Word will never fail.

When you face uncertainty or feel like the world is shifting beneath your feet, remember that God's Word is a firm foundation. His promises are unchanging, and you can stand on them with confidence. No matter what happens, God's Word will guide, comfort, and sustain you.

Call to Action: Spend time reading God's Word today, focusing on a promise that you need to hold onto.

Prayer: Lord, thank You for the power and truth of Your Word. Help me trust in its promises and rely on it as my foundation. Amen.

January 26
God's Strength Never Fails

Verse: *"But those who hope in the Lord will renew their strength. They will soar on wings like eagles; they will run and not grow weary, they will walk and not be faint."*

(Isaiah 40:31, NIV)

Message: When we place our hope in God, He renews our strength. Instead of relying on our own abilities, which often leave us exhausted, we can trust in the Lord's limitless power. God promises that when we wait on Him, we will find the strength to keep going, no matter how difficult the journey.

In Isaiah 40, the prophet speaks to a weary people, reminding them that even the strongest of humans grow tired. But God never grows weary, and He gives power to the weak. By trusting in God and waiting on Him, we can experience supernatural strength—strength that helps us soar above life's difficulties and persevere in the race set before us.

As you face challenges, remember that God's strength is available to you. When you feel like you can't take another step, trust that He will renew your energy and help you move forward. Just as an eagle soars effortlessly in the sky, God will lift you up and give you the power to overcome every obstacle.

Call to Action: If you're feeling weary, take time to wait on the Lord in prayer, asking Him to renew your strength.

Prayer: Lord, thank You for the strength You give when I wait on You. Renew my energy today and help me soar above life's challenges. Amen.

January 27
God's Promises Are True

Verse: *"Not one of all the Lord's good promises to Israel failed; every one was fulfilled."*

(Joshua 21:45, NIV)

Message: God's promises are trustworthy. In the history of Israel, every promise God made to His people came to pass. He did not forget a single word He spoke, and His faithfulness was evident in their lives. The same is true for us today—God is faithful to fulfill every promise He has made to His people.

In Joshua 21, after the Israelites had settled in the Promised Land, the Bible records that not one of God's promises to them failed. Whether it was deliverance from their enemies, provision in the wilderness, or a future of hope, God fulfilled every word. This serves as a reminder that we, too, can trust God to keep His promises to us.

Whatever promises you are holding onto—whether for healing, provision, or peace—know that God is faithful. He doesn't forget His Word, and He will bring it to pass in your life. Trust in His timing and His faithfulness, knowing that not one of His promises will fail.

Call to Action: Write down a promise from God's Word that you are waiting to see fulfilled. Pray for faith and patience as you wait on His perfect timing.

Prayer: Lord, thank You for Your faithfulness in keeping Your promises. Help me trust You as I wait for Your promises to be fulfilled in my life. Amen.

January 28
God's Peace Guards Your Heart

Verse: *"And the peace of God, which transcends all understanding, will guard your hearts and your minds in Christ Jesus."*

(Philippians 4:7, NIV)

Message: God offers us a peace that goes beyond human understanding. His peace is not dependent on circumstances but is rooted in His presence. When we turn our anxieties over to God in prayer, He fills our hearts and minds with a peace that shields us from fear and worry. This peace guards us, protecting us from the turmoil around us.

In Philippians 4, Paul encourages believers to present their requests to God with thanksgiving, and in return, God's peace will guard their hearts. Paul himself experienced this peace while in prison, facing uncertain and difficult circumstances. Yet, despite his situation, he could still write about the peace of God that transcends understanding.

When life feels overwhelming, and anxiety creeps in, remember that God's peace is available to you. As you bring your concerns to Him in prayer, He will replace your worry with His peace. This peace will guard your heart and mind, giving you the strength to face whatever comes your way with calm assurance.

Call to Action: Spend time in prayer today, bringing your worries and anxieties to God. Ask Him to fill you with His peace.

Prayer: Lord, thank You for the peace that guards my heart and mind. Help me trust You with my worries and rest in Your perfect peace. Amen.

January 29
God is Faithful to Forgive

Verse: *"If we confess our sins, He is faithful and just and will forgive us our sins and purify us from all unrighteousness."*

(1 John 1:9, NIV)

Message: God's forgiveness is always available to us. When we confess our sins to Him, He is faithful to forgive us and cleanse us from all unrighteousness. His forgiveness is not something we earn—it is a gift of grace. No matter what we've done, God's mercy is greater, and He offers us a fresh start when we turn to Him.

The story of the Prodigal Son in Luke 15 illustrates this beautifully. The son had squandered his inheritance and hit rock bottom. Yet, when he returned to his father, expecting rejection, he was met with open arms and a celebration. This parable reminds us that no matter how far we've strayed, God is always ready to forgive and welcome us back into His embrace.

God's forgiveness is available to you today. Whatever guilt or shame you're carrying, you can bring it to Him in confession, and He will forgive you. His love wipes away your sins and gives you a clean slate, allowing you to walk in freedom and grace.

Call to Action: Spend time in confession today, bringing any sin or burden to God, and receive His forgiveness and cleansing.

Prayer: Lord, thank You for Your faithful forgiveness. Help me walk in the freedom of Your grace, knowing that I am forgiven and loved. Amen.

January 30
God is the Light of the World

Verse: *"When Jesus spoke again to the people, He said, 'I am the light of the world. Whoever follows me will never walk in darkness, but will have the light of life.'"*

(John 8:12, NIV)

Message: Jesus is the light of the world, and when we follow Him, we no longer have to walk in darkness. His light illuminates the path before us, guiding us in truth and righteousness. In a world filled with confusion and sin, Jesus brings clarity, hope, and the light of life. As we follow Him, His light shines through us, allowing us to reflect His love to others.

In John 8, Jesus spoke these words to the people, declaring that He is the source of light in a dark world. Just as the sun gives light and life to the earth, Jesus gives light and life to our souls. When we walk in His light, we are no longer bound by the darkness of sin and fear.

If you're feeling lost or confused, turn to Jesus, the light of the world. He will guide you out of the darkness and into His light. His presence brings hope and direction, and as you follow Him, you will experience the life that only He can give.

Call to Action: Reflect on an area of your life where you need God's light to shine. Ask Him to guide you and bring clarity and truth to that situation.

Prayer: Lord, thank You for being the light of the world. Guide me out of darkness and help me walk in Your light every day. Amen.

January 31
Trusting in God's Unfailing Love

Verse: *"But I trust in Your unfailing love; my heart rejoices in Your salvation."*

(Psalm 13:5, NIV)

Message: God's love is unfailing, and we can place our trust in it no matter what life brings. His love never gives up, never runs out, and never changes. Even when we face difficulties or feel distant from God, we can rest in the assurance that His love remains constant. Trusting in His unfailing love fills our hearts with joy and gives us hope in every circumstance.

David, who wrote Psalm 13, often faced trials and hardships, yet he consistently trusted in God's love. In this psalm, David begins by crying out in anguish but ends by declaring his trust in God's unfailing love. This shows us that even in moments of despair, we can turn to God and find peace in His love.

No matter what you're going through, God's love is a firm foundation. It is the anchor that holds you steady when everything else is uncertain. As you trust in His unfailing love, you will find joy and hope, knowing that God is with you and His love will never fail.

Call to Action: Spend time reflecting on God's unfailing love. Thank Him for His constant love and ask Him to help you trust in it more fully.

Prayer: Father, thank You for Your unfailing love. Help me trust in Your love more deeply, and let my heart rejoice in the salvation You provide. Amen.

February

God's Love and Our Identity

February 1
Loved by God

Verse: "See what great love the Father has lavished on us, that we should be called children of God! And that is what we are!"

(1 John 3:1, NIV)

Message: God's love for us is overwhelming and unconditional. He has lavished His love on us, calling us His children. We are not just followers or servants—we are sons and daughters of the living God. This love is not something we earn; it is freely given by a Father who delights in us. Our identity begins with understanding that we are loved by God simply because we belong to Him.

In 1 John 3:1, the apostle reminds believers of their true identity. We are not defined by our past mistakes, failures, or the world's opinions. We are defined by God's love. The moment we accept His love, we become part of His family, and this new identity shapes everything about how we live, think, and interact with others. We are not only loved; we are called His children, and that truth empowers us to live confidently.

Live today knowing that you are deeply loved by the Father. Let this love shape your identity, and remember that you are not defined by your circumstances but by God's amazing love.

Call to Action: Spend time today reflecting on the truth that you are loved by God. Let that love shape your thoughts, actions, and how you see yourself.

Prayer: Father, thank You for Your incredible love. Help me remember that I am Your child and that my identity is secure in You. Let Your love shape everything about who I am. Amen.

February 2
Nothing Can Separate Us from God's Love

Verse: *"For I am convinced that neither death nor life, neither angels nor demons, neither the present nor the future, nor any powers... will be able to separate us from the love of God that is in Christ Jesus our Lord."*

(Romans 8:38-39, NIV)

Message: God's love for us is unbreakable. Nothing in this world or beyond can separate us from His love. We often face challenges that make us doubt if God still loves us, but the truth is that His love is constant, unwavering, and eternal. Whether we feel it or not, God's love surrounds us, and no power can pull us away from it.

In Romans 8, Paul expresses his deep conviction that nothing—no hardship, trial, or spiritual force—can separate us from God's love. This love is secure in Christ, meaning that no matter what happens in our lives, God's love remains unshakable. When we understand that God's love is not based on our performance but on His grace, we can live in freedom, knowing that we are secure in Him.

When you face challenges or doubts today, remind yourself of God's unwavering love. Trust that nothing can separate you from His love, no matter what comes your way.

Call to Action: Write down the things in your life that make you feel separated from God. Bring them to Him in prayer, and trust in His promise that nothing can separate you from His love.

Prayer: Lord, thank You for Your unbreakable love. Help me trust in the truth that nothing can separate me from Your love, and let that love give me confidence and peace today. Amen.

February 3
Fearfully and Wonderfully Made

Verse*: "I praise You because I am fearfully and wonderfully made; Your works are wonderful, I know that full well."*

(Psalm 139:14, NIV)

Message: Your identity is shaped by God's careful and intentional creation. You are fearfully and wonderfully made by the Creator of the universe, who knows you intimately. Every part of you was designed with purpose and love. God does not make mistakes, and your unique personality, abilities, and appearance are a reflection of His creativity and love for you.

In Psalm 139, David praises God for the intricate and beautiful way he was created. This truth applies to each of us. You are not a product of chance; you were designed by God Himself, and He sees you as a masterpiece. Often, we struggle with our self-image or compare ourselves to others, but God sees you as precious and wonderfully made.

Today, embrace the truth that you are God's creation—fearfully and wonderfully made. Let go of comparisons, and live confidently in the identity God has given you.

Call to Action: Spend time thanking God for the way He created you. Reflect on your unique qualities and abilities, and embrace the truth that you are wonderfully made by Him.

Prayer: Father, thank You for making me fearfully and wonderfully. Help me see myself through Your eyes and embrace the unique person You've created me to be. Amen.

February 4
God's Love Casts Out Fear

Verse*: "There is no fear in love. But perfect love drives out fear, because fear has to do with punishment. The one who fears is not made perfect in love."*

(1 John 4:18, NIV)

Message: God's perfect love has the power to cast out fear. Fear is a crippling emotion that can keep us from living fully in the freedom that God offers. When we experience the fullness of God's love, fear loses its grip on our hearts. His love reminds us that we are safe, forgiven, and accepted, so we no longer need to live in fear of judgment or failure.

John's words in 1 John 4:18 reveal a profound truth: fear cannot coexist with the perfect love of God. God's love is perfect, and it removes the fear of punishment or rejection. We often live in fear of not being good enough, but God's love assures us that we are accepted because of who He is, not because of what we do. When we rest in this love, fear is replaced with peace and confidence.

If fear is holding you back today, invite God's love to fill your heart. Let His perfect love drive out your fear, and walk in the freedom He offers.

Call to Action: Identify areas in your life where fear is holding you back. Bring those fears to God in prayer, asking Him to fill your heart with His perfect love and remove your fear.

Prayer: Lord, thank You for Your perfect love that drives out fear. Help me rest in Your love today, trusting that I am fully accepted by You and that I no longer need to live in fear. Amen.

February 5
Chosen and Appointed by God

Verse: *"You did not choose Me, but I chose you and appointed you so that you might go and bear fruit—fruit that will last—and so that whatever you ask in My name the Father will give you."*

(John 15:16, NIV)

Message: You are chosen by God. Long before you sought after Him, He chose you to be part of His family and to bear lasting fruit. This means that your life has a divine purpose. God has appointed you for a unique role in His Kingdom, and His love for you is the foundation of this calling. You are not here by accident—you are here by God's choosing, and He has a plan for your life.

In John 15:16, Jesus reminds His disciples that He chose them and appointed them to bear lasting fruit. This is true for us today as well. We didn't earn our place in God's family; He chose us out of love and called us to live lives that make an eternal impact. Knowing that we are chosen by God gives us confidence and purpose. We can trust that God has a specific plan for our lives, and His love equips us to fulfill that plan.

Live today knowing that you are chosen and appointed by God. Trust in His love and purpose for your life, and seek to bear fruit that reflects His Kingdom.

Call to Action: Reflect on how God has chosen and appointed you to bear lasting fruit. Ask Him to show you ways to live out His purpose and to trust in His plan for your life.

Prayer: Father, thank You for choosing me and appointing me to bear fruit. Help me walk confidently in Your love, knowing that You have a purpose for my life and that I am here for a reason. Amen.

February 6
Made in God's Image

Verse: *"So God created mankind in His own image, in the image of God He created them; male and female He created them."*

(Genesis 1:27, NIV)

Message: You were created in the image of God. This is a foundational truth of our identity. Being made in God's image means that you carry a reflection of His nature within you. You were designed to represent His character—His creativity, love, justice, and holiness. This truth gives us immense value and worth because our identity is directly tied to the Creator Himself.

In Genesis 1:27, we see that God's design for humanity was intentional. Both men and women are made in His image, carrying the unique responsibility and honor of reflecting Him in the world. This doesn't mean we are perfect like God, but it means that we are set apart from the rest of creation. We are His image-bearers, created with purpose and dignity. Knowing this helps us understand that our identity is not based on external factors but on the fact that we are made in the image of God.

As you go through your day, remember that you bear the image of your Creator. Let this truth shape how you see yourself and how you interact with the world around you.

Call to Action: Reflect on what it means to be made in God's image. Consider how this truth shapes your sense of identity and how you can reflect God's character in your everyday life.

Prayer: Lord, thank You for creating me in Your image. Help me reflect Your love, kindness, and character in my life, and remind me daily of the worth and dignity You've given me. Amen.

February 7
God Delights in You

Verse: *"The Lord your God is with you, the Mighty Warrior who saves. He will take great delight in you; in His love He will no longer rebuke you, but will rejoice over you with singing."*

(Zephaniah 3:17, NIV)

Message: God delights in you. Often, we think of God as being far off or indifferent, but Zephaniah 3:17 reveals the opposite. God is near, He is with you, and He delights in who you are. He rejoices over you with singing. This shows that God's love for you is not just duty-bound or obligatory—it is joyful, affectionate, and deeply personal.

The image of God rejoicing over His people is a beautiful expression of His love. He is not a distant or disinterested Father. He takes great pleasure in who you are. This truth can transform how we see ourselves, knowing that we bring joy to the heart of God. Even in our imperfections, God delights in us because of His great love. He is the Mighty Warrior who saves, and He sings over us with joy.

Let today be a reminder that you are someone God rejoices over. Live in the confidence of His delight and let His love fill your heart with joy.

Call to Action: Reflect on how knowing that God delights in you changes the way you view yourself. Take time to thank Him for His joyful love over your life.

Prayer: Father, thank You for delighting in me and rejoicing over me with singing. Help me live in the confidence of Your love and find joy in the fact that You care for me so deeply. Amen.

February 8
Accepted in Christ

Verse: *"To the praise of His glorious grace, which He has freely given us in the One He loves."*

(Ephesians 1:6, NIV)

Message: In Christ, you are fully accepted. God's grace is freely given to us through Jesus, and it is through Him that we are brought into a place of acceptance before God. Often, we may feel like we need to earn approval or acceptance from others or even from God. But the truth is, because of what Jesus has done, you are already fully accepted by the Father.

Paul's message to the Ephesians is a powerful reminder of God's grace. It is not something we work for; it is freely given. In Christ, we are loved and accepted, not because of our own efforts but because of God's great love for us. This truth is foundational to our identity as believers. We don't have to strive for God's approval—we already have it through Christ. Knowing this brings freedom and confidence to live as God's beloved children.

Today, rest in the truth that you are accepted in Christ. Let go of the pressure to earn God's approval and instead embrace the grace that has been freely given to you.

Call to Action: Reflect on areas of your life where you may feel pressure to earn acceptance. Surrender those to God and rest in the truth that you are already fully accepted in Christ.

Prayer: Lord, thank You for accepting me in Christ. Help me live in the freedom of Your grace, knowing that I don't have to earn Your love. Thank You for the acceptance I have in You. Amen.

February 9
You Are God's Masterpiece

Verse: *"For we are God's handiwork, created in Christ Jesus to do good works, which God prepared in advance for us to do."*

(Ephesians 2:10, NIV)

Message: You are God's masterpiece, His handiwork. This means that you are uniquely created with purpose and intention. God doesn't create anything without meaning, and your life has been crafted with great care. Not only are you His creation, but you were created for a purpose—to do good works that He has already prepared for you to do.

Ephesians 2:10 reminds us that we are not an accident or the result of random chance. We are the handiwork of God, created with specific gifts, talents, and callings that are meant to be used for His glory. God has already prepared good works for you to do, and He has equipped you to fulfill the purpose He has set for your life. Embracing this truth changes how we view ourselves and how we approach our lives.

Today, embrace your identity as God's masterpiece. Trust that He has prepared good works for you, and step into the purpose He has designed for you.

Call to Action: Reflect on the truth that you are God's handiwork. Ask God to show you the good works He has prepared for you, and seek opportunities to walk in the purpose He has given you.

Prayer: Father, thank You for creating me as Your masterpiece. Help me walk confidently in the good works You have prepared for me, and let my life bring glory to Your name. Amen.

February 10
Adopted Into God's Family

Verse: *"The Spirit you received does not make you slaves, so that you live in fear again; rather, the Spirit you received brought about your adoption to sonship. And by Him we cry, 'Abba, Father.'"*

(Romans 8:15, NIV)

Message: As believers, we have been adopted into God's family. We are no longer slaves to fear or sin—we are sons and daughters of God, with all the rights and privileges that come with being His children. Through the Holy Spirit, we have a close and intimate relationship with God, and we can call Him "Abba, Father," which expresses the deep bond between us and our Heavenly Father.

Romans 8:15 speaks of the incredible truth of our adoption into God's family. We are not just followers of God; we are His children. This means we have access to His love, His protection, and His provision. We are not orphans or outsiders; we belong to God. This identity as His children frees us from fear and gives us the confidence to approach Him with our needs and desires.

Today, live in the truth that you are God's child, adopted into His family. Let this truth fill you with confidence and peace, knowing that you belong to Him.

Call to Action: Spend time reflecting on what it means to be adopted into God's family. Thank Him for the privilege of being His child, and approach Him with confidence, knowing that He loves you as His own.

Prayer: Lord, thank You for adopting me into Your family. Help me live in the freedom and confidence that comes from being Your child, and let me draw near to You as my loving Father. Amen.

February 11

God Knows You by Name

Verse: *"But now, this is what the Lord says—*
He who created you, Jacob, He who formed you, Israel:
'Do not fear, for I have redeemed you; I have
summoned you by name; you are mine.'"

(Isaiah 43:1, NIV)

Message: God knows you personally. He calls you by name and claims you as His own. In a world where we often feel overlooked or unknown, this truth brings incredible comfort. The Creator of the universe knows you intimately and personally. He formed you, redeemed you, and calls you His. You are not forgotten or insignificant—you belong to God.

In Isaiah 43:1, God speaks to Israel, but this truth applies to each of us as His children. God knows your name and calls you His own. This means that your life is of great value to Him. He doesn't just see you as part of a crowd—He sees you individually, with all your uniqueness, and He has a special purpose for you. His love for you is personal, and you can trust that He is deeply invested in every detail of your life.

Live today knowing that God knows your name and calls you His own. Let this truth give you confidence in His love and care for you.

Call to Action: Take a moment to reflect on the fact that God knows you by name. Spend time thanking Him for His personal love for you and trust that He is with you in every situation.

Prayer: Father, thank You for knowing me by name and for calling me Your own. Help me rest in Your personal love and trust that You are always with me, guiding and protecting me. Amen.

February 12
God's Love Is Unfailing

Verse: "But I trust in Your unfailing love; my heart rejoices in Your salvation."

(Psalm 13:5, NIV)

Message: God's love for you is unfailing. It never runs out, never gives up, and never wavers. Human love may disappoint or fade, but God's love is constant and dependable. In times of uncertainty or difficulty, we can place our trust in His unfailing love, knowing that it will always sustain us. His love brings joy and salvation, even in the darkest times.

In Psalm 13, David expresses his trust in God's unfailing love, even while going through hardship. This love is the anchor that holds us steady when life feels uncertain. We don't have to earn it or worry that it will fade—God's love is steadfast, and it carries us through every situation. Trusting in God's love allows us to rejoice, knowing that He is always working for our good, even when we can't see the full picture.

If you are feeling uncertain today, remind yourself of God's unfailing love. Trust in it, and let it fill your heart with peace and joy.

Call to Action: Reflect on a situation where you need to trust in God's unfailing love. Bring it to Him in prayer, and ask Him to fill your heart with joy and peace as you trust in His love.

Prayer: Lord, thank You for Your unfailing love. Help me trust in that love, even when I don't understand what's happening around me. Let Your love fill my heart with joy and peace today. Amen.

February 13

Chosen Before the Foundation of the World

Verse: *"For He chose us in Him before the creation of the world to be holy and blameless in His sight. In love He predestined us for adoption to sonship through Jesus Christ, in accordance with His pleasure and will."*

(Ephesians 1:4-5, NIV)

Message: Before the world was even created, God chose you. You were not an afterthought or a backup plan. In His love, God predestined you for adoption into His family through Jesus Christ. This means that God has had a plan for your life from the beginning of time, and He has always desired to bring you into a relationship with Him. Your identity is rooted in the fact that God chose you out of love, not because of anything you have done but because of who He is.

In Ephesians 1, Paul reminds believers that their adoption into God's family was part of God's eternal plan. This truth should give us incredible confidence and peace, knowing that our identity is secure in Christ. We are not here by accident, and our lives have a purpose that was established by God long before we were born. God's love for us is eternal, and His plans for us are filled with His goodness and grace.

Live today with the assurance that you were chosen by God before the foundation of the world. Let this truth give you confidence in your identity and purpose.

Call to Action: Reflect on the truth that God chose you before the creation of the world. Thank Him for His eternal love and ask Him to help you live out the purpose He has set for your life.

Prayer: Father, thank You for choosing me before the foundation of the world. Help me live in the confidence of Your love and fulfill the purpose You have for my life. Amen.

February 14
The Depth of God's Love

> **Verse:** *"And I pray that you, being rooted and established in love, may have power, together with all the Lord's holy people, to grasp how wide and long and high and deep is the love of Christ."*
>
> *(Ephesians 3:17-18, NIV)*

Message: God's love for you is immeasurable. It is wider, longer, higher, and deeper than anything we can fully comprehend. Paul's prayer in Ephesians is that believers would have the power to grasp the vastness of Christ's love. This love is beyond human understanding, but it is something that we are called to experience and live in every day. God's love is not limited by circumstances, and it reaches every part of our lives.

The love of Christ is a foundation for our faith and our identity. When we are rooted and established in this love, we are able to stand firm, no matter what comes our way. The depth of God's love provides security, peace, and joy. As we grow in our understanding of this love, we are drawn closer to God and more confident in His care for us.

Today, take time to meditate on the vastness of God's love for you. Let it fill your heart with peace, and trust that His love surrounds you in every situation.

Call to Action: Spend time reflecting on the width, length, height, and depth of God's love. Ask Him to help you experience His love in a deeper way today.

Prayer: Lord, thank You for the vastness of Your love. Help me grasp how deep, wide, and long Your love for me truly is. Let me be rooted and established in Your love, knowing that it will never fail. Amen.

February 15
You Are God's Beloved

Verse: *"As the Father has loved Me, so have I loved you. Now remain in My love."*

(John 15:9, NIV)

Message: You are God's beloved. Jesus tells us in John 15:9 that the same love the Father has for Him is the love He has for us. This is a profound truth that reveals how deeply we are loved by God. Jesus invites us to remain in His love, to rest in it and let it be the source of our identity and strength. His love is not conditional or temporary—it is constant and perfect, and it is the foundation of who we are as His children.

Jesus' words remind us that our identity is rooted in His love. We are not defined by our failures, achievements, or the opinions of others. We are defined by the love of Christ, which is the same love that the Father has for Him. This truth gives us security and peace, knowing that we are fully loved and accepted by God. Remaining in His love means trusting in it, relying on it, and allowing it to shape every part of our lives.

Today, live in the reality that you are God's beloved. Remain in His love and let it be the foundation of your identity and your strength.

Call to Action: Spend time today reflecting on the love of Christ for you. Ask Him to help you remain in His love and to let that love shape your identity and actions.

Prayer: Father, thank You for loving me with the same love You have for Your Son. Help me remain in that love and live each day in the confidence of being Your beloved. Amen.

February 16
God's Love Never Fails

Verse: *"Give thanks to the Lord, for He is good. His love endures forever."*

(Psalm 136:1, NIV)

Message: God's love is eternal, and it never fails. The love of people may come and go, but God's love for us remains constant and unwavering. It endures through every season of life, every trial, and every moment of uncertainty. God's love is rooted in His goodness, and because He is unchanging, His love for you is unchanging as well.

Psalm 136 is a beautiful reminder of God's enduring love. Over and over, it declares that His love endures forever. This repetition is meant to drive home the point that no matter what happens, God's love remains. This truth should give us incredible confidence. We don't have to worry that God's love will run out or that it depends on our performance. His love endures through all things, and we can trust that it will never fail.

As you go through your day, rest in the assurance that God's love for you endures forever. No matter what you face, His love is constant and reliable.

Call to Action: Reflect on the unchanging nature of God's love. Thank Him for His enduring love, and trust that it will never fail you, no matter what you are going through.

Prayer: Father, thank You that Your love endures forever. Help me rest in the truth that Your love will never fail and that it is with me through every season of life. Amen.

February 17

You Are a New Creation in Christ

Verse: *"Therefore, if anyone is in Christ, the new creation has come: The old has gone, the new is here!"*

(2 Corinthians 5:17, NIV)

Message: When you accept Christ, you become a new creation. Your old identity, marked by sin and brokenness, is gone. In its place, God gives you a new identity—one rooted in His love and redemption. You are no longer defined by your past or your failures. In Christ, you have been made new, and this new identity is marked by freedom, grace, and purpose.

In 2 Corinthians 5:17, Paul reminds us that being "in Christ" changes everything. The old you is gone, and a new creation has come. This is more than just a fresh start—it's a complete transformation. God is not just fixing the broken pieces of your old life; He is making you entirely new. Your identity now comes from being in Christ, and with that comes the freedom to live in His grace and love.

Today, embrace your new identity in Christ. Let go of the old and live in the freedom and purpose that comes with being a new creation in Him.

Call to Action: Reflect on areas of your life where you may still be holding on to your old identity. Surrender those to God, and ask Him to help you fully embrace your new identity as a new creation in Christ.

Prayer: Lord, thank You for making me a new creation in Christ. Help me live in the freedom and purpose of my new identity, letting go of the past and embracing the life You have for me. Amen.

February 18
God's Love Has Redeemed You

> ***Verse:*** *"In Him we have redemption through His blood, the forgiveness of sins, in accordance with the riches of God's grace."*
>
> ***(Ephesians 1:7, NIV)***

Message: God's love is a redeeming love. Through Christ's sacrifice on the cross, you have been redeemed—set free from sin and brought into a new relationship with God. Redemption means that your past no longer defines you. You are forgiven, and God's grace now covers your life. His love is rich in mercy, and because of it, you can walk in freedom and forgiveness.

In Ephesians 1:7, Paul reminds us of the incredible gift of redemption. Christ's blood paid the price for our sins, and through His sacrifice, we are forgiven. This redemption is not based on anything we have done but on the riches of God's grace. We are no longer slaves to sin or defined by our past mistakes. God's love has redeemed us and given us a new identity—one marked by freedom and grace.

Live today in the freedom that comes from knowing you are redeemed by God's love. Let go of any guilt or shame from the past, and walk confidently in the grace He has given you.

Call to Action: Reflect on the redemption you have through Christ. Spend time in prayer, thanking God for His forgiveness and asking Him to help you walk in the freedom of His grace.

Prayer: Father, thank You for redeeming me through the blood of Jesus. Help me live in the freedom of Your forgiveness and grace, knowing that I am no longer bound by sin or my past. Amen.

February 19
You Are More Than a Conqueror

Verse: *"No, in all these things we are more than conquerors through Him who loved us."*

(Romans 8:37, NIV)

Message: In Christ, you are more than a conqueror. This means that through God's love, you not only have victory over life's challenges, but you are empowered to overcome them in a way that glorifies God. God's love gives you the strength to face any difficulty with confidence, knowing that He is with you and that He has already won the victory on your behalf.

Romans 8:37 is a powerful reminder of the strength and victory we have in Christ. Because of God's love, we are more than conquerors. This doesn't mean we won't face challenges or difficulties, but it does mean that we don't have to face them alone. God's love empowers us to overcome, to rise above the obstacles we encounter, and to live in the victory that Christ has already secured for us.

If you are facing challenges today, remember that you are more than a conqueror through Christ. Trust in His love to give you the strength and courage to overcome whatever comes your way.

Call to Action: Reflect on a challenge you are currently facing. Pray and declare the truth that you are more than a conqueror through Christ. Trust in His love to carry you through.

Prayer: Lord, thank You for making me more than a conqueror through Your love. Help me face every challenge with confidence, knowing that You are with me and that the victory is already won in You. Amen.

FEBRUARY 20
GOD'S LOVE GIVES YOU STRENGTH

Verse: *"The Lord is my strength and my shield; my heart trusts in Him, and He helps me. My heart leaps for joy, and with my song I praise Him."*

(Psalm 28:7, NIV)

Message: God's love is your source of strength. When you feel weak or overwhelmed, you can trust in Him to be your strength and your shield. He is your protector and your helper, always ready to lift you up when you need it. Because of His love, you don't have to rely on your own strength—you can draw from His infinite power and find joy in knowing that He is with you.

In Psalm 28:7, David expresses his trust in the Lord as his strength and shield. This is the confidence we can have as believers—knowing that God is our source of strength in every situation. His love is not just a feeling; it is an active, powerful force that strengthens and protects us. When we trust in Him, we find joy even in the midst of difficulty, because we know that He is our helper and our defender.

If you are feeling weak or overwhelmed, turn to God as your strength. Let His love empower you and give you the strength you need for today.

Call to Action: Reflect on a situation where you need God's strength. Bring it to Him in prayer, trusting that He will be your strength and shield, and that His love will carry you through.

Prayer: Lord, thank You for being my strength and shield. Help me trust in Your love to sustain me, and let my heart find joy in knowing that You are my helper and protector. Amen.

February 21
You Are God's Workmanship

Verse: *"For we are God's handiwork, created in Christ Jesus to do good works, which God prepared in advance for us to do."*

(Ephesians 2:10, NIV)

Message: You are God's handiwork, crafted with purpose and intention. Every detail of your life, your personality, and your gifts were carefully designed by the Creator of the universe. You were not only created by God but created for a purpose. In Christ, you are empowered to do the good works that God has already prepared for you. You are a masterpiece, designed to reflect God's love and goodness in the world.

In Ephesians 2:10, Paul reminds us that we are not self-made. We are God's creation, and He has crafted us for specific purposes. This truth gives us confidence in our identity and reminds us that our lives have meaning and direction. God's love for us is reflected in the fact that He not only created us but also has plans for our lives that will bring Him glory and bless others.

Today, live in the truth that you are God's masterpiece. Trust that He has prepared good works for you to do and that your life has a divine purpose in His plan.

Call to Action: Reflect on the good works God has prepared for you. Ask Him to reveal how He wants to use your gifts and talents to fulfill His purpose in your life.

Prayer: Father, thank You for creating me as Your handiwork. Help me walk in the good works You have prepared for me and live out my purpose with confidence in Your love. Amen.

February 22
God's Love Gives You Confidence

Verse: *"In Him and through faith in Him we may approach God with freedom and confidence."*

(Ephesians 3:12, NIV)

Message: God's love gives you the freedom and confidence to approach Him without fear or hesitation. Through faith in Jesus, you have access to the Father, and you can come before Him with boldness, knowing that He loves you and desires a relationship with you. This confidence comes not from who we are, but from who Christ is and what He has done for us.

Ephesians 3:12 reminds us that we have direct access to God because of Christ. We don't need to be afraid or feel unworthy. God invites us to come to Him freely, with the confidence that we are His beloved children. This access to God's presence is one of the most beautiful expressions of His love for us. We don't have to hide or feel distant—God wants us to draw near to Him with boldness and trust.

Today, approach God with confidence. Know that His love has made a way for you to be in His presence, and He is always ready to listen and respond.

Call to Action: Spend time in prayer today, approaching God with confidence. Bring your needs, concerns, and desires to Him, trusting in His love and knowing that He hears you.

Prayer: Lord, thank You for giving me the confidence to approach You through Christ. Help me draw near to You in faith, knowing that You love me and are always ready to hear my prayers. Amen.

February 23
God's Love Makes You His Child

Verse: *"Yet to all who did receive Him, to those who believed in His name, He gave the right to become children of God."*

(John 1:12, NIV)

Message: When you receive Jesus, you become a child of God. This is one of the most powerful aspects of your identity—you are not just a follower of God, but His beloved child. Through faith in Jesus, you are brought into the family of God and given all the rights and privileges that come with being His child. This identity is not earned but received as a gift through God's love.

John 1:12 emphasizes the profound truth that through believing in Jesus, we are given the right to become children of God. This is more than just a title—it means we have an intimate relationship with the Father. We are no longer distant or separated from Him; we are part of His family. Being a child of God means we are loved, cared for, and valued beyond measure.

Today, live in the reality that you are a child of God. Let this truth shape your identity and how you see yourself in the world.

Call to Action: Reflect on what it means to be a child of God. Spend time in prayer, thanking Him for adopting you into His family, and live confidently in that identity.

Prayer: Father, thank You for making me Your child through Jesus. Help me live in the security and joy of being part of Your family, knowing that I am loved and accepted by You. Amen.

February 24
God's Love Is Steadfast

Verse: *"The steadfast love of the Lord never ceases; His mercies never come to an end; they are new every morning; great is Your faithfulness."*

(Lamentations 3:22-23, NIV)

Message: God's love for you is steadfast and unchanging. It never fades, weakens, or ceases. No matter what happens in your life, God's love remains constant, and His mercies are new every morning. His faithfulness is great, and you can trust that His love will carry you through every situation. Even in the hardest times, God's love is a solid foundation that will never fail.

Lamentations 3:22-23 is a beautiful reminder of the enduring nature of God's love. Even in times of difficulty or pain, His love remains steadfast. His mercies are new every day, which means that each morning brings a fresh outpouring of His grace and love for us. No matter what challenges we face, we can trust that God's love will never run out.

Today, take comfort in the steadfast love of God. Trust that His love will never fail you, and lean on His faithfulness in every situation.

Call to Action: Reflect on God's steadfast love in your life. Thank Him for His faithfulness and for the new mercies He gives you each day, and trust Him to carry you through every challenge.

Prayer: Lord, thank You for Your steadfast love that never ceases. Help me trust in Your faithfulness and rest in Your love, knowing that Your mercies are new every morning. Amen.

February 25
God's Love Gives You Peace

Verse: *"Peace I leave with you; My peace I give you. I do not give to you as the world gives. Do not let your hearts be troubled and do not be afraid."*

(John 14:27, NIV)

Message: God's love gives you peace—peace that is unlike anything the world can offer. Jesus promised His disciples that He would give them His peace, a peace that would guard their hearts and minds and protect them from fear. This peace comes from knowing that God is in control, that His love surrounds us, and that He is working all things for our good. When we trust in God's love, we can experience this deep, lasting peace, even in the midst of chaos.

In John 14:27, Jesus speaks words of comfort to His disciples. He knows that they will face trials and challenges, but He assures them that His peace will be with them. This peace is a gift that comes from God's love, and it guards our hearts from fear and worry. When we focus on God's love and trust in His promises, we can experience the peace that surpasses all understanding.

If you are feeling anxious or troubled, lean on God's love and let His peace fill your heart. Trust that He is in control and that His love will sustain you.

Call to Action: Spend time in prayer, asking God to fill your heart with His peace. Reflect on areas where you need to trust Him more and let His love bring you peace in the midst of uncertainty.

Prayer: Father, thank You for the peace that comes from Your love. Help me trust in You and let go of fear, knowing that Your peace guards my heart and mind. Amen.

FEBRUARY 26
YOU ARE CHOSEN AND PRECIOUS

Verse: "But you are a chosen people, a royal priesthood, a holy nation, God's special possession, that you may declare the praises of Him who called you out of darkness into His wonderful light."

(1 Peter 2:9, NIV)

Message: You are chosen by God and precious in His sight. As His special possession, you are set apart to declare His glory and live in the light of His love. This verse reminds us that we are not only loved but chosen with a purpose. God called you out of darkness into His light so that your life would reflect His goodness and grace. Your identity is rooted in being God's beloved and cherished possession, uniquely chosen to be part of His Kingdom.

In 1 Peter 2:9, we see a beautiful description of who we are in Christ. We are chosen, set apart, and given the responsibility and privilege of declaring God's praises. Our lives are meant to be a testimony of His love, not only in what we say but also in how we live. Being God's special possession means we are valued beyond measure, and this truth should fill us with confidence and joy.

Today, walk in the knowledge that you are chosen and precious to God. Let this truth shape your identity and inspire you to live a life that reflects His light and love.

Call to Action: Reflect on what it means to be God's chosen and special possession. Thank Him for choosing you and ask Him to show you how to live out this calling in your everyday life.

Prayer: Father, thank You for choosing me and calling me out of darkness into Your light. Help me live as Your special possession, declaring Your praises and reflecting Your love. Amen.

February 27
God's Love Makes You Whole

Verse: *"He heals the brokenhearted and binds up their wounds."*
(Psalm 147:3, NIV)

Message: God's love has the power to heal the deepest wounds and make you whole. Whether you have experienced pain, rejection, or loss, God sees your brokenness and offers healing through His love. He doesn't just patch up our wounds—He binds them and restores us completely. His love brings wholeness to every part of our lives, healing our hearts and making us new.

Psalm 147:3 is a comforting reminder of God's tender care for those who are hurting. His love reaches into the broken places of our hearts and brings restoration. We often carry wounds from past experiences, but God's love has the power to heal and make us whole again. He doesn't leave us in our brokenness but invites us into a journey of healing and wholeness through His love and grace.

If you are feeling broken or wounded, bring your heart to God and let His love heal you. Trust that He sees your pain and that His love is strong enough to restore you completely.

Call to Action: Reflect on areas in your life where you need God's healing. Bring those wounds to Him in prayer, asking Him to heal your heart and make you whole through His love.

Prayer: Lord, thank You for Your love that heals the brokenhearted. Help me trust in Your healing power and bring my wounds to You, knowing that You will make me whole. Amen.

February 28
Your Identity Is Secure in Christ

Verse: *"For you died, and your life is now hidden with Christ in God."*

(Colossians 3:3, NIV)

Message: Your identity is secure in Christ. When you place your faith in Him, your old life dies, and you are given a new life that is hidden with Christ in God. This means that your true identity is found in your relationship with Jesus, not in your past, your mistakes, or the opinions of others. In Christ, you are fully loved, fully accepted, and fully secure. Nothing can shake this identity because it is anchored in God's unchanging love.

In Colossians 3:3, Paul reminds us that our lives are now hidden with Christ. This means that when God looks at you, He sees Jesus. Your identity is no longer tied to the things of this world but to your relationship with Christ. This gives you incredible security and confidence because you know that your identity is rooted in the One who is eternal and unchanging. You are safe and secure in God's love, no matter what life brings.

As you close out this month, remember that your identity is secure in Christ. Let go of any insecurity or fear, and live confidently in the truth that you are hidden with Christ in God.

Call to Action: Reflect on areas of insecurity or doubt in your life. Surrender those to God, and trust that your true identity is secure in Christ, hidden in His love and grace.

Prayer: Father, thank You that my identity is secure in Christ. Help me live confidently in this truth, knowing that I am fully loved, fully accepted, and fully secure in You. Amen.

March

Walking by Faith, Not by Sight

March 1
Faith is Confidence in What We Hope For

Verse: *"Now faith is confidence in what we hope for and assurance about what we do not see."*

(Hebrews 11:1, NIV)

Message: Faith is the confident assurance that what we hope for in God's promises will come to pass, even when we cannot see it. Faith is not based on what is visible or tangible; it is rooted in trust in God's character and His Word. This kind of faith requires us to believe in God's goodness and faithfulness, even when the circumstances around us seem uncertain or confusing.

Hebrews 11:1 defines faith in powerful terms—confidence and assurance. This type of faith doesn't depend on seeing results or understanding every detail; it is a trust that God will fulfill what He has promised. Throughout Scripture, we see examples of men and women who lived by faith, trusting in God even when they couldn't see how things would work out. This same faith is available to us as we walk with God.

Today, choose to live by faith, trusting in what you hope for even when you cannot see the full picture. Believe that God is at work, even in the unseen, and rest in the assurance of His promises.

Call to Action: Reflect on an area in your life where you need to exercise faith. Pray for confidence and assurance, trusting that God's promises will be fulfilled, even when you can't yet see the outcome.

Prayer: Lord, thank You for the gift of faith. Help me trust in what I cannot see and have confidence in Your promises, knowing that You are always faithful to fulfill Your Word. Amen.

March 2
Fixing Our Eyes on the Unseen

Verse: *"So we fix our eyes not on what is seen, but on what is unseen, since what is seen is temporary, but what is unseen is eternal."*

(2 Corinthians 4:18, NIV)

Message: Faith teaches us to fix our eyes on the unseen rather than the temporary things of this world. While the world around us is filled with distractions, trials, and uncertainties, the things of God—His promises, His kingdom, His love—are eternal. When we focus on what is unseen, we are able to keep an eternal perspective, trusting that God's plans go far beyond our current circumstances.

In 2 Corinthians 4:18, Paul encourages believers to look beyond the visible and focus on the eternal realities of God's kingdom. The challenges we face in this life are temporary, but the promises of God are everlasting. Walking by faith means trusting in the things we cannot yet see—God's perfect plan, His promises of restoration, and the hope of eternal life with Him. This perspective brings peace and strength as we navigate life's uncertainties.

If you are feeling overwhelmed by what you see around you, fix your eyes on the unseen promises of God. Trust that what is eternal is far greater than the temporary challenges you face today.

Call to Action: Spend time reflecting on what it means to fix your eyes on the unseen. Ask God to help you focus on His eternal promises rather than the temporary things of this world.

Prayer: Father, thank You for the eternal promises that are found in You. Help me fix my eyes on what is unseen and trust in Your kingdom, knowing that what is eternal will never fade. Amen.

March 3
Faith Overcomes Fear

Verse: *"When I am afraid, I put my trust in You."*

(Psalm 56:3, NIV)

Message: Faith is the antidote to fear. When we face situations that cause anxiety or uncertainty, we are called to put our trust in God. Fear can paralyze us, making us doubt God's promises or feel overwhelmed by our circumstances. But faith invites us to trust that God is in control, even when we are afraid. When we place our trust in Him, fear loses its grip on our hearts, and we are able to move forward in confidence.

In Psalm 56:3, David expresses his faith in the midst of fear. Instead of allowing fear to dictate his actions, he chose to trust in God's protection and provision. We, too, can overcome fear by placing our trust in God's sovereignty and love. Fear may still come, but faith gives us the courage to face it, knowing that God is with us and that He will never leave us or forsake us.

If fear is holding you back today, take a step of faith by putting your trust in God. Let go of the fear, and trust that God is bigger than any challenge you are facing.

Call to Action: Identify an area of your life where fear is present. Bring it to God in prayer, asking Him to help you trust in His protection and provision.

Prayer: Lord, thank You for being my refuge and strength. When I am afraid, help me put my trust in You, knowing that You are always with me and that I have nothing to fear. Amen.

March 4
Walking by Faith, Not by Sight

Verse: *"For we live by faith, not by sight."*

(2 Corinthians 5:7, NIV)

Message: As believers, we are called to live by faith, not by sight. This means that we don't base our decisions or outlook on what we can see or understand. Instead, we trust God's wisdom, guidance, and promises. Walking by faith requires surrendering our desire for control and certainty and choosing to trust that God is leading us, even when the path ahead is unclear.

2 Corinthians 5:7 encourages us to live in a way that is not dictated by our physical circumstances but by our trust in God's plan. Throughout Scripture, we see examples of people who stepped out in faith, even when they didn't know where they were going. Abraham left his homeland, not knowing his destination, trusting in God's promise. This kind of faith calls us to trust God's unseen work in our lives and to walk forward, believing that He is guiding our steps.

Today, choose to walk by faith, not by sight. Trust that God is working in ways you cannot see, and surrender your need for control, allowing Him to guide you.

Call to Action: Reflect on an area in your life where you need to walk by faith rather than relying on what you can see. Ask God for the courage to trust Him, even when the path is unclear.

Prayer: Father, help me live by faith, trusting in Your guidance and promises. Even when I can't see the way forward, I know You are leading me. Give me the courage to walk by faith, not by sight. Amen.

March 5
Faith That Trusts in God's Timing

Verse: *"The Lord is not slow in keeping His promise, as some understand slowness. Instead, He is patient with you, not wanting anyone to perish, but everyone to come to repentance."*

(2 Peter 3:9, NIV)

Message: Faith involves trusting in God's timing. Often, we want immediate answers or results, but God's plans unfold according to His perfect timeline. What may seem like a delay to us is often part of God's greater plan. He is never slow or late—He is always right on time. Walking by faith means believing that God's timing is better than our own and trusting that He is working behind the scenes, even when we can't see it.

In 2 Peter 3:9, we are reminded that God's timing is patient and purposeful. He desires that all come to repentance, and His delays are often for a greater purpose that we cannot yet see. When we trust in God's timing, we surrender our need for immediate results and rest in the knowledge that His plans are good and perfect. Faith means trusting that He knows what is best, even when we don't understand the wait.

If you're waiting on God's promises, trust in His timing. Believe that He is working all things together for your good, and rest in the peace that comes from trusting in His perfect plan.

Call to Action: Reflect on a situation where you are waiting on God's timing. Surrender your impatience to Him, and ask for the faith to trust in His perfect timing and plan.

Prayer: Lord, thank You for Your perfect timing. Help me trust in Your plans and wait patiently for Your promises to be fulfilled, knowing that You are always working for my good. Amen.

March 6
Faith That Pleases God

Verse: *"And without faith it is impossible to please God, because anyone who comes to Him must believe that He exists and that He rewards those who earnestly seek Him."*

(Hebrews 11:6, NIV)

Message: Faith is foundational to our relationship with God. It's impossible to please God without it, because faith is the bridge that connects us to His heart. When we trust in Him, we demonstrate that we believe in His goodness, His presence, and His promises. Faith invites us to seek God earnestly, knowing that He rewards those who pursue Him. This kind of faith is not about seeing immediate results—it's about trusting that God is who He says He is, even when we can't see the whole picture.

In Hebrews 11:6, we are reminded that faith is not just about believing that God exists—it's about trusting in His character and His promises. God desires a relationship with us that is built on trust and dependence on Him. As we seek Him, He rewards us with His presence, His peace, and His guidance. Faith pleases God because it shows that we believe in His goodness and His ability to work in our lives, even when we don't have all the answers.

Today, seek God with faith, trusting that He rewards those who earnestly pursue Him. Believe that your faith pleases Him and that He is working in your life in ways you cannot yet see.

Call to Action: Reflect on how you are seeking God in your daily life. Ask Him to strengthen your faith and help you trust in His goodness and His promises.

Prayer: Father, thank You for the gift of faith. Help me seek You earnestly, knowing that You reward those who trust in You. Strengthen my faith so that I may please You in all that I do. Amen.

March 7
Faith in God's Provision

Verse: "And my God will meet all your needs according to the riches of His glory in Christ Jesus."
(Philippians 4:19, NIV)

Message: Faith means trusting in God's provision, knowing that He is able to meet all our needs. Often, we face situations where we feel uncertain about how things will work out, but God promises to provide for us according to His riches in glory. His provision is not limited by our circumstances—He is the God of abundance, and He knows exactly what we need, when we need it.

In Philippians 4:19, Paul assures believers that God will meet all their needs, not just some of them. This is a promise that we can hold onto, especially in times of uncertainty. Faith in God's provision means that we trust Him to supply everything we need—whether physical, emotional, or spiritual—out of His infinite resources. We may not always know how or when His provision will come, but we can trust that it will.

If you're facing a need today, trust in God's provision. Believe that He sees your situation and will supply exactly what you need, according to His perfect timing.

Call to Action: Reflect on a current need in your life. Bring it before God in prayer, asking Him to provide for you, and trust that He will meet your need according to His riches in glory.

Prayer: Lord, thank You for Your promise to meet all my needs. Help me trust in Your provision and rest in the assurance that You will supply everything I need according to Your riches in glory. Amen.

March 8

Faith in the Power of Prayer

Verse: *"Therefore I tell you, whatever you ask for in prayer, believe that you have received it, and it will be yours."*

(Mark 11:24, NIV)

Message: Faith is key to powerful prayer. Jesus teaches us that when we pray, we should believe that we have received what we ask for, trusting that God hears our prayers and is able to answer them according to His will. This kind of faith is not about wishful thinking—it's about trusting in the power of God to act and knowing that He responds to the prayers of His people.

In Mark 11:24, Jesus encourages us to approach prayer with faith, believing that God is not only able to answer but is already working on our behalf. This kind of faith requires us to trust in God's timing and His wisdom, knowing that He will answer in the way that is best for us. Faith-filled prayer is not just about asking—it's about believing that God is moving, even when we don't immediately see the results.

Today, approach prayer with faith. Trust that God hears your prayers and that He is working in ways you may not yet see. Believe that His answers are already on the way.

Call to Action: Spend time in prayer, bringing your requests before God with faith. Trust that He hears you and is answering according to His will.

Prayer: Father, thank You for the power of prayer. Help me pray with faith, trusting that You hear me and that You are already working on my behalf. Strengthen my belief in Your power to answer my prayers. Amen.

March 9
Faith That Overcomes Doubt

Verse: *"Immediately the boy's father exclaimed, 'I do believe; help me overcome my unbelief!'"*

(Mark 9:24, NIV)

Message: Faith and doubt often coexist, but God calls us to trust Him even in the midst of uncertainty. The father in Mark 9 believed in Jesus' power to heal his son, but he also admitted his struggle with doubt. His honesty is a reminder that it's okay to bring our doubts to God. He can handle them, and He helps us overcome our unbelief as we continue to trust Him.

The father's cry—"I do believe; help me overcome my unbelief"—is something many of us can relate to. We want to have faith, but we also face moments of doubt and uncertainty. Jesus didn't rebuke the father for his doubt; instead, He responded with compassion and healed the boy. God understands our struggles with faith, and He invites us to bring our doubts to Him, trusting that He will strengthen our belief as we walk with Him.

If you're struggling with doubt, bring it to God. Ask Him to help you overcome your unbelief and strengthen your faith, trusting that He is able to work through even the smallest seed of faith.

Call to Action: Reflect on an area where you are struggling with doubt. Bring it to God in prayer, asking Him to help you overcome your unbelief and to grow your faith.

Prayer: Lord, I believe, but I also struggle with doubt. Help me overcome my unbelief and trust in Your power, even when I don't see the full picture. Strengthen my faith in You. Amen.

March 10
Faith That Moves Mountains

Verse: *"Truly I tell you, if you have faith as small as a mustard seed, you can say to this mountain, 'Move from here to there,' and it will move. Nothing will be impossible for you."*

(Matthew 17:20, NIV)

Message: Even a small amount of faith can accomplish great things. Jesus tells His disciples that if they have faith as small as a mustard seed, they can move mountains. This is a powerful reminder that it's not the size of our faith that matters but the greatness of the God in whom we place our faith. Even when our faith feels small or weak, God is able to work through it to do the impossible.

In Matthew 17:20, Jesus encourages us to have even the smallest amount of faith, knowing that God can move mountains on our behalf. Faith doesn't have to be perfect or without doubt—it just has to be genuine. God is not limited by the size of our faith; He is able to work through even the tiniest seed of belief to accomplish great things. When we trust in His power, we can see the impossible become possible.

If you're facing a challenge that feels like a mountain, remember that even a small amount of faith can move it. Trust in God's power, and believe that He is able to do the impossible in your life.

Call to Action: Reflect on an area where you need God to move a "mountain." Pray with faith, even if it feels small, and trust that God is able to do the impossible.

Prayer: Father, thank You for the power of faith, even when it's as small as a mustard seed. Help me trust in Your ability to move mountains in my life and believe that nothing is impossible with You. Amen.

March 11
Faith That Perseveres

Verse: *"Let us not become weary in doing good, for at the proper time we will reap a harvest if we do not give up."*

(Galatians 6:9, NIV)

Message: Faith requires perseverance. Sometimes we may feel weary, especially when we don't see immediate results or when life's challenges feel overwhelming. But God calls us to keep going, trusting that in due time, we will reap a harvest. Persevering in faith means holding onto God's promises, even when the journey is long or difficult. It means believing that He is at work, even when we don't see the fruits of our labor right away.

In Galatians 6:9, Paul encourages believers to continue doing good and to persevere in faith, trusting that God's timing is perfect. The harvest comes in "due time"—God's appointed time—not necessarily when we expect it. Persevering in faith means trusting that God sees our efforts, knows our struggles, and will reward our faithfulness. It's about continuing to trust Him, even when the answers aren't immediate.

If you're feeling weary today, take heart. Keep going in faith, trusting that God is working behind the scenes, and that in His time, you will see the harvest.

Call to Action: Reflect on an area of your life where you need to persevere. Ask God for the strength to keep going and trust that He is bringing a harvest in His perfect timing.

Prayer: Lord, thank You for the promise of a harvest in Your timing. Help me persevere in faith, even when I feel weary, and trust that You are at work, bringing about good in due time. Amen.

March 12
Faith That Trusts in God's Plan

Verse: "For I know the plans I have for you," declares the Lord, "plans to prosper you and not to harm you, plans to give you hope and a future."

(Jeremiah 29:11, NIV)

Message: Faith is trusting in God's plan, even when it doesn't align with our own. God has a purpose for each of our lives, and His plans are always for our good. This doesn't mean we won't face challenges or detours along the way, but it does mean that God is always working toward a greater purpose. Walking by faith means trusting in His plan, even when the future feels uncertain or different from what we expected.

In Jeremiah 29:11, God reassures the Israelites that He has plans to prosper them and give them hope, even though they were in exile at the time. This promise applies to us as well. God's plans are not meant to harm us, but to bring us hope and a future. Faith means letting go of our need to control every aspect of our lives and trusting that God's plans are better than our own. He sees the bigger picture, and His timing is perfect.

Today, trust that God's plan for your life is good, even if it looks different from what you expected. Believe that He is leading you into a future filled with hope.

Call to Action: Reflect on an area of your life where you are struggling to trust God's plan. Pray and ask Him to give you the faith to surrender your plans and trust in His purpose for your life.

Prayer: Father, thank You for Your plans to give me hope and a future. Help me trust in Your purpose for my life, even when it looks different from what I expected. Strengthen my faith in Your perfect plan. Amen.

March 13
Faith That Overcomes Obstacles

Verse: "Jesus looked at them and said, 'With man this is impossible, but with God all things are possible.'"

(Matthew 19:26, NIV)

Message: Faith allows us to overcome obstacles that seem impossible. When we rely on our own strength or resources, we may feel limited, but with God, nothing is impossible. Faith invites us to trust in God's power to do what we cannot. Whether we face challenges, limitations, or difficult circumstances, we can have faith that God is able to make a way, even when the situation feels hopeless.

In Matthew 19:26, Jesus reminds His disciples that what is impossible for man is possible for God. This truth applies to every area of our lives. There is no obstacle too great for God to overcome. Faith means trusting in God's ability to work beyond our limitations and believing that He can accomplish the impossible. When we place our faith in Him, we open the door for His power to move in our lives.

If you're facing an obstacle today that feels impossible, remember that with God, all things are possible. Trust in His power to overcome whatever challenges you face.

Call to Action: Reflect on an obstacle you're currently facing. Bring it to God in prayer, asking Him to move in ways that only He can. Trust that He is able to do the impossible in your life.

Prayer: Lord, thank You for reminding me that with You, all things are possible. Help me trust in Your power to overcome the obstacles in my life, and give me the faith to believe in the impossible. Amen.

March 14

Faith That Sees Beyond the Present

Verse: "For I consider that our present sufferings are not worth comparing with the glory that will be revealed in us."

(Romans 8:18, NIV)

Message: Faith helps us see beyond the present moment and focus on the glory that is yet to come. Life often brings suffering, hardship, and pain, but these are not the final word. Faith teaches us to look forward to the glory that God will reveal in us, both in this life and in eternity. No matter what we are going through, the hope of God's promises gives us strength to endure and a reason to persevere.

In Romans 8:18, Paul encourages believers to keep an eternal perspective. The suffering we experience now is temporary, but the glory that awaits us in Christ is eternal. This doesn't minimize our pain, but it gives us hope in the midst of it. Faith allows us to endure suffering because we know that something far greater is coming. The promises of God are a light that guides us through dark times, reminding us that His glory will ultimately be revealed.

If you're going through a difficult season, keep your eyes on the glory that is to come. Trust that God is working in and through your suffering, and that His promises will be fulfilled.

Call to Action: Reflect on the eternal promises of God. Let them give you strength and hope as you navigate your current challenges, trusting that the glory that awaits is far greater than any present suffering.

Prayer: Father, thank You for the hope of the glory that will be revealed in me. Help me keep an eternal perspective and trust that my present suffering is temporary compared to the eternal promises You have for me. Amen.

March 15
Faith That Produces Action

Verse: *"As the body without the spirit is dead, so faith without deeds is dead."*

(James 2:26, NIV)

Message: True faith produces action. It's not enough to simply believe in God or trust in His promises—our faith should be evident in the way we live. Faith without action is incomplete. When we truly trust in God, our lives will reflect that trust through the choices we make, the way we treat others, and the steps we take in obedience to His Word.

In James 2:26, we are reminded that faith without deeds is dead. This doesn't mean that we earn our salvation through works, but that genuine faith naturally leads to action. Our faith in God should inspire us to love others, serve those in need, and live out the teachings of Jesus in practical ways. Faith that produces action is alive and active, making a difference in our lives and the lives of those around us.

Today, let your faith move you to action. Ask God to show you how you can live out your faith in tangible ways, serving others and reflecting His love in everything you do.

Call to Action: Reflect on how your faith is producing action in your life. Pray and ask God to help you live out your faith through deeds that reflect His love and truth.

Prayer: Lord, thank You for the gift of faith. Help me live out my faith in action, serving others and walking in obedience to Your Word. Let my life be a reflection of the faith I have in You. Amen.

March 16
Faith That Trusts in God's Strength

Verse: *"But those who hope in the Lord will renew their strength. They will soar on wings like eagles; they will run and not grow weary, they will walk and not be faint."*

(Isaiah 40:31, NIV)

Message: Faith teaches us to trust in God's strength rather than our own. When we place our hope in the Lord, He renews our strength. Life can often make us feel weary or overwhelmed, but God's power never runs out. As we rely on Him, we are given the strength to keep moving forward, even when we feel weak. Faith allows us to draw from God's endless supply of strength, enabling us to soar like eagles and persevere through life's challenges.

Isaiah 40:31 reminds us that when we hope in the Lord, we are not limited by our own strength. God's strength is more than enough to sustain us, and He promises to renew us when we feel worn down. Faith is trusting that God's strength is available to us at all times. When we rely on His power rather than our own, we are able to run without growing weary and walk without fainting, knowing that He is carrying us.

If you are feeling weary today, put your hope in the Lord and trust that He will renew your strength. Lean on His power and allow Him to sustain you in every situation.

Call to Action: Reflect on an area of your life where you need to rely on God's strength. Pray and ask God to renew your strength and help you trust in His power rather than your own.

Prayer: Lord, thank You for being my source of strength. Help me place my hope in You and trust in Your power to sustain me. Renew my strength today, and give me the endurance to keep moving forward in faith. Amen.

March 17
Faith That Trusts in God's Protection

Verse: *"The Lord is my light and my salvation—whom shall I fear? The Lord is the stronghold of my life—of whom shall I be afraid?"*

(Psalm 27:1, NIV)

Message: Faith gives us the confidence to trust in God's protection. When the Lord is our light and our salvation, we have no reason to fear. He is the stronghold of our lives, our refuge and defender. No matter what dangers or threats we may face, God's protection surrounds us, and we can trust that He is watching over us at all times. Faith in God's protection means that we don't have to live in fear—we can rest in the assurance that He is with us, shielding us from harm.

In Psalm 27:1, David declares his trust in God's protection. His confidence wasn't in his own abilities but in the power and strength of the Lord. This same confidence is available to us. Faith allows us to face life's uncertainties without fear because we know that God is our protector. He is our stronghold, and nothing can come against us without first passing through His hands.

If fear is creeping into your heart today, remember that the Lord is your stronghold. Trust in His protection and live confidently, knowing that He is always with you.

Call to Action: Reflect on an area where you are struggling with fear. Bring it to God in prayer, asking Him to help you trust in His protection and live with confidence in His care.

Prayer: Father, thank You for being my protector and stronghold. Help me trust in Your protection and live without fear, knowing that You are always with me, shielding me from harm. Amen.

March 18
Faith That Trusts in God's Guidance

Verse: *"Trust in the Lord with all your heart and lean not on your own understanding; in all your ways submit to Him, and He will make your paths straight."*

(Proverbs 3:5-6, NIV)

Message: Faith means trusting in God's guidance, even when we don't fully understand the path ahead. Proverbs 3:5-6 encourages us to trust the Lord with all our hearts, not relying on our own understanding. God's wisdom is far greater than ours, and when we submit to His guidance, He promises to make our paths straight. Faith involves letting go of our need to control every detail and trusting that God is directing our steps.

In Proverbs 3, we are reminded that when we acknowledge God in all our ways, He will guide us and make our paths clear. This doesn't mean the journey will always be easy, but it does mean that God's direction is always right. Walking by faith means trusting that God knows the best way forward, even when we can't see the full picture. When we submit our plans to Him, He leads us on the path that leads to life and blessing.

If you're unsure of the direction to take in your life, trust in God's guidance. Submit your plans to Him, and have faith that He is leading you on the path that is best for you.

Call to Action: Reflect on a decision or direction you are unsure of. Bring it to God in prayer, asking for His guidance, and trust that He will make your path straight.

Prayer: Lord, thank You for Your wisdom and guidance. Help me trust in You with all my heart and lean not on my own understanding. Lead me on the right path and give me the faith to follow Your direction. Amen.

March 19
Faith That Trusts in God's Promises

Verse: *"Let us hold unswervingly to the hope we profess, for He who promised is faithful."*

(Hebrews 10:23, NIV)

Message: Faith holds tightly to God's promises, knowing that He is faithful to fulfill every word He has spoken. When life is uncertain, when challenges arise, and when we face delays, we can stand firm in the hope we have in God's promises. His faithfulness is unchanging, and He will never break a single promise He has made. Faith means trusting that God will do what He says, even when the timing or the outcome doesn't look as we expect.

Hebrews 10:23 encourages us to hold unswervingly to our hope in God's promises. This means that no matter what comes our way, we can trust that God will keep His word. His faithfulness never wavers, and His promises are true. Faith allows us to cling to hope in every season of life, trusting that God is working all things together for our good, just as He promised.

Today, hold on tightly to the promises of God. Trust that He is faithful, and that in His perfect timing, He will fulfill every promise He has made.

Call to Action: Reflect on a promise from God's Word that you are holding onto. Spend time in prayer, asking God to strengthen your faith and help you trust in His faithfulness to fulfill that promise.

Prayer: Father, thank You for Your faithfulness to keep every promise. Help me hold unswervingly to the hope I have in You, trusting that You are always true to Your Word. Strengthen my faith as I wait for Your promises to be fulfilled. Amen.

March 20
Faith That Trusts God's Love

Verse: *"And so we know and rely on the love God has for us. God is love. Whoever lives in love lives in God, and God in them."*

(1 John 4:16, NIV)

Message: Faith is rooted in God's love. We are called to know and rely on the love that God has for us, trusting that His love never fails. God is love, and when we live in love, we live in God. This kind of faith is not just intellectual belief—it's a deep trust in the character of God as a loving Father who cares for us, protects us, and provides for us. Relying on God's love means that we trust Him with every part of our lives, knowing that His love is always working for our good.

In 1 John 4:16, we are reminded that God is love, and living in His love brings us into a close relationship with Him. Faith in God's love means that we don't have to fear or worry because we are held in the hands of a loving Father. His love is steadfast, and it is the foundation of our faith. When we rely on God's love, we can walk confidently through life, knowing that He is always with us, guiding us with His love.

If you're feeling uncertain or fearful, remember that God's love surrounds you. Trust in His love, and let it be the foundation of your faith and the source of your confidence.

Call to Action: Reflect on the ways God has shown His love for you. Spend time in prayer, thanking Him for His love, and ask Him to help you rely on that love in every area of your life.

Prayer: Lord, thank You for Your unfailing love. Help me rely on Your love in every situation, knowing that You are always with me. Let Your love be the foundation of my faith and my confidence. Amen.

March 21
Faith That Trusts God's Grace

Verse: "But He said to me, 'My grace is sufficient for you, for My power is made perfect in weakness.' Therefore I will boast all the more gladly about my weaknesses, so that Christ's power may rest on me."

(2 Corinthians 12:9, NIV)

Message: Faith trusts in God's grace, knowing that His power is perfected in our weakness. We often feel the pressure to be strong, but God's grace invites us to rest in His strength rather than our own. His grace is more than enough to carry us through every situation, and when we rely on it, we find that God's power shines through our weaknesses. Faith is not about having it all together—it's about trusting that God's grace is sufficient in every moment.

In 2 Corinthians 12:9, Paul shares the profound truth that God's grace is sufficient in all circumstances. God doesn't ask us to be perfect; He asks us to trust in His grace. When we recognize our own weakness, we make room for God's strength to work in us. Faith means relying on His grace every day, knowing that His power is made perfect in our weakness.

If you're feeling weak today, trust in God's grace. Know that His grace is more than enough to sustain you, and that His power is at work in your life, even in your weakest moments.

Call to Action: Reflect on an area of your life where you feel weak or inadequate. Bring it to God in prayer, asking Him to fill you with His grace and allow His power to work through your weakness.

Prayer: Lord, thank You for Your sufficient grace. Help me trust in Your strength, especially in my weakness. Let Your grace sustain me and Your power work through me in every situation. Amen.

March 22
Faith That Believes Without Seeing

Verse: *"Then Jesus told him, 'Because you have seen Me, you have believed; blessed are those who have not seen and yet have believed.'"*
(John 20:29, NIV)

Message: Faith is believing in God's promises even when we cannot see them. Jesus commended those who believe without seeing, highlighting the blessing that comes with trusting in what we cannot yet perceive with our eyes. Walking by faith means relying on God's Word and His character, trusting that He is at work even when we don't see immediate results. This kind of faith pleases God because it shows that we trust in Him rather than in our circumstances.

In John 20:29, Jesus speaks to Thomas, who needed to see physical evidence of the resurrection in order to believe. While Jesus graciously showed Thomas the scars in His hands, He declared a special blessing for those who believe without seeing. This is the faith we are called to—a faith that believes in God's promises, even when they are not yet visible. It's a trust that goes beyond what we can see and relies on the truth of who God is.

If you are waiting on a promise from God, choose to believe even when you can't see. Trust that God is faithful and that His promises will come to pass in His perfect timing.

Call to Action: Reflect on an area of your life where you need to believe without seeing. Ask God to strengthen your faith and help you trust in His promises, even when the outcome is not yet visible.

Prayer: Father, thank You for Your promises. Help me believe without seeing, trusting in Your Word and Your faithfulness. Strengthen my faith as I wait for Your promises to be fulfilled in my life. Amen.

March 23
Faith That Walks in Obedience

Verse: *"By faith Abraham, when called to go to a place he would later receive as his inheritance, obeyed and went, even though he did not know where he was going."*

(Hebrews 11:8, NIV)

Message: Faith leads to obedience, even when we don't fully understand the path ahead. Abraham is a powerful example of walking by faith, as he obeyed God's call without knowing where it would lead. This kind of faith requires trust in God's plan, even when we don't have all the details. Obedience is a demonstration of our faith—it shows that we trust God's direction more than our own understanding.

In Hebrews 11:8, we see that Abraham's faith was not passive—it was active and obedient. He followed God's call, even though the destination was unknown. This is the essence of walking by faith: stepping out in obedience, trusting that God knows the way, even when we don't. Faith means believing that God's plans are good, even when we can't see the full picture.

If God is calling you to step out in faith, take that step in obedience. Trust that He is leading you, and have faith that His plans for you are greater than you can imagine.

Call to Action: Reflect on an area where God is calling you to step out in obedience. Pray for the faith to trust Him and the courage to follow His direction, even when the path is unclear.

Prayer: Lord, thank You for Your guidance and direction. Help me walk in obedience, even when I don't know the full picture. Give me the faith to trust that Your plans are good and that You are leading me. Amen.

March 24
Faith That Waits on God

Verse: *"Wait for the Lord; be strong and take heart and wait for the Lord."*

(Psalm 27:14, NIV)

Message: Faith often requires waiting on God's timing. We live in a world that values immediacy, but God's timing is perfect, and it often involves waiting. Waiting on the Lord is not passive; it's an active trust in His plan and His timing. It's choosing to be strong and take heart, knowing that God is at work even when we can't see it. Waiting in faith is an act of surrender, trusting that God's timing is better than our own.

Psalm 27:14 encourages us to wait on the Lord with strength and courage. This kind of waiting is not filled with anxiety or frustration—it's filled with trust. Faith means believing that God is working behind the scenes, even when we don't have all the answers. When we wait on the Lord, we can take heart, knowing that He will fulfill His promises in the right time and in the right way.

If you're in a season of waiting, trust that God's timing is perfect. Be strong and take heart, knowing that the Lord is working on your behalf.

Call to Action: Reflect on an area of your life where you are waiting on God. Pray for the strength and courage to trust in His timing, and ask Him to help you wait with faith.

Prayer: Father, thank You for Your perfect timing. Help me wait on You with strength and courage, trusting that You are working behind the scenes and that Your timing is always best. Amen.

March 25
Faith That Overcomes Trials

Verse: "Consider it pure joy, my brothers and sisters, whenever you face trials of many kinds, because you know that the testing of your faith produces perseverance."

(James 1:2-3, NIV)

Message: Faith is strengthened through trials. James encourages us to consider it pure joy when we face difficulties because those trials test and refine our faith. It's not that the trials themselves are joyful, but that through them, our faith grows stronger. Trials teach us to trust in God more deeply and to rely on His strength rather than our own. Faith that has been tested through trials is resilient and produces perseverance, enabling us to endure and overcome.

In James 1:2-3, we are reminded that the testing of our faith produces perseverance. Trials are not meant to defeat us; they are opportunities for growth. When we face challenges, we have a choice—to allow them to weaken our faith or to use them as opportunities to grow in our trust in God. Faith that endures trials becomes stronger, and we are better equipped to face future challenges with confidence in God's faithfulness.

If you're facing a trial today, consider it an opportunity for your faith to grow. Trust that God is using this season to strengthen your perseverance and draw you closer to Him.

Call to Action: Reflect on a current or past trial in your life. Ask God to show you how this trial is strengthening your faith, and pray for the perseverance to continue trusting in Him through the challenge.

Prayer: Lord, thank You for the trials that refine and strengthen my faith. Help me see my challenges as opportunities to grow in perseverance, and give me the faith to trust in You through every trial. Amen.

March 26

Faith That Overcomes the World

Verse: *"For everyone born of God overcomes the world. This is the victory that has overcome the world, even our faith."*

(1 John 5:4, NIV)

Message: Faith in God gives us the power to overcome the world and all its challenges. As believers, we are not bound by the limitations of this world because we have victory in Christ. Faith is the key to this victory. Through faith, we are able to rise above the temptations, struggles, and fears that try to pull us down. It is through our trust in God's power and promises that we are able to live as overcomers.

In 1 John 5:4, John reminds us that our faith in Christ is the victory that overcomes the world. This victory is not just for eternity; it's for our daily lives. We are not meant to live in defeat or fear—we are called to live in the victory that Christ has already won for us. Faith enables us to walk in this victory, knowing that God has overcome every obstacle we face.

If you feel overwhelmed by the challenges of this world, remember that your faith gives you the victory. Trust in Christ's power to overcome, and walk confidently in the victory He has won for you.

Call to Action: Reflect on a current challenge or fear that feels overwhelming. Bring it to God in prayer, and declare by faith that you are an overcomer through Christ.

Prayer: Lord, thank You for the victory that I have through faith in Christ. Help me walk as an overcomer, trusting in Your power to overcome every challenge and temptation in this world. Amen.

March 27
Faith That Grows Through God's Word

Verse: *"Consequently, faith comes from hearing the message, and the message is heard through the word about Christ."*

(Romans 10:17, NIV)

Message: Faith grows as we immerse ourselves in God's Word. The more we hear and understand the message of Christ, the more our faith is strengthened. God's Word is not just information—it is living and active, able to transform our hearts and minds. By regularly reading and meditating on Scripture, we allow God's truth to take root in us, building our faith and helping us trust Him more fully.

Romans 10:17 teaches that faith comes from hearing the message of Christ. This means that our faith grows as we spend time in God's Word, listening to His promises and letting them shape our lives. When we face challenges, it's God's Word that reminds us of His faithfulness and gives us the strength to keep going. Faith is not something we muster on our own—it is cultivated through our relationship with God, especially as we engage with His Word.

If you want your faith to grow, spend time in God's Word. Let His truth fill your heart and mind, and watch as your trust in Him deepens.

Call to Action: Set aside time each day to read and meditate on God's Word. As you do, ask God to increase your faith and help you trust in His promises more fully.

Prayer: Father, thank You for the power of Your Word to grow my faith. Help me be diligent in reading and meditating on Scripture, allowing Your truth to shape my life and deepen my trust in You. Amen.

March 28
Faith That Trusts in God's Promises

Verse: "The Lord is faithful to all His promises and loving toward all He has made."

(Psalm 145:13, NIV)

Message: Faith means trusting that God will keep His promises. Throughout Scripture, we see that God is always faithful to fulfill what He has spoken. His promises are sure and unchanging, and He is loving toward everything He has created. Even when circumstances seem uncertain, we can trust that God will be true to His Word. Faith holds onto God's promises, knowing that He is faithful and will never fail.

In Psalm 145:13, we are reminded of God's faithfulness to His promises. This truth gives us confidence, even when we face challenges or delays. Faith is not about wishful thinking—it's about trusting that what God has promised, He will do. His love and faithfulness are the foundation of our hope, and we can stand firm in the knowledge that He will fulfill every promise He has made.

If you're waiting on God to fulfill a promise, trust in His faithfulness. Believe that He is true to His Word, and hold onto the hope that His promises will come to pass in His perfect timing.

Call to Action: Reflect on a promise from God's Word that you are holding onto. Pray and thank God for His faithfulness, and ask Him to help you trust in His promises, even in times of waiting.

Prayer: Lord, thank You for Your faithfulness to every promise. Help me trust in Your Word and hold onto the hope that You will fulfill what You have spoken. Strengthen my faith as I wait on You. Amen.

March 29
Faith That Moves Us to Action

Verse: *"Show me your faith without deeds, and I will show you my faith by my deeds."*

(James 2:18, NIV)

Message: Genuine faith moves us to action. Faith is not just something we believe—it is something we live out in our daily lives. James challenges us to show our faith through our actions, reminding us that faith without deeds is dead. True faith is active, showing itself in the way we love, serve, and live for God. When we have faith, it compels us to act, trusting that God will work through our obedience.

In James 2:18, we see that faith is demonstrated through our actions. It's not enough to say we have faith if our lives don't reflect it. Faith that pleases God is faith that leads to action—whether it's serving others, stepping out in obedience, or sharing the gospel. Our actions don't earn God's love, but they do reflect the depth of our trust in Him. Faith and action go hand in hand, and together, they make a powerful testimony of God's work in our lives.

Today, let your faith move you to action. Look for opportunities to serve, love, and step out in obedience, showing the world that your faith in God is real and alive.

Call to Action: Reflect on how your faith is being demonstrated in your actions. Ask God to show you areas where you can put your faith into practice, and take steps to live out your faith today.

Prayer: Father, thank You for the gift of faith. Help me live out my faith in action, showing the world that my trust in You is real. Guide me to opportunities where I can serve and love others in Your name. Amen.

March 30
Faith That Trusts in God's Provision

Verse: *"And my God will meet all your needs according to the riches of His glory in Christ Jesus."*

(Philippians 4:19, NIV)

Message: Faith trusts that God will provide for all our needs. Whether we are facing financial difficulties, emotional challenges, or spiritual drought, we can trust that God knows exactly what we need and will supply it from His abundant resources. His provision is not limited by our circumstances—He is able to meet every need according to His glorious riches in Christ Jesus.

Philippians 4:19 reminds us that God is a faithful provider. He sees every need in our lives, and He is more than able to meet those needs. Faith means trusting in God's provision, even when we don't see how it will happen. It means believing that God's resources are limitless and that He cares deeply for us, providing for us in His perfect timing and way.

If you are facing a need today, bring it to God in faith. Trust that He will provide for you according to His glorious riches, and rest in the assurance that He is your provider.

Call to Action: Reflect on a current need in your life. Bring it to God in prayer, asking Him to meet your need, and trust that He will provide in His perfect way.

Prayer: Lord, thank You for Your promise to meet all my needs. Help me trust in Your provision and believe that You will supply everything I need according to Your riches in Christ Jesus. Amen.

March 31
Faith That Endures to the End

Verse: *"Blessed is the one who perseveres under trial because, having stood the test, that person will receive the crown of life that the Lord has promised to those who love Him."*

(James 1:12, NIV)

Message: Faith endures to the end, even through trials and difficulties. James tells us that those who persevere under trial are blessed and will receive the crown of life. Trials test our faith, but they also strengthen it, helping us grow in perseverance and trust in God. Faith that endures is faith that holds onto God's promises, even when life is hard. It's a faith that looks beyond the present suffering to the eternal reward that awaits those who love God.

James 1:12 reminds us that trials are not the end of the story. For those who persevere in faith, there is a reward—the crown of life that God has promised. This eternal perspective helps us endure the challenges of life, knowing that our faith is being refined and strengthened. Faith that endures is faith that trusts in God's goodness, even when we can't see the outcome.

If you're going through a trial, keep persevering in faith. Trust that God is with you, strengthening you, and that there is a crown of life awaiting you as you endure to the end.

Call to Action: Reflect on a trial you are currently facing. Ask God for the strength to persevere, and trust that He will reward your faith with the crown of life.

Prayer: Lord, thank You for the promise of the crown of life. Help me endure in faith through every trial, trusting that You are with me and that You will reward my perseverance. Amen.

APRIL

TRUSTING GOD'S PLAN

April 1
God's Plan is Perfect

Verse*: "For I know the plans I have for you," declares the Lord, "plans to prosper you and not to harm you, plans to give you hope and a future."*

(Jeremiah 29:11, NIV)

Message: God's plan for your life is perfect. He knows every detail of your future, and His intentions are always for your good. Often, we might not understand why certain things happen or why certain doors close, but we can trust that God is working everything according to His divine plan. His plans are not to harm us, but to give us hope and a future, which means that whatever we face, we can trust that He is leading us toward His best for our lives.

Jeremiah 29:11 reminds us that even when life feels uncertain, God is sure of His plan for us. The Israelites were in exile when these words were spoken, facing great difficulty, yet God's promise was that His plans were good and full of hope. This same promise applies to us today. No matter what season of life you're in—whether a time of difficulty or success—God's plan is still working for your good, and His ultimate purpose is to bring you closer to Him.

If you're questioning the path you're on, trust that God's plan is perfect. Surrender your fears and anxieties to Him, knowing that His plan will always bring you hope and a future.

Call to Action: Reflect on an area of your life where you need to trust God's plan. Surrender your worries to Him and ask for peace as you trust in His perfect plan.

Prayer: Father, thank You for the promise that Your plans are always for my good. Help me trust in Your perfect plan, even when I don't understand my circumstances. Give me peace and hope as I walk in Your will. Amen.

April 2
Trusting God in the Waiting

Verse: *"Wait for the Lord; be strong and take heart and wait for the Lord."*

(Psalm 27:14, NIV)

Message: Waiting is often difficult, but it's an essential part of trusting God's plan. While we may want answers immediately, God's timing is perfect, and sometimes He asks us to wait as He prepares the way for us. Waiting is not passive—it's a time of strengthening our faith, learning to trust God more deeply, and allowing Him to work in ways we cannot see. In the waiting, God is shaping us, teaching us patience, and reminding us that His plans are worth waiting for.

In Psalm 27:14, David encourages us to "wait for the Lord," with strength and courage. Waiting on God doesn't mean we do nothing—it means we actively trust Him to bring about His plans in the right time. Whether you're waiting for direction, provision, or an answer to prayer, know that God is working in the waiting. His plan is still unfolding, and His timing is always perfect, even when it seems slow to us.

If you're in a season of waiting, be encouraged that God is working behind the scenes. Trust that His timing is perfect and that the waiting is part of His plan for your growth.

Call to Action: Reflect on a time when waiting felt difficult but God showed up in His perfect timing. Pray for patience and faith as you wait for His plan to unfold in your current circumstances.

Prayer: Lord, thank You for being with me in the waiting. Help me trust Your timing and have faith that Your plan is unfolding perfectly. Give me the strength to wait with hope and confidence in You. Amen.

April 3
Trusting God Through Uncertainty

Verse: "Trust in the Lord with all your heart and lean not on your own understanding; in all your ways submit to Him, and He will make your paths straight."

(Proverbs 3:5-6, NIV)

Message: Life often brings uncertainty, but God calls us to trust in Him with all our hearts. When we face situations we don't understand, we are tempted to lean on our own wisdom, but God invites us to trust in His greater understanding. He sees the bigger picture, and when we submit to His plan, He promises to make our paths straight. Faith means trusting in God's wisdom, even when we don't know what the future holds.

Proverbs 3:5-6 is a reminder that trusting God means surrendering our desire to control every detail. Instead of relying on our limited understanding, we can rest in the assurance that God is leading us. His ways are higher than ours, and His plans are always good. When we let go of our need for certainty and allow God to guide us, we find peace in knowing that He is directing our steps.

If you're facing uncertainty, choose to trust God's plan. Lean not on your own understanding, and submit your path to Him, knowing that He will lead you in the right direction.

Call to Action: Reflect on an area of your life where you feel uncertain. Pray for the strength to trust God with that uncertainty and ask Him to guide you on the right path.

Prayer: Father, thank You for Your guidance and wisdom. Help me trust in You with all my heart, especially in times of uncertainty. Lead me on the path that You have prepared for me, and give me peace as I trust in Your plan. Amen.

April 4
Trusting God in Seasons of Change

Verse: *"The Lord Himself goes before you and will be with you; He will never leave you nor forsake you. Do not be afraid; do not be discouraged."*

(Deuteronomy 31:8, NIV)

Message: Change can be unsettling, but God is always with us in seasons of transition. Whether you are entering a new chapter of life, starting a new job, or facing an unexpected change, you can trust that God has already gone ahead of you. He promises to be with you every step of the way and never to leave you. Knowing this allows us to face change with confidence, knowing that God's plan is unfolding even when things seem uncertain.

In Deuteronomy 31:8, God reassures Joshua and the Israelites that He will go before them as they enter the Promised Land. This same promise applies to us today—no matter what changes we face, God is already there, preparing the way for us. His presence is constant, and He will never leave us to navigate change alone. Trusting in God's plan during times of transition means believing that He is in control and that He will carry us through to the other side.

If you're going through a season of change, take comfort in knowing that God is with you. Trust that He has gone before you and that His plan is leading you into a future filled with hope.

Call to Action: Reflect on a recent or upcoming change in your life. Ask God to give you peace in the midst of that change and to help you trust that He is leading you.

Prayer: Lord, thank You for being with me in every season of change. Help me trust that You have gone before me and that You are guiding me through every transition. Give me the confidence to face change with faith in Your plan. Amen.

April 5
Trusting God's Plan in Difficult Times

> ***Verse***: *"And we know that in all things God works for the good of those who love Him, who have been called according to His purpose."*
>
> *(Romans 8:28, NIV)*

Message: Even in difficult times, God's plan is still at work. Life is filled with challenges, but God promises that He is working all things for the good of those who love Him. This doesn't mean we won't face hardship, but it means that God is using every circumstance to shape us and fulfill His purpose in our lives. Faith means trusting that God's plan is good, even when we can't see how things will work out.

Romans 8:28 is a powerful reminder that nothing in our lives is wasted. Every trial, every setback, and every challenge is part of God's greater plan for our good. His ways are higher than ours, and while we may not always understand why we go through difficult seasons, we can trust that God is working behind the scenes. He is turning everything around for our good, using even the hardest times to bring about His purpose in our lives.

If you're in a difficult season, trust that God's plan is still good. Surrender your worries and fears to Him, knowing that He is working all things for your good and His glory.

Call to Action: Reflect on a difficult time in your life when God worked things out for good. Spend time in prayer, thanking Him for His faithfulness and asking Him to help you trust His plan in your current situation.

Prayer: Father, thank You for working all things for my good, even in difficult times. Help me trust in Your plan, knowing that You are using every challenge to shape me and fulfill Your purpose in my life. Amen.

April 6
Trusting God's Plan When It's Unclear

Verse: "*Your word is a lamp for my feet, a light on my path.*"

(Psalm 119:105, NIV)

Message: Sometimes God's plan may seem unclear or uncertain, but He promises to guide us step by step. His Word is like a lamp for our feet, illuminating just enough for us to take the next step in faith. God may not reveal the entire plan all at once, but as we trust Him, He shows us the way forward, little by little. Walking by faith means trusting God even when the path ahead isn't fully visible, knowing that He will guide us where we need to go.

In Psalm 119:105, we are reminded that God's Word is our guide. Just as a lamp lights the way in the darkness, God's Word shines a light on our path, giving us the wisdom and direction we need. While we may want to see the whole journey laid out before us, God often asks us to trust Him with the next step. His guidance is always available through His Word, and as we follow Him, He leads us along the path He has prepared.

If you're feeling unsure about what's next in your life, trust that God is guiding you. Lean on His Word for wisdom, and take each step in faith, knowing that He is leading you forward.

Call to Action: Spend time reading God's Word today, asking Him to guide you through any areas of uncertainty. Trust that He will show you the next step in His plan.

Prayer: Father, thank You for Your Word that lights my path. Help me trust in Your guidance, even when I can't see the whole picture. Lead me step by step as I walk in faith, trusting in Your perfect plan. Amen.

April 7
Trusting God's Plan in Seasons of Change

Verse: *"There is a time for everything, and a season for every activity under the heavens."*

(Ecclesiastes 3:1, NIV)

Message: Life is full of different seasons, and God is sovereign over them all. Whether you are entering a season of growth, transition, or waiting, you can trust that God is working in each one. Every season has a purpose, and God uses each phase of our lives to teach us, grow us, and draw us closer to Him. Trusting God's plan means embracing the season you are in, knowing that He is using it for His glory and your good.

In Ecclesiastes 3:1, we are reminded that there is a time for everything under heaven. God is in control of the seasons of our lives, and He knows exactly what we need in each one. Whether you're in a time of joy or a time of challenge, trust that God's timing is perfect and that He is with you through every change. Seasons may shift, but God's presence and His plan for your life remain constant.

If you're going through a season of change, trust that God is in control. Embrace the lessons He is teaching you, and know that He is working all things together according to His perfect plan.

Call to Action: Reflect on the current season of your life. Ask God to help you trust His plan for this season and give you peace, knowing that He is using it for His purpose.

Prayer: Lord, thank You for being with me in every season. Help me trust in Your plan, whether I am in a season of growth, waiting, or change. Teach me what You want me to learn, and give me peace as I walk through each season with You. Amen.

April 8
Trusting God's Plan for Your Future

Verse: *"In their hearts humans plan their course, but the Lord establishes their steps."*

(Proverbs 16:9, NIV)

Message: We often make plans for our future, but ultimately, it is the Lord who directs our steps. While it's good to have dreams and goals, we must always submit them to God, trusting that His plan is greater than anything we could imagine. God's wisdom and foresight far exceed our own, and when we allow Him to guide our steps, we experience His perfect will for our lives. Trusting God's plan for the future means surrendering our desires and trusting that He will lead us in the right direction.

Proverbs 16:9 reminds us that while we may plan our course, it is God who establishes our steps. We don't have to worry about the future because God is already there, preparing the way for us. He knows the path we should take, and when we trust Him to guide us, we experience the peace that comes from walking in His will. God's plan for your future is good, and you can trust Him to lead you every step of the way.

If you're anxious about your future, trust that God is directing your steps. Submit your plans to Him and ask Him to guide you as you follow His plan for your life.

Call to Action: Reflect on your plans for the future. Surrender them to God in prayer, asking Him to establish your steps and lead you into His perfect plan for your life.

Prayer: Father, thank You for guiding my steps and establishing my path. Help me surrender my plans to You and trust in Your perfect will for my future. Lead me in the direction You want me to go, and give me peace as I trust in Your plan. Amen.

April 9
Trusting God's Plan in the Midst of Trials

Verse*: "Consider it pure joy, my brothers and sisters, whenever you face trials of many kinds, because you know that the testing of your faith produces perseverance."*

(James 1:2-3, NIV)

Message: Trials are a part of life, but even in the midst of difficulties, we can trust that God's plan is at work. James encourages us to consider it pure joy when we face trials, not because trials are enjoyable, but because they produce perseverance in us. God uses challenges to strengthen our faith, build our character, and draw us closer to Him. Trusting God's plan means believing that He is using every trial to refine us and bring us into a deeper relationship with Him.

In James 1:2-3, we are reminded that trials are not meaningless—they are opportunities for growth. God is not absent in our suffering; He is actively using it to shape us and strengthen our faith. When we trust God's plan in the midst of trials, we can endure with hope, knowing that He is working for our good and His glory. Our trials may test us, but they also produce perseverance, making us stronger in our faith.

If you are going through a trial, trust that God is using it for a greater purpose. Lean on Him for strength, and believe that He is working all things for your good.

Call to Action: Reflect on a current or past trial in your life. Pray for the strength to trust in God's plan during difficult times and ask Him to help you grow through the challenge.

Prayer: Lord, thank You for using every trial to strengthen my faith. Help me trust in Your plan, even when I face challenges, and give me the perseverance to endure with hope and faith in You. Amen.

April 10
Trusting God's Plan When You Don't Understand

Verse: *"As the heavens are higher than the earth, so are My ways higher than your ways and My thoughts than your thoughts."*
(Isaiah 55:9, NIV)

Message: God's ways are higher than ours, and there will be times when we don't fully understand His plan. Yet, even in those moments, we are called to trust in His wisdom and sovereignty. God sees the bigger picture, and His thoughts are far beyond what we can comprehend. Trusting in God's plan means accepting that we won't always understand why things happen the way they do, but we can have confidence that God is working for our good and His glory.

In Isaiah 55:9, God reminds us that His ways and thoughts are higher than ours. We may not always understand why certain things happen or why God leads us down specific paths, but we can trust that His wisdom is perfect. Faith is not about having all the answers; it's about trusting in the One who does. When we surrender our need to understand and instead place our trust in God's higher ways, we find peace in the midst of uncertainty.

If you're struggling to understand God's plan, trust that His ways are higher than yours. Surrender your need for answers, and rest in the assurance that He is in control.

Call to Action: Reflect on a situation where you don't understand God's plan. Surrender it to Him in prayer, trusting that His ways are higher and that He is working for your good.

Prayer: Father, thank You for Your wisdom that is far beyond my understanding. Help me trust in Your higher ways, even when I don't understand Your plan. Give me the faith to surrender my need for answers and to rest in Your perfect will. Amen.

April 11
Trusting God When the Path is Difficult

Verse: *"The righteous person may have many troubles, but the Lord delivers him from them all."*

(Psalm 34:19, NIV)

Message: Following God's plan does not mean life will always be easy. There will be challenges, hardships, and trials along the way, but we can trust that God is with us in every difficulty. Psalm 34:19 reminds us that though the righteous may face many troubles, God is faithful to deliver them. Trusting God's plan means that even when the path is difficult, we have the assurance that He will see us through every challenge.

David, the author of Psalm 34, experienced countless trials—fleeing from Saul, hiding in caves, and facing overwhelming enemies. Yet through it all, he trusted in God's deliverance. God doesn't promise that we won't face trouble, but He does promise to be with us and to bring us through it. We may not understand why the road is hard, but we can be confident that God's plan includes deliverance, strength, and ultimate victory over every difficulty we encounter.

If you're facing difficulties today, trust that God will deliver you. He is with you, and His plan will bring you through even the hardest challenges you face.

Call to Action: Reflect on a difficulty you are currently facing. Pray and ask God to give you the strength to trust in His deliverance, knowing that He is with you and will guide you through.

Prayer: Father, thank You for being with me in times of trouble. Help me trust in Your plan, even when the path is difficult. Give me the strength to endure, knowing that You will deliver me and guide me through every challenge. Amen.

April 12
Trusting God's Plan for Provision

Verse: *"And God is able to bless you abundantly, so that in all things at all times, having all that you need, you will abound in every good work."*

(2 Corinthians 9:8, NIV)

Message: God's plan for your life includes provision for everything you need. He is a generous and faithful provider, blessing you abundantly so that you can abound in every good work. Sometimes, we may worry about whether we will have enough—whether that's financially, emotionally, or spiritually—but God promises that He will provide what we need to fulfill His purpose. Trusting God's plan means resting in the knowledge that He knows your needs and will supply them according to His riches.

In 2 Corinthians 9:8, Paul assures believers that God is able to provide all that we need, at all times, in all things. This doesn't just refer to material provision but also includes strength, wisdom, and grace for the tasks He has called us to. We may not always understand how or when God's provision will come, but we can trust that it will come. His resources are limitless, and His blessings enable us to abound in every good work He has prepared for us.

If you're concerned about provision, trust that God's plan includes everything you need. Rely on His faithfulness, knowing that He will supply abundantly for every area of your life.

Call to Action: Reflect on an area of your life where you need God's provision. Surrender your worries to Him, and trust that He will provide what you need to fulfill His plan for you.

Prayer: Lord, thank You for being my provider. Help me trust in Your abundant provision, knowing that You will supply everything I need for the work You have called me to. Give me faith to rest in Your generosity and grace. Amen.

April 13
Trusting God's Plan When Doors Close

Verse: *"The heart of man plans his way, but the Lord establishes his steps."*

(Proverbs 16:9, NIV)

Message: Sometimes, trusting God's plan means accepting closed doors. We may have our own plans and ideas for how life should go, but God, in His wisdom, sometimes closes doors to guide us in a different direction. While it can be disappointing or confusing when things don't go as we hoped, we can trust that God is directing our steps. His closed doors are often a way of protecting us or preparing us for something better.

Proverbs 16:9 reminds us that while we may plan our way, it is ultimately the Lord who establishes our steps. When God closes a door, it is not because He is withholding good from us—it is because He has something better in mind. Trusting in His plan means believing that every closed door is part of His greater purpose for our lives. What may seem like a setback is often a divine redirection, guiding us toward His perfect will.

If a door has recently closed in your life, trust that God is guiding you toward something better. Have faith that He is establishing your steps and leading you in the direction He has planned for you.

Call to Action: Reflect on a door that has recently closed in your life. Ask God for peace and clarity as you trust that He is guiding you toward something better.

Prayer: Father, thank You for Your wisdom in directing my steps. Help me trust Your plan, even when doors close. Give me faith to believe that You are guiding me toward something greater, and help me rest in Your perfect will. Amen.

April 14
Trusting God's Timing

Verse: *"He has made everything beautiful in its time."*

(Ecclesiastes 3:11, NIV)

Message: God's timing is perfect, even when it feels slow to us. Trusting in His plan means trusting in His timing, knowing that He makes everything beautiful at the right moment. We often want things to happen quickly, but God works according to His divine schedule, which is always for our ultimate good. His timing may not align with our own desires, but it is always perfect.

In Ecclesiastes 3:11, we are reminded that God makes everything beautiful in its time. This verse encourages us to trust that God is working, even when we don't see immediate results. Whether you are waiting on a promise, a breakthrough, or a dream, know that God is orchestrating everything according to His perfect timing. He is never late, and His plan will unfold in a way that is far more beautiful than anything we could arrange on our own.

If you're struggling with waiting, trust in God's timing. He is never early or late—He is always on time, and He is making everything beautiful in its season.

Call to Action: Reflect on something you are waiting for in your life. Ask God for the patience to trust in His timing and the faith to believe that He is making everything beautiful in His time.

Prayer: Lord, thank You for Your perfect timing. Help me trust in Your plan, even when I'm waiting. Give me the patience and faith to believe that You are making everything beautiful in its time. Amen.

April 15
Trusting God's Plan for Healing

Verse: *"He heals the brokenhearted and binds up their wounds."*

(Psalm 147:3, NIV)

Message: God's plan includes healing—whether that's physical, emotional, or spiritual healing. He is the One who heals the brokenhearted and binds up our wounds. We live in a broken world, and each of us will experience pain, loss, or brokenness at some point. But God's desire is to bring healing to every area of our lives. Trusting His plan means believing that He is able to restore what is broken and heal what is wounded.

In Psalm 147:3, we are reminded that God is not distant from our pain. He sees our wounds and is actively working to bring healing. Whether you're dealing with grief, a broken relationship, or physical illness, trust that God's plan includes healing for you. His healing may come in ways we don't expect, but His promise is to be with us in our pain and to bring restoration to every broken part of our lives.

If you're in need of healing, trust that God is working to heal your heart, your body, and your soul. Believe that He is with you in your brokenness and that His plan includes complete restoration.

Call to Action: Reflect on an area of your life where you need healing. Bring it to God in prayer, asking for His healing touch, and trust that He is working to bring restoration.

Prayer: Father, thank You for being the Healer of my heart, soul, and body. Help me trust in Your plan for healing, and give me the faith to believe that You are restoring every broken area of my life. Amen.

April 16
Trusting God in the Unknown

Verse: *"When I am afraid, I put my trust in You."*
(Psalm 56:3, NIV)

Message: Life often leads us into the unknown, where we can feel uncertain and afraid. But in these moments, God invites us to trust in Him. He knows every detail of our journey, even when we do not. Trusting God's plan in the unknown requires us to lay down our fears and place our confidence in Him, knowing that He is guiding us, even when the path ahead is unclear. His plan is still good, even when we don't know what comes next.

David, the writer of Psalm 56, faced many unknowns and dangers, yet he consistently chose to place his trust in God. When fear rises, faith calls us to turn to God and rely on His wisdom and protection. God doesn't leave us to navigate the unknown alone; He is with us every step of the way, guiding us in ways we can't always see. Faith is trusting that God knows the end from the beginning and that we are safe in His hands.

If you are facing uncertainty, choose to trust God today. Bring your fears to Him and believe that His plan for you is sure, even when you can't see what's ahead.

Call to Action: Reflect on an area of your life where you feel uncertain or afraid. Surrender your fears to God in prayer and trust Him to guide you through the unknown.

Prayer: Lord, thank You for being with me in times of uncertainty. Help me trust in Your plan, even when I don't know what comes next. Give me faith to believe that You are guiding my steps and that Your plan for me is good. Amen.

April 17
Trusting God's Plan for Your Relationships

Verse: *"As iron sharpens iron, so one person sharpens another."*

(Proverbs 27:17, NIV)

Message: Relationships are an essential part of God's plan for our lives. Whether it's friendships, family, or marriage, God uses relationships to shape us, teach us, and help us grow in our faith. Proverbs 27:17 reminds us that as iron sharpens iron, so one person sharpens another. Trusting God's plan for your relationships means seeking His guidance in who you surround yourself with and how you invest in those relationships. He uses the people in our lives to refine us and to draw us closer to Him.

Throughout the Bible, we see how God uses relationships to fulfill His purposes. David had Jonathan as a loyal friend, Paul had Barnabas as a companion in ministry, and Jesus had His disciples to support Him during His time on earth. God's plan for your relationships is intentional, and He places people in your life for specific reasons. Trusting His plan means seeking relationships that encourage you to grow in faith and being open to the sharpening process that happens through community.

If you're seeking clarity in your relationships, trust that God has a plan. Ask Him to guide you in forming relationships that will help you grow and bring Him glory.

Call to Action: Reflect on the relationships in your life. Ask God to show you how you can invest in and nurture these relationships for His glory, and pray for wisdom in choosing those who will sharpen your faith.

Prayer: Father, thank You for the gift of relationships. Help me trust Your plan for the people in my life, and guide me in building relationships that strengthen my faith and bring You glory. Amen.

April 18
Trusting God's Plan for Your Purpose

Verse: *"For we are God's handiwork, created in Christ Jesus to do good works, which God prepared in advance for us to do."*

(Ephesians 2:10, NIV)

Message: God has a unique purpose for each of us. As His handiwork, we are created for good works that He prepared in advance for us to do. Trusting God's plan means believing that He has a purpose for your life that goes beyond your own plans and ambitions. He has created you with specific gifts, talents, and passions, all designed to fulfill His purpose for your life and bring glory to Him.

In Ephesians 2:10, Paul reminds us that we are God's workmanship, carefully crafted for a purpose. This means that God has already planned the good works He wants you to do, and He will equip you to accomplish them. Trusting God's plan for your purpose means seeking Him first in all things, allowing Him to guide you into the works He has prepared for you. It also means trusting that God's purpose is greater than your own and that He is leading you toward a future that brings Him glory.

If you're wondering about your purpose, trust that God has already prepared the good works He wants you to do. Seek Him for direction, and trust that He will lead you into the purpose He has for your life.

Call to Action: Reflect on the ways God has gifted and called you. Pray for clarity and trust as you seek to live out the purpose He has prepared for you.

Prayer: Lord, thank You for creating me with a purpose. Help me trust in Your plan for my life and seek You in all things. Guide me into the good works You have prepared for me, and let my life bring glory to You. Amen.

April 19
Trusting God's Plan in Times of Doubt

Verse: *"Immediately the boy's father exclaimed, 'I do believe; help me overcome my unbelief!'"*

(Mark 9:24, NIV)

Message: Faith is not always easy, and there are moments when doubt creeps in. Even when we trust God's plan, we may struggle with unbelief, wondering if things will really work out as He promises. In these moments, we can take comfort in knowing that we are not alone. In Mark 9:24, a father asks Jesus to help his son, but he also honestly admits his struggle with unbelief. Jesus responds with compassion, showing that even in our doubts, God is still faithful.

The father's cry in Mark 9 is something we can all relate to—believing but still struggling with doubts. Trusting God's plan in times of doubt means bringing our uncertainties to Him and asking for His help. God understands our struggles and is patient with us as we grow in faith. He invites us to come to Him, doubts and all, and trust that He is still working, even when we can't fully see the way forward.

If you are struggling with doubt, bring it to God in prayer. Trust that He is faithful, even when your faith feels weak, and ask Him to help you overcome your unbelief.

Call to Action: Reflect on an area where you are experiencing doubt. Bring it to God in prayer, asking Him to help you trust His plan and to strengthen your faith in the process.

Prayer: Lord, thank You for being patient with me in times of doubt. Help me trust in Your plan, even when I struggle with unbelief. Strengthen my faith and help me overcome any doubts that I have about Your goodness and Your promises. Amen.

April 20
Trusting God's Plan for Rest

Verse: *"Come to me, all you who are weary and burdened, and I will give you rest."*

(Matthew 11:28, NIV)

Message: Rest is a vital part of God's plan for our lives. In a world that glorifies busyness and constant activity, God invites us to find true rest in Him. Jesus extends a personal invitation in Matthew 11:28, calling the weary and burdened to come to Him for rest. Trusting God's plan for rest means acknowledging that we are not meant to carry the weight of life on our own. He offers us rest for our souls when we surrender our burdens to Him.

In Matthew 11, Jesus calls us to find rest in His presence. This rest is not just physical but also spiritual. It's a rest that refreshes our souls and restores our strength. When we trust in God's plan for rest, we recognize that it is not selfish or lazy to take time to recharge—it is essential. Rest is part of God's design, allowing us to be renewed in His presence and empowered to continue the work He has called us to do.

If you're feeling weary, trust in God's invitation to rest. Take time to be still before Him, knowing that He will restore your soul and renew your strength.

Call to Action: Take some time today to rest in God's presence. Surrender your burdens to Him in prayer and trust that He will give you the rest you need.

Prayer: Father, thank You for the gift of rest. Help me trust in Your plan for my life, which includes rest for my soul. Teach me to surrender my burdens to You and to find peace and restoration in Your presence. Amen.

April 21
Trusting God's Plan for Spiritual Growth

Verse: "But grow in the grace and knowledge of our Lord and Savior Jesus Christ. To Him be glory both now and forever! Amen."

(2 Peter 3:18, NIV)

Message: Spiritual growth is part of God's plan for our lives. He doesn't just save us and leave us as we are—He desires for us to grow in grace and knowledge of Jesus Christ. This growth comes through spending time in God's Word, prayer, and learning to walk in step with the Holy Spirit. Trusting God's plan means trusting that He is continually working in us to shape us more into the image of Christ, even through life's challenges.

In 2 Peter 3:18, Peter encourages believers to continue growing in grace and in the knowledge of Christ. This is not a one-time event but a lifelong journey. God uses various experiences, both joyful and difficult, to mature us in our faith. Trusting God's plan for spiritual growth means surrendering to His refining process and allowing Him to stretch us in ways that deepen our relationship with Him. Each season, whether easy or hard, has the potential to grow us closer to Christ if we remain open to what He is teaching us.

If you feel stagnant in your spiritual growth, ask God to renew your passion for knowing Him more. Trust that He is at work in your heart, shaping you daily through His grace.

Call to Action: Reflect on your spiritual growth journey. Ask God to help you grow deeper in your relationship with Christ, and seek His guidance in areas where you need to mature in your faith.

Prayer: Father, thank You for the privilege of growing in grace and knowledge of Jesus. Help me trust in Your plan for my spiritual growth and lead me into a deeper relationship with You each day. Amen.

April 22
Trusting God in Times of Change

Verse: *"I the Lord do not change. So you, the descendants of Jacob, are not destroyed."*

(Malachi 3:6, NIV)

Message: In a world that is constantly changing, we can trust that God remains the same. While life may shift in unexpected ways—through job changes, moves, or new seasons—God's character is steadfast. He is unchanging in His love, faithfulness, and goodness. Trusting God's plan means anchoring ourselves in His unchanging nature, even when everything else around us feels unstable.

In Malachi 3:6, God declares that He does not change. This truth gives us security in times of change because we know that the same God who was faithful in the past will continue to be faithful in the future. When life feels uncertain, we can trust that God's plan remains constant, rooted in His unchanging love for us. He is our rock, and He will guide us through every change with wisdom and grace.

If you're going through a season of change, trust that God is the same yesterday, today, and forever. His plan is secure, and He is with you through every transition.

Call to Action: Reflect on how God's unchanging nature has been a source of strength for you in times of change. Pray for faith to trust Him through whatever changes you are facing.

Prayer: Lord, thank You for being unchanging in a world of constant change. Help me trust in Your plan and Your steady hand, no matter what shifts in my life. Give me peace as I navigate new seasons, knowing that You are always the same. Amen.

April 23
Trusting God's Plan in Seasons of Waiting

Verse: *"The Lord is good to those whose hope is in Him, to the one who seeks Him; it is good to wait quietly for the salvation of the Lord."*

(Lamentations 3:25-26, NIV)

Message: Waiting can be one of the most challenging parts of trusting God's plan, but it is often in the waiting that our faith is strengthened the most. God uses seasons of waiting to refine us, teach us patience, and deepen our dependence on Him. Lamentations 3:25-26 reminds us that waiting for the Lord is good, and those who put their hope in Him will see His goodness in His perfect time.

The prophet Jeremiah, who wrote Lamentations, endured great suffering and uncertainty, yet he learned to trust in the goodness of God even in times of waiting. Trusting God's plan in seasons of waiting means believing that He is at work, even when we can't see immediate results. God's timing is always perfect, and He is never late. In the waiting, we grow closer to Him as we learn to trust His ways and surrender our own timelines.

If you are in a season of waiting, remember that God is good and faithful. Trust that His plan is unfolding in His perfect timing, and allow this time to deepen your relationship with Him.

Call to Action: Reflect on a time when you had to wait for God's timing. Pray for patience and faith as you wait on His plan to unfold, trusting that He is working for your good.

Prayer: Lord, thank You for the seasons of waiting that teach me to trust in Your timing. Help me wait with hope and faith, knowing that You are good and that Your plan is perfect. Amen.

April 24
Trusting God's Plan for Guidance

Verse: "Your word is a lamp for my feet, a light on my path."

(Psalm 119:105, NIV)

Message: God's Word is our guide in every step we take. When we trust in His plan, we allow His Word to direct our paths and give us clarity for the decisions we need to make. Whether we are facing a major life choice or simply navigating daily life, God's Word illuminates the way. Trusting God's plan means seeking His guidance through Scripture, knowing that He will provide the wisdom we need at the right time.

Psalm 119:105 reminds us that God's Word is a lamp for our feet and a light on our path. This means that God often reveals His plan step by step, giving us just enough light to move forward in faith. We may not see the whole picture, but as we trust in God's Word and follow His direction, He faithfully guides us on the right path. Trusting God's plan means relying on His wisdom and allowing His Word to shape our decisions.

If you're seeking guidance, turn to God's Word and trust that He will light your way. Trust that He will give you clarity and wisdom for every decision you face.

Call to Action: Spend time reading and meditating on God's Word today. Ask Him to guide you in the decisions you are facing, and trust that His Word will illuminate your path.

Prayer: Father, thank You for Your Word that guides me in every area of my life. Help me trust in Your plan and seek Your guidance through Scripture. Give me the wisdom I need for the decisions ahead, and light my path with Your truth. Amen.

April 25
Trusting God's Plan for Your Future

Verse: *"For I know the plans I have for you," declares the Lord, "plans to prosper you and not to harm you, plans to give you hope and a future."*

(Jeremiah 29:11, NIV)

Message: God's plan for your future is good. He knows every detail of your life and has designed a future filled with hope and purpose. While we may not always understand the twists and turns of life, we can trust that God's plan is always for our good. He is the author of our lives, and His plans are to prosper us and lead us into a future that reflects His glory. Trusting God's plan for the future means letting go of fear and worry and resting in the knowledge that He holds your future securely in His hands.

Jeremiah 29:11 is a promise that reminds us of God's faithfulness to His people, even in times of uncertainty. The Israelites were in exile when God spoke these words to them, yet He assured them that His plan was still for their good. This same promise applies to us today. No matter what circumstances you face, you can trust that God's plan for your future is full of hope. His purpose for your life is greater than anything you could imagine, and He is leading you toward His perfect plan.

If you're uncertain about the future, trust that God's plan is for your good. Surrender your fears and anxieties to Him, and rest in the assurance that He has a bright future prepared for you.

Call to Action: Reflect on any fears or worries you have about the future. Surrender them to God in prayer, and trust that He has a good and hopeful plan for your life.

Prayer: Lord, thank You for the promise that Your plans for me are good. Help me trust in Your plan for my future and let go of any fear or worry. Give me the faith to believe that You are leading me into a future filled with hope and purpose. Amen.

April 26
Trusting God's Plan for Peace

Verse: *"You will keep in perfect peace those whose minds are steadfast, because they trust in You."*

(Isaiah 26:3, NIV)

Message: True peace comes from trusting in God's plan. When we fix our minds on Him and trust in His goodness, He promises to keep us in perfect peace. Life can be filled with stress, anxiety, and uncertainty, but God offers us peace that transcends our circumstances. This peace is not based on the absence of problems, but on the presence of God. When we trust Him, He calms our hearts and minds, giving us peace that the world cannot offer.

In Isaiah 26:3, we are reminded that God's peace comes when we remain steadfast in our trust in Him. This means that even in the midst of chaos or difficult circumstances, we can experience the calm assurance that God is in control. Trusting in God's plan allows us to release our worries and rest in the peace that only He can provide. His peace guards our hearts and minds, helping us stay focused on His promises rather than our problems.

If you are feeling overwhelmed or anxious, trust that God's plan includes peace for you. Fix your mind on Him, and allow His perfect peace to guard your heart and mind today.

Call to Action: Reflect on areas in your life where you are lacking peace. Surrender those anxieties to God, and ask Him to fill your heart with His perfect peace as you trust in His plan.

Prayer: Lord, thank You for the promise of peace that comes from trusting in You. Help me fix my mind on You, and fill me with Your perfect peace, even in the midst of uncertainty. Amen.

April 27
Trusting God's Plan for Strength

Verse: *"But those who hope in the Lord will renew their strength. They will soar on wings like eagles; they will run and not grow weary, they will walk and not be faint."*

(Isaiah 40:31, NIV)

Message: When we trust in God's plan, He renews our strength. Life can be exhausting, and there are times when we feel weak and weary. But God promises that when we place our hope in Him, He will give us the strength we need to keep going. Trusting in His plan means depending on His power rather than our own. He gives us the endurance to run the race before us and the ability to walk through difficult seasons without growing faint.

Isaiah 40:31 is a beautiful promise of renewed strength for those who hope in the Lord. Like eagles that soar above the storms, God gives us the ability to rise above the challenges of life when we place our trust in Him. He doesn't promise that the road will always be easy, but He does promise to be our source of strength. When we trust in His plan, we find the endurance we need to keep moving forward, no matter how difficult the journey may be.

If you're feeling weary, trust that God will renew your strength. Place your hope in Him, and allow Him to give you the energy and perseverance to soar above the challenges you are facing.

Call to Action: Reflect on an area of your life where you feel weary or weak. Surrender it to God in prayer, asking Him to renew your strength and give you the endurance to keep going.

Prayer: Father, thank You for being the source of my strength. Help me trust in Your plan and rely on Your power to renew my strength. Give me the endurance to soar above the challenges I face, trusting that You are with me every step of the way. Amen.

April 28
Trusting God's Plan in Times of Testing

Verse: *"Consider it pure joy, my brothers and sisters, whenever you face trials of many kinds, because you know that the testing of your faith produces perseverance."*

(James 1:2-3, NIV)

Message: Trusting God's plan doesn't mean we won't face trials, but it does mean that those trials have a purpose. James encourages us to consider it pure joy when we face trials, not because the trials are enjoyable, but because they test our faith and produce perseverance. Every challenge we face is an opportunity for growth and spiritual maturity. Trusting in God's plan during times of testing means believing that He is refining our faith and building our endurance.

James 1:2-3 reminds us that trials are not meaningless—they serve a purpose in God's plan for our lives. They test our faith, strengthen our character, and produce perseverance. When we face difficulties, we can trust that God is using them to shape us into the people He has called us to be. He doesn't waste a single hardship, and through every test, He is working for our good.

If you are going through a trial, trust that God is using it to refine your faith. Lean on Him for strength, and believe that He is producing perseverance in you through every challenge.

Call to Action: Reflect on a trial you are currently facing. Ask God to help you see how He is using this season to test and strengthen your faith, and trust that He is working for your good.

Prayer: Lord, thank You for using every trial to refine my faith. Help me trust in Your plan during times of testing, knowing that You are producing perseverance in me. Strengthen my faith and help me endure with joy, even in the midst of challenges. Amen.

April 29
Trusting God's Plan for Joy

Verse: "The joy of the Lord is your strength."

(Nehemiah 8:10, NIV)

Message: True joy comes from trusting in God's plan. The joy of the Lord is not dependent on our circumstances—it is a deep, abiding joy that comes from knowing we are loved, cared for, and secure in God's hands. Nehemiah 8:10 reminds us that the joy of the Lord is our strength. When we trust in His plan, even in difficult seasons, we can experience a joy that strengthens us and carries us through life's challenges.

In the book of Nehemiah, the people of Israel were rebuilding their lives after exile, and they faced many difficulties. Yet in the midst of these challenges, they were reminded to find their strength in the joy of the Lord. This joy was not based on their circumstances but on the knowledge that God was with them and working for their good. Trusting in God's plan allows us to experience this same joy, knowing that He is faithful and that His plans for us are good.

If you're struggling to find joy, remember that the joy of the Lord is your strength. Trust in His plan, and allow His joy to fill your heart, even in difficult circumstances.

Call to Action: Reflect on how you can find joy in God, regardless of your circumstances. Spend time in prayer, asking God to fill you with His joy and to strengthen you through it.

Prayer: Father, thank You for the joy that comes from trusting in You. Help me find my strength in Your joy, even in difficult times. Fill my heart with Your joy and help me walk in the confidence of knowing that You are working for my good. Amen.

April 30
Trusting God's Plan for Your Future

Verse: *"Trust in the Lord with all your heart and lean not on your own understanding; in all your ways submit to Him, and He will make your paths straight."*

(Proverbs 3:5-6, NIV)

Message: Trusting God's plan for your future means surrendering your own understanding and relying on His wisdom. We may not always understand the path that God leads us on, but we can trust that He knows the way. Proverbs 3:5-6 encourages us to trust in the Lord with all our hearts and to submit our plans to Him. When we do this, He promises to make our paths straight, guiding us according to His perfect plan.

In Proverbs 3, we are reminded that our own understanding is limited, but God's wisdom is infinite. Trusting His plan means letting go of our desire to control the future and instead submitting our lives to His guidance. He knows the best path for us, and when we trust Him, we can walk in confidence, knowing that He is directing our steps. God's plan for our future is good, and when we trust in Him, He will lead us exactly where we need to go.

If you're unsure about the future, trust that God is leading you. Surrender your plans to Him, and believe that He will make your path straight as you trust in His wisdom.

Call to Action: Reflect on an area of your life where you need to trust God with your future. Submit it to Him in prayer, and trust that He is guiding you in the way you should go.

Prayer: Lord, thank You for Your wisdom and guidance. Help me trust in Your plan for my future and lean not on my own understanding. Lead me on the path You have prepared for me, and give me faith to follow where You lead. Amen.

May

The Power of Prayer

May 1
Prayer Changes Everything

Verse: *"The prayer of a righteous person is powerful and effective."*
(James 5:16, NIV)

Message: Prayer is not just a ritual or routine—it is a powerful tool that can change everything. When we pray, we are communicating directly with God, and He hears and responds. James 5:16 tells us that the prayer of a righteous person is powerful and effective, meaning that our prayers have the ability to impact our circumstances, bring about healing, and align our hearts with God's will. Prayer is a vital part of the Christian life because it invites God's power into every situation.

In the Bible, we see countless examples of how prayer changes things. From Elijah praying for rain and seeing it stop and start, to Hannah praying for a child and receiving Samuel, God shows us that prayer is powerful. Whether we are praying for healing, provision, or wisdom, we can trust that God hears us. While His answers may come in different forms, prayer always moves the hand of God. It is a reminder that He is intimately involved in our lives and that nothing is too small or too big to bring before Him in prayer.

If you are facing a challenge today, remember the power of prayer. Don't underestimate the impact of bringing your needs before God, and trust that He is working powerfully through your prayers.

Call to Action: Take a moment to reflect on a situation in your life that needs change. Bring it before God in prayer and believe that He is working powerfully through your faith.

Prayer: Lord, thank You for the gift of prayer. Help me trust in the power of prayer and believe that You are working in every situation I bring before You. Strengthen my faith as I pray, knowing that You hear me and that my prayers are powerful and effective. Amen.

May 2
Praying in Faith

Verse: *"Therefore I tell you, whatever you ask for in prayer, believe that you have received it, and it will be yours."*

(Mark 11:24, NIV)

Message: Prayer is rooted in faith. When we come before God in prayer, we are called to believe that He hears us and is able to answer. Mark 11:24 teaches us that when we pray, we should believe that we have already received what we ask for. This kind of faith-filled prayer requires us to trust in God's power and goodness, knowing that He can do far more than we could ever imagine. Faith is the foundation of powerful prayer, and when we pray with belief, we open the door for God to move in miraculous ways.

In Mark 11, Jesus is teaching His disciples about the importance of faith in prayer. He emphasizes that believing in God's ability to answer is key to receiving. This doesn't mean we get everything we ask for immediately, but it does mean that we trust God's plan and timing. Praying in faith means releasing our doubts and fully trusting that God is able to answer according to His will. Our faith is not in the outcome but in God Himself, who is faithful and capable of doing the impossible.

If you are praying for something today, pray with faith. Believe that God hears you and that He is able to answer in ways that are beyond what you can see.

Call to Action: Reflect on a prayer you've been lifting up to God. Ask Him to strengthen your faith as you wait for His answer, and trust that He is working in ways you may not yet see.

Prayer: Father, thank You for teaching me to pray with faith. Help me believe in Your power and goodness, trusting that You are able to answer my prayers. Strengthen my faith and help me trust in Your timing and plan. Amen.

May 3
Praying with Persistence

Verse: *"Then Jesus told His disciples a parable to show them that they should always pray and not give up."*
(Luke 18:1, NIV)

Message: Prayer requires persistence. Jesus taught His disciples the importance of praying continually and not giving up, even when the answer doesn't come right away. In Luke 18, Jesus shares a parable about a widow who persistently asked for justice, and eventually, her request was granted. This story illustrates the power of persistence in prayer. God invites us to keep coming to Him in prayer, trusting that He hears us and will answer in His perfect time.

The widow in Jesus' parable did not give up, even when it seemed like her request was being ignored. Her persistence paid off, and she received what she asked for. In the same way, we are called to persist in prayer, not losing heart when the answer doesn't come immediately. God values perseverance, and as we continue to pray, our faith grows stronger. Persistent prayer shows that we trust God enough to keep asking, seeking, and knocking, even when the answer seems delayed.

If you've been praying for something for a long time, don't give up. Keep coming before God with persistence, knowing that He hears every prayer and will answer in His perfect timing.

Call to Action: Think about a prayer that you've been persistent in lifting up to God. Ask Him for the strength to keep praying with faith, trusting that He is working behind the scenes.

Prayer: Lord, thank You for teaching me the importance of persistence in prayer. Help me keep praying and not give up, knowing that You hear every prayer and will answer in Your perfect time. Strengthen my faith as I continue to seek You. Amen.

May 4
The Power of Intercessory Prayer

Verse: *"I urge, then, first of all, that petitions, prayers, intercession, and thanksgiving be made for all people."*

(1 Timothy 2:1, NIV)

Message: Intercessory prayer is a powerful way to stand in the gap for others, lifting up their needs before God. When we pray for others, we are partnering with God in His work in their lives. Paul encourages Timothy to pray for all people, urging believers to engage in prayer not only for their own needs but also for the needs of others. Intercession is an act of love and faith, believing that God is able to move powerfully in the lives of those we pray for.

Throughout Scripture, we see examples of intercessory prayer. Moses prayed for the Israelites, asking God to spare them from judgment. Jesus interceded for His disciples, praying for their protection and unity. Intercession is a way we can show love to others and participate in God's plan for their lives. As we pray for others, we trust that God is working in their situations, even when we don't see immediate results.

If someone in your life needs prayer, take time today to lift them up before God. Trust that your prayers are making a difference, and believe that God is working in their life.

Call to Action: Think of someone who needs prayer and spend time interceding for them. Ask God to move powerfully in their life and trust that He hears your prayers for them.

Prayer: Father, thank You for the privilege of praying for others. Help me be faithful in intercessory prayer, lifting up those who need Your grace, healing, and provision. I trust that You are working in their lives as I pray. Amen.

May 5
Praying with Thanksgiving

Verse: *"Do not be anxious about anything, but in every situation, by prayer and petition, with thanksgiving, present your requests to God."*

(Philippians 4:6, NIV)

Message: Prayer and thanksgiving go hand in hand. Paul encourages us to present our requests to God with thanksgiving, even before we see the answer. When we approach God with a heart of gratitude, we acknowledge His goodness and faithfulness, trusting that He is already at work. Thanksgiving shifts our focus from our problems to God's provision, and it reminds us of all that He has already done in our lives.

In Philippians 4:6, Paul instructs us not to be anxious but to bring our needs before God with thanksgiving. This is a powerful way to combat worry—by focusing on God's faithfulness rather than our concerns. When we pray with thanksgiving, we express our confidence in God's ability to provide and care for us. It's an act of faith that declares, "God, I trust You, and I am grateful for what You are doing, even if I don't see it yet."

If you are feeling anxious, turn your worries into prayers and thank God for His faithfulness. Trust that He is working on your behalf, and let gratitude fill your heart as you pray.

Call to Action: Reflect on a situation that is causing you anxiety. Bring it before God in prayer, and thank Him for His faithfulness and provision, trusting that He is working even when you don't see the results yet.

Prayer: Lord, thank You for Your faithfulness in my life. Help me approach You in prayer with a heart full of thanksgiving, trusting that You are already at work in every situation. Calm my anxieties and fill my heart with peace as I pray with gratitude. Amen.

May 6
Praying for Wisdom

> ***Verse:*** *"If any of you lacks wisdom, you should ask God, who gives generously to all without finding fault, and it will be given to you."*
>
> *(James 1:5, NIV)*

Message: When we are faced with difficult decisions or feel uncertain about what to do, we can turn to God in prayer and ask for wisdom. James 1:5 promises that God will give wisdom generously to those who ask. This means that whenever we need guidance, God is ready and willing to provide the wisdom we need. We don't have to figure things out on our own—God invites us to seek Him in prayer, trusting that He will lead us in the right direction.

Solomon, the wisest man who ever lived, started his journey by asking God for wisdom. Instead of requesting wealth or power, Solomon prayed for discernment to govern God's people well. God answered his prayer by giving him extraordinary wisdom. In the same way, God delights in answering our prayers for wisdom. When we pray for wisdom, we acknowledge our dependence on God and open ourselves to His perfect guidance.

If you need wisdom today, bring your request to God in prayer. Trust that He will provide the guidance you need and lead you in the way you should go.

Call to Action: Reflect on an area of your life where you need wisdom. Bring it before God in prayer and trust that He will provide the insight and clarity you need.

Prayer: Father, thank You for Your promise to give wisdom generously to those who ask. I come before You now, seeking wisdom and guidance for the decisions I need to make. Lead me in Your ways, and give me the clarity I need to follow Your plan. Amen.

May 7
Praying with Confidence

Verse: *"This is the confidence we have in approaching God: that if we ask anything according to His will, He hears us."*

(1 John 5:14, NIV)

Message: When we pray according to God's will, we can approach Him with confidence, knowing that He hears us. Prayer is not just a wishful hope—it is a confident declaration of our trust in God's ability to act. 1 John 5:14 assures us that when we align our prayers with God's will, we can be sure that He hears and answers. This gives us boldness in our prayers, trusting that God is both willing and able to respond.

Jesus modeled this kind of confident prayer when He prayed in the Garden of Gethsemane, saying, "Not My will, but Yours be done." Even as He faced the cross, Jesus trusted His Father's will completely. When we pray with confidence in God's will, we surrender our desires and trust that God knows what is best for us. His plans are always good, and when we pray with this understanding, we can approach Him with boldness and assurance.

If you are struggling to pray with confidence, remember that God hears you. Align your heart with His will, and trust that He is working for your good, even in ways you cannot see.

Call to Action: Spend time in prayer today, asking God to align your heart with His will. Pray with confidence, trusting that He hears you and will answer according to His perfect plan.

Prayer: Lord, thank You for the confidence I can have in prayer. Help me align my prayers with Your will and trust that You hear me. Give me boldness in my prayers, knowing that You are always working for my good and Your glory. Amen.

May 8
Praying for Healing

> **Verse**: *"Is anyone among you sick? Let them call the elders of the church to pray over them and anoint them with oil in the name of the Lord. And the prayer offered in faith will make the sick person well; the Lord will raise them up."*
>
> *(James 5:14-15, NIV)*

Message: God calls us to pray for healing, both for ourselves and for others. James 5:14-15 teaches us that the prayer offered in faith can bring healing and restoration. While we may not always understand how or when healing comes, we can trust that God hears our prayers and is able to bring healing according to His will. Prayer is a powerful way to seek God's intervention in our physical, emotional, and spiritual health.

In the Gospels, we see many instances where Jesus healed the sick in response to faith-filled prayers. Whether it was the woman who touched the hem of His garment or the blind man who cried out for mercy, Jesus responded to their prayers with compassion and healing. Today, we are invited to pray in the same way, trusting that God is able to heal and restore. While the timing and method of healing are in His hands, we are called to pray in faith, believing that nothing is impossible for God.

If you or someone you know needs healing, lift that need to God in prayer. Trust that He is able to bring healing and restoration in His perfect way and timing.

Call to Action: Reflect on someone in your life who needs healing, whether physical, emotional, or spiritual. Spend time praying for them, asking God to bring His healing power into their life.

Prayer: Lord, thank You for Your power to heal. I come before You now, praying for healing for those who are sick and in need of restoration. I trust in Your ability to heal and ask that You bring wholeness and peace according to Your will. Amen.

May 9
Praying in the Spirit

Verse: *"And pray in the Spirit on all occasions with all kinds of prayers and requests. With this in mind, be alert and always keep on praying for all the Lord's people."*

(Ephesians 6:18, NIV)

Message: Praying in the Spirit means allowing the Holy Spirit to guide our prayers and align them with God's will. The Holy Spirit knows the deepest desires of our hearts and helps us pray in ways that we may not even have words for. Ephesians 6:18 encourages us to pray in the Spirit on all occasions, staying alert and persistent in our prayers. When we rely on the Holy Spirit in our prayer life, we are empowered to pray effectively and in line with God's heart.

Paul, who wrote Ephesians, understood the importance of prayer being guided by the Holy Spirit. The Spirit not only helps us pray but also intercedes for us when we don't know what to say (Romans 8:26). Praying in the Spirit involves sensitivity to the Spirit's leading, being open to praying beyond our own understanding. Whether we are praying in moments of worship, asking for guidance, or interceding for others, the Holy Spirit enables us to connect more deeply with God through prayer.

If you're unsure how to pray in certain situations, invite the Holy Spirit to guide your prayers. Trust that He will lead you and help you pray according to God's will.

Call to Action: Spend time in prayer today, asking the Holy Spirit to guide your prayers. Be sensitive to His leading as you pray for yourself and others, trusting that He is helping you pray according to God's will.

Prayer: Father, thank You for the gift of the Holy Spirit, who helps me pray. I ask that You guide my prayers by Your Spirit, aligning my heart with Your will. Lead me as I intercede for others, and help me pray in a way that honors You. Amen.

May 10
Praying for Peace

Verse: *"Do not be anxious about anything, but in every situation, by prayer and petition, with thanksgiving, present your requests to God. And the peace of God, which transcends all understanding, will guard your hearts and your minds in Christ Jesus."*

(Philippians 4:6-7, NIV)

Message: One of the greatest gifts we receive through prayer is peace. When we bring our anxieties and worries to God in prayer, He exchanges them for His peace. Philippians 4:6-7 tells us not to be anxious but to present our requests to God with thanksgiving, trusting that His peace will guard our hearts and minds. This peace is not based on circumstances but on the presence of God in our lives. It transcends all understanding and keeps us grounded in His love and faithfulness.

Throughout the Bible, we see how prayer brings peace to God's people. When Daniel faced the lion's den, he prayed and trusted God for protection, and God's peace sustained him. When Jesus faced the cross, He prayed in the Garden of Gethsemane, and despite the agony of the situation, He was strengthened to fulfill His mission. In the same way, prayer brings peace to our hearts as we trust God with every situation we face.

If you're feeling anxious or overwhelmed, bring your concerns to God in prayer. Trust that He will replace your anxiety with His perfect peace, guarding your heart and mind in Christ Jesus.

Call to Action: Reflect on an area of your life that is causing anxiety or worry. Bring it to God in prayer, and ask Him to fill you with His peace, trusting that He is in control.

Prayer: Lord, thank You for the peace that comes through prayer. I bring my anxieties and worries before You, trusting that You will guard my heart and mind with Your perfect peace. Help me rest in Your presence and know that You are in control of every situation. Amen.

May 11
Praying for Protection

Verse: *"The Lord will keep you from all harm—He will watch over your life; the Lord will watch over your coming and going both now and forevermore."*

(Psalm 121:7-8, NIV)

Message: Prayer is one of the most powerful ways we seek God's protection over our lives. Psalm 121:7-8 reminds us that God is our protector, watching over every aspect of our lives. Whether we are facing physical danger, spiritual attack, or emotional challenges, God promises to guard us. Through prayer, we ask for His covering and trust that He is our shield, keeping us safe from harm.

Throughout Scripture, we see examples of God's protection through prayer. Daniel was protected from the lions, Shadrach, Meshach, and Abednego were protected in the fiery furnace, and David was protected from Saul's pursuit. In all of these stories, God's protection was present because they trusted in His power and sought Him in prayer. Today, we can come to God and ask for His protection, knowing that He is watching over our lives at all times.

If you are seeking protection for yourself or someone you love, bring that need before God in prayer. Trust that He is your refuge and that He will watch over your coming and going, both now and forevermore.

Call to Action: Reflect on an area of your life where you need God's protection. Pray for His covering, asking Him to guard you and keep you safe in every situation.

Prayer: Lord, thank You for being my protector and my shield. I ask for Your protection over my life and the lives of my loved ones. Guard us from all harm, and watch over our coming and going. I trust in Your power to keep us safe. Amen.

May 12
Praying with Surrender

Verse*: "Not my will, but Yours be done."*

(Luke 22:42, NIV)

Message: True power in prayer comes when we surrender our will to God's will. In Luke 22:42, Jesus prays this powerful prayer of surrender in the Garden of Gethsemane, knowing the difficult path that lay ahead of Him. Jesus shows us that the heart of prayer is not just asking for what we want but submitting ourselves to God's greater plan. When we pray with surrender, we trust that God's will is better than our own, even when it requires sacrifice or challenges.

In the Garden, Jesus faced the ultimate test of surrender as He prepared to go to the cross. Yet, He trusted in the Father's plan and surrendered His will for the sake of God's greater purpose. This kind of surrender in prayer is not easy, but it is powerful. When we let go of our need to control and trust in God's plan, we experience the peace and power that come from aligning ourselves with His will. God's ways are higher than ours, and when we surrender to His will, we can trust that He is working for our good.

If you're struggling to surrender a specific area of your life to God, bring it before Him in prayer. Ask Him for the strength to trust in His will and the courage to follow where He leads.

Call to Action: Reflect on an area of your life where you need to surrender your will to God's will. Pray for the strength to let go and trust that His plan is greater than your own.

Prayer: Father, thank You for showing me the power of surrender through Jesus' example. Help me surrender my will to Yours, trusting that Your plan is better than mine. Give me the faith to follow where You lead, even when it's difficult. Amen.

May 13
Praying in Times of Fear

Verse: "When I am afraid, I put my trust in You."

(Psalm 56:3, NIV)

Message: Prayer is a powerful way to combat fear. When we face situations that cause us anxiety or fear, God invites us to bring those fears to Him in prayer. Psalm 56:3 teaches us to put our trust in God whenever we are afraid, knowing that He is our refuge and strength. Through prayer, we can shift our focus from our fears to the One who is greater than any fear we face.

David, who wrote Psalm 56, was no stranger to fear. He faced enemies, threats, and danger throughout his life, but he consistently chose to trust in God. Prayer was his way of turning his fears over to God and finding peace in the midst of uncertainty. When we pray in times of fear, we remind ourselves that God is in control and that He is with us. Our fears may not disappear immediately, but through prayer, we experience God's presence and peace, even in the most fearful situations.

If you are feeling afraid today, bring your fears to God in prayer. Trust that He is with you and that His presence is greater than any fear you face.

Call to Action: Think about a fear that is currently weighing on your heart. Bring it to God in prayer, asking Him to replace your fear with trust in His power and protection.

Prayer: Lord, thank You for being with me in times of fear. I bring my fears to You now, trusting that You are greater than any challenge I face. Help me put my trust in You, knowing that You are my refuge and strength. Amen.

May 14
Praying for Forgiveness

Verse: *"If we confess our sins, He is faithful and just and will forgive us our sins and purify us from all unrighteousness."*

(1 John 1:9, NIV)

Message: Prayer is the way we seek forgiveness and restoration with God. 1 John 1:9 reminds us that if we confess our sins to God, He is faithful and just to forgive us and cleanse us from all unrighteousness. God's forgiveness is a gift, freely given to those who come to Him in repentance. Through prayer, we confess our sins and receive the cleansing that only Jesus can provide.

In the Bible, we see many examples of people coming to God in prayer to seek forgiveness. David, after his sin with Bathsheba, prayed earnestly for God's forgiveness and restoration (Psalm 51). The tax collector in Jesus' parable prayed for mercy, and he went home justified. God is always ready to forgive those who come to Him with a repentant heart. When we pray for forgiveness, we experience the freedom that comes from being washed clean by God's grace.

If there is any sin weighing on your heart, bring it before God in prayer. Confess it to Him, and trust that He is faithful to forgive and cleanse you from all unrighteousness.

Call to Action: Spend time in prayer today, confessing any sins that may be weighing on your heart. Ask God for forgiveness and trust that He is faithful to cleanse you and restore you to righteousness.

Prayer: Father, thank You for Your promise of forgiveness. I confess my sins to You now, trusting in Your faithfulness to cleanse me from all unrighteousness. Help me walk in the freedom and forgiveness that You have given me through Jesus. Amen.

May 15
Praying for Courage

Verse: "Have I not commanded you? Be strong and courageous. Do not be afraid; do not be discouraged, for the Lord your God will be with you wherever you go."

(Joshua 1:9, NIV)

Message: Prayer empowers us with the courage we need to face life's challenges. In Joshua 1:9, God commands Joshua to be strong and courageous, reminding him that the Lord would be with him wherever he went. This same promise is available to us today. When we pray for courage, we invite God's strength into our lives, trusting that He is with us in every situation. Prayer gives us the boldness to step out in faith, knowing that God is by our side.

Joshua faced the daunting task of leading the Israelites into the Promised Land, but he relied on God's presence and strength to guide him. Through prayer, we can ask for the same courage and boldness to take on the tasks that God has called us to. Whether it's stepping into a new season, facing a difficult decision, or overcoming fear, we can trust that God is with us, giving us the courage we need to move forward.

If you need courage today, bring that request to God in prayer. Trust that He is with you, strengthening you for every challenge you face.

Call to Action: Reflect on an area of your life where you need courage. Pray for boldness and strength, trusting that God will empower you to face whatever lies ahead.

Prayer: Lord, thank You for the courage You give through Your presence. Help me be strong and courageous, knowing that You are with me wherever I go. Strengthen me for the challenges ahead, and help me step out in faith, trusting in Your power. Amen.

May 16
Praying for Guidance

Verse: "Trust in the Lord with all your heart and lean not on your own understanding; in all your ways submit to Him, and He will make your paths straight."

(Proverbs 3:5-6, NIV)

Message: One of the greatest blessings of prayer is the ability to seek God's guidance in every decision. Proverbs 3:5-6 encourages us to trust in the Lord with all our hearts and not rely on our own understanding. When we submit our plans to Him in prayer, He promises to direct our paths. Prayer invites God's wisdom into our lives, helping us make decisions that align with His will. Instead of being overwhelmed by choices, we can find peace in knowing that God is leading us.

In the Bible, we see examples of people who sought God's guidance through prayer. Moses prayed for direction as he led the Israelites, David prayed for guidance in battle, and the early church prayed for wisdom in spreading the gospel. Each time, God provided the direction they needed. Today, we can trust that God will guide us in the same way. Through prayer, we align our hearts with His and allow Him to direct our steps toward the path He has prepared for us.

If you are facing a decision or need direction, bring it to God in prayer. Trust that He will lead you and make your path clear as you submit your plans to Him.

Call to Action: Reflect on an area where you need guidance. Spend time in prayer, asking God to give you clarity and direction, and trust that He will make your path straight.

Prayer: Father, thank You for being my guide. I bring my plans and decisions before You, trusting that You will direct my path. Help me rely on Your wisdom, not my own, and give me the clarity I need to follow Your will. Amen.

May 17
Praying for Strength

Verse: *"I can do all this through Him who gives me strength."*
(Philippians 4:13, NIV)

Message: Life's challenges can often feel overwhelming, but through prayer, we tap into God's limitless strength. Philippians 4:13 reminds us that we can do all things through Christ, who strengthens us. This promise means that no matter what we face, God is with us, empowering us to endure, overcome, and succeed according to His will. Prayer is our way of receiving this strength and relying on God rather than on our own abilities.

Paul, the writer of Philippians, knew what it was like to face hardship—imprisonment, persecution, and challenges in ministry. Yet, through prayer and dependence on Christ, he found the strength to persevere. When we pray for strength, we are acknowledging our need for God's power in our lives. We are admitting that we cannot do it on our own but need His strength to sustain us. Prayer is where we exchange our weakness for God's strength, allowing Him to carry us through every difficulty.

If you're feeling weak or overwhelmed, pray for God's strength today. Trust that through Christ, you can do all things, and He will give you the power to overcome every challenge you face.

Call to Action: Reflect on an area of your life where you need strength. Bring it to God in prayer, asking for His strength to sustain you, and trust that He will empower you.

Prayer: Lord, thank You for the strength You provide through Christ. I bring my weakness to You now, asking for Your power to sustain me. Help me rely on Your strength in every challenge, trusting that You will enable me to do all things. Amen.

May 18
Praying with a Heart of Gratitude

Verse: *"Give thanks in all circumstances; for this is God's will for you in Christ Jesus."*

(1 Thessalonians 5:18, NIV)

Message: Gratitude is a powerful aspect of prayer. 1 Thessalonians 5:18 encourages us to give thanks in all circumstances, recognizing that gratitude aligns our hearts with God's will. When we pray with a heart of gratitude, we shift our focus from our problems to God's goodness. Gratitude reminds us that no matter what we are facing, God is faithful, and He is working for our good. Prayer filled with thanksgiving brings joy and peace, even in the midst of trials.

Paul wrote these words to the Thessalonians while facing persecution, yet he still urged them to give thanks in all circumstances. Gratitude in prayer is not about ignoring our struggles but about recognizing God's presence and provision in every situation. When we choose to thank God, even in difficult times, we are declaring our trust in His plan and His faithfulness. Gratitude transforms our perspective, helping us see God's hand at work, no matter the circumstances.

If you're struggling today, take time to thank God for His faithfulness. Pray with a heart of gratitude, and trust that He is working in every situation, even when you can't see it.

Call to Action: Spend time in prayer today, thanking God for the blessings in your life. Focus on His faithfulness, and allow gratitude to fill your heart, no matter your circumstances.

Prayer: Father, thank You for Your faithfulness and goodness in my life. Help me cultivate a heart of gratitude, even in difficult times. I choose to give thanks in all circumstances, trusting that You are working for my good and Your glory. Amen.

May 19
Praying for Others

Verse: "*And pray in the Spirit on all occasions with all kinds of prayers and requests. With this in mind, be alert and always keep on praying for all the Lord's people.*"

(Ephesians 6:18, NIV)

Message: Prayer is not only about our own needs but also about lifting up others in intercession. Ephesians 6:18 encourages us to pray on all occasions for all the Lord's people. When we pray for others, we are partnering with God in His work in their lives. Intercession is an act of love, where we bring the needs of others before God, trusting that He is able to move in their situations. Through prayer, we support and encourage others in their faith journeys.

Throughout Scripture, we see examples of people who prayed for others. Moses interceded for the Israelites, asking God to spare them from judgment. Paul constantly prayed for the churches he planted, asking God to strengthen and protect them. Jesus Himself prayed for His disciples and for all believers. We are called to follow this example, lifting up our brothers and sisters in Christ, knowing that our prayers make a difference in their lives.

If you know someone who is in need of prayer, take time today to intercede for them. Trust that God hears your prayers and is working in their lives in ways you may not see.

Call to Action: Think of someone who needs prayer today—whether it's a family member, friend, or fellow believer. Spend time interceding for them, asking God to move in their life and meet their needs.

Prayer: Lord, thank You for the privilege of praying for others. I lift up those in my life who need Your touch. Strengthen them, provide for them, and move in their situations according to Your will. Help me be faithful in intercession, trusting that You hear and respond to every prayer. Amen.

May 20
Praying for God's Will to Be Done

Verse*: "Your kingdom come, Your will be done, on earth as it is in heaven."*

(Matthew 6:10, NIV)

Message: One of the most important aspects of prayer is aligning ourselves with God's will. In the Lord's Prayer, Jesus teaches us to pray, "Your kingdom come, Your will be done," reminding us that prayer is about seeking God's will above our own. When we pray for God's will to be done, we surrender our desires and trust that His plan is better than anything we could imagine. Prayer is a powerful way to invite God's kingdom to work in our lives and in the world around us.

Jesus modeled this kind of prayer in the Garden of Gethsemane when He prayed, "Not My will, but Yours be done." Even though He knew the suffering that lay ahead, He trusted the Father's plan. When we pray for God's will to be done, we are acknowledging that His ways are higher than ours and that His plans are perfect. This kind of prayer requires faith and surrender, but it also brings peace, knowing that God's will is always for our good and His glory.

If you're facing a difficult decision or situation, pray for God's will to be done. Trust that His plan is perfect, and surrender your desires to His greater purpose.

Call to Action: Reflect on an area of your life where you need to surrender your will to God's. Pray for His will to be done, trusting that His plan is better than your own.

Prayer: Father, thank You for teaching me to pray for Your will to be done. Help me surrender my desires and trust in Your perfect plan. Let Your kingdom come and Your will be done in my life and in the world around me. Amen.

May 21
Praying in Times of Temptation

Verse: *"Watch and pray so that you will not fall into temptation. The spirit is willing, but the flesh is weak."*

(Matthew 26:41, NIV)

Message: Prayer is essential when we face temptation. Jesus warned His disciples to stay alert and pray so they wouldn't fall into temptation. He knew that while our spirits may be willing, our flesh is weak. Temptation can come in many forms, and without prayer, it's easy to fall into traps that lead us away from God's will. Through prayer, we ask for God's strength to resist temptation and walk in the Spirit rather than giving in to the desires of the flesh.

In the Garden of Gethsemane, Jesus urged His disciples to pray, knowing that they were about to face the greatest challenge of their faith. He understood the power of temptation and how easily we can fall when we rely on our own strength. Through prayer, we stay connected to God's power, which enables us to stand firm against temptation. Prayer keeps us alert, strengthens our resolve, and helps us resist the enemy's schemes.

If you are facing temptation, bring it to God in prayer. Ask Him for the strength to resist and for the wisdom to walk in His ways.

Call to Action: Reflect on an area where you are struggling with temptation. Pray for strength and ask God to help you resist and remain faithful to His Word.

Prayer: Lord, thank You for the strength You give to resist temptation. I ask for Your help in areas where I struggle, knowing that my flesh is weak but Your power is great. Help me stay alert and pray continually so that I may stand firm in Your will. Amen.

May 22
Praying for Provision

Verse: *"And my God will meet all your needs according to the riches of His glory in Christ Jesus."*

(Philippians 4:19, NIV)

Message: God promises to meet all our needs, and we can trust Him as our provider. Philippians 4:19 assures us that God will provide for us according to His glorious riches in Christ Jesus. Prayer is a way for us to bring our needs before God, trusting that He will provide in His time and way. Whether it's financial provision, emotional support, or spiritual strength, God is faithful to meet every need when we seek Him in prayer.

Throughout the Bible, we see how God provides for His people. He provided manna in the desert for the Israelites, oil for the widow, and daily bread for His disciples. Today, God continues to be our provider. Prayer is the way we acknowledge our dependence on Him and invite Him to supply everything we need. While His provision may come in unexpected ways, we can trust that God knows exactly what we need and when we need it.

If you have a need today, bring it to God in prayer. Trust that He will provide according to His riches in Christ, and thank Him for His faithfulness.

Call to Action: Reflect on a specific need in your life, whether physical, emotional, or spiritual. Bring it before God in prayer, trusting that He will provide according to His perfect plan.

Prayer: Father, thank You for being my provider. I bring my needs before You now, trusting that You will meet every need according to Your glorious riches in Christ Jesus. Help me trust in Your timing and Your provision in every area of my life. Amen.

May 23
Praying for Peace in the Storm

Verse: *"He got up, rebuked the wind and said to the waves, 'Quiet! Be still!' Then the wind died down and it was completely calm."*

(Mark 4:39, NIV)

Message: When we face storms in life, we can turn to Jesus, the One who calms the winds and the waves. In Mark 4:39, Jesus speaks to a violent storm and commands it to be still, bringing peace and calm to His fearful disciples. Prayer is our way of turning to Jesus in the midst of life's storms. He hears our cries for help and has the power to bring peace, even in the most chaotic situations.

In this story, the disciples were terrified by the storm, but Jesus was asleep in the boat, completely at peace. When they woke Him, He rebuked the storm and brought calm. This is a reminder that no matter how big the storm, Jesus is bigger. Through prayer, we invite His peace into our lives, trusting that He is in control. Even if the circumstances don't change right away, we can experience the peace that comes from knowing Jesus is with us in the storm.

If you're in the midst of a storm, turn to Jesus in prayer. Ask Him to speak peace over your situation, and trust that He is in control, no matter how strong the winds may be.

Call to Action: Reflect on a storm you are currently facing, whether physical, emotional, or spiritual. Bring it to Jesus in prayer, asking Him to calm your heart and bring peace to your situation.

Prayer: Lord, thank You for being the One who calms the storms in my life. I bring my fears and anxieties to You, trusting that You are in control. Speak peace over my situation, and help me find rest in Your presence, no matter what storms may come. Amen.

May 24
Praying for a Heart of Forgiveness

> **Verse:** *"And when you stand praying, if you hold anything against anyone, forgive them, so that your Father in heaven may forgive you your sins."*
>
> *(Mark 11:25, NIV)*

Message: Forgiveness is a key part of our prayer life. Jesus taught that when we pray, we should forgive others, just as God has forgiven us. Holding onto unforgiveness can hinder our prayers and block the flow of God's grace in our lives. Through prayer, we ask God to help us release any bitterness, anger, or resentment we may be holding onto. Forgiveness frees our hearts to experience God's love more fully and to walk in His peace.

In Mark 11:25, Jesus emphasizes the importance of forgiving others when we pray. Forgiveness is not always easy, but it is essential for our spiritual health. Just as we have been forgiven by God, we are called to extend that same forgiveness to others. Through prayer, we ask for God's help to forgive, knowing that forgiveness is a choice and a process. As we release others from the debt of offense, we experience the freedom that comes from living in God's grace.

If you are struggling to forgive someone, bring that situation to God in prayer. Ask Him to give you a heart of forgiveness and to help you release any bitterness or anger you may be holding.

Call to Action: Reflect on any area of your life where you may be holding onto unforgiveness. Spend time in prayer, asking God to help you forgive and release the situation into His hands.

Prayer: Father, thank You for the forgiveness You have extended to me. I bring my heart before You now, asking for Your help to forgive those who have wronged me. Help me release any bitterness, anger, or resentment, and fill my heart with Your love and grace. Amen.

May 25
Praying for Revival

Verse: *"If My people, who are called by My name, will humble themselves and pray and seek My face and turn from their wicked ways, then I will hear from heaven, and I will forgive their sin and will heal their land."*

(2 Chronicles 7:14, NIV)

Message: Revival begins with prayer. In 2 Chronicles 7:14, God promises that if His people humble themselves, pray, seek His face, and turn from their wicked ways, He will hear from heaven, forgive their sins, and heal their land. Revival starts in the hearts of God's people as we turn back to Him in prayer and repentance. When we seek God wholeheartedly, we invite His presence to move powerfully in our lives, our churches, and our communities.

Throughout history, we have seen revivals break out when God's people come together in prayer, seeking His face and asking for a fresh outpouring of His Spirit. Revival is not just a one-time event; it's a continual renewal of our hearts as we turn to God in repentance and prayer. As we pray for revival, we ask God to awaken our hearts, fill us with His Spirit, and bring transformation to our lives and the world around us.

If you are longing for revival in your heart, your church, or your community, spend time praying and seeking God. Ask Him to bring healing, renewal, and revival according to His will.

Call to Action: Reflect on your desire for revival in your life and community. Spend time in prayer, asking God to move powerfully and bring about renewal and transformation.

Prayer: Lord, thank You for Your promise to bring healing and revival when we humble ourselves and pray. I come before You now, seeking Your face and asking for a fresh outpouring of Your Spirit. Heal my heart, heal my community, and bring revival according to Your will. Amen.

May 26
Praying for Renewal

Verse: "Create in me a pure heart, O God, and renew a steadfast spirit within me."

(Psalm 51:10, NIV)

Message: Renewal begins with prayer. Psalm 51:10 is a heartfelt cry from David, asking God to cleanse him and renew his spirit after a time of personal failure. This verse reminds us that when we feel spiritually dry or distant from God, we can come to Him in prayer, asking for renewal and restoration. God is faithful to revive our hearts when we humbly seek His forgiveness and grace.

David's prayer in Psalm 51 came after he had sinned, and he realized his need for God's cleansing and renewal. In the same way, we can pray for spiritual renewal when we feel distant from God or weighed down by sin or fatigue. Through prayer, we ask God to renew our hearts, strengthen our spirits, and fill us afresh with His presence. Renewal happens as we surrender our hearts to God and allow Him to restore us.

If you feel in need of renewal, bring your heart to God in prayer. Ask Him to create in you a clean heart and renew a steadfast spirit, knowing that He is able to restore your soul.

Call to Action: Spend time in prayer, asking God to renew your heart and strengthen your spirit. Reflect on areas of your life where you need spiritual renewal and surrender them to Him.

Prayer: Father, thank You for Your renewing power. I ask that You create in me a pure heart and renew a steadfast spirit within me. Restore my joy and strengthen me to walk in Your ways. Amen.

May 27
Praying for Strength in Weakness

Verse: *"But He said to me, 'My grace is sufficient for you, for My power is made perfect in weakness.'"*

(2 Corinthians 12:9, NIV)

Message: God's power is made perfect in our weakness, and prayer is how we invite His strength into our lives. In 2 Corinthians 12:9, Paul shares how God reminded him that His grace is sufficient and that His power is most evident when we are weak. This truth encourages us to come to God in prayer, not hiding our weaknesses but embracing them, knowing that God's strength will carry us through. Prayer is where we acknowledge our limitations and invite God's unlimited power to work in us and through us.

Paul experienced many trials and hardships, yet he learned to rely on God's grace and strength rather than his own. When we feel weak—whether physically, emotionally, or spiritually—we can bring our weakness to God in prayer, trusting that He will give us the strength we need. His power is at work in our lives, especially when we are at our weakest. Prayer allows us to lean on God's strength and find the grace to endure whatever we are facing.

If you are feeling weak today, bring your weakness to God in prayer. Trust that His grace is sufficient and that His strength will carry you through.

Call to Action: Reflect on an area of your life where you feel weak or inadequate. Bring it to God in prayer, asking for His strength to sustain you and for His grace to empower you.

Prayer: Lord, thank You for Your grace that is sufficient for me. I bring my weakness to You, trusting that Your power is made perfect in my weakness. Strengthen me with Your grace, and help me rely on Your strength in every situation. Amen.

May 28
Praying for God's Presence

Verse: "The Lord replied, 'My Presence will go with you, and I will give you rest.'"

(Exodus 33:14, NIV)

Message: The presence of God is the most precious gift we can experience, and through prayer, we invite His presence into our lives. In Exodus 33:14, God reassured Moses that His presence would go with him and give him rest. This promise applies to us today as well. When we pray, we enter into God's presence, and it is in His presence that we find peace, rest, and the strength to face whatever lies ahead.

Moses knew that without God's presence, he could not lead the Israelites or fulfill God's calling on his life. He longed for the assurance that God would be with him every step of the way. In the same way, we need God's presence to guide us, comfort us, and strengthen us. Through prayer, we connect with God and experience the peace and rest that only His presence can provide. No matter what challenges we face, God's presence is the key to peace and rest.

If you long for a deeper experience of God's presence, take time to seek Him in prayer. Trust that as you draw near to Him, He will draw near to you, filling you with His peace and rest.

Call to Action: Spend time in quiet prayer today, inviting God's presence into your heart and life. Rest in His presence, knowing that He is with you and will give you peace.

Prayer: Lord, thank You for the gift of Your presence. I seek You today, asking for Your peace and rest to fill my heart. Help me draw near to You in prayer and experience the comfort and strength that comes from being in Your presence. Amen.

May 29
Praying for a Spirit of Unity

Verse: *"Make every effort to keep the unity of the Spirit through the bond of peace."*

(Ephesians 4:3, NIV)

Message: Prayer plays a vital role in maintaining unity within the body of Christ. Ephesians 4:3 calls us to make every effort to keep the unity of the Spirit through the bond of peace. When we pray for unity, we ask God to soften our hearts, help us forgive one another, and bring healing to relationships. Prayer fosters an environment of peace and unity, where believers can work together for God's kingdom.

The early church experienced the power of unity as they prayed together, shared life together, and served one another. This unity was not just a human effort—it was the work of the Holy Spirit. Through prayer, the Holy Spirit helps us maintain unity by cultivating love, patience, and forgiveness in our hearts. Unity is a reflection of God's heart, and as we pray for it, we experience the joy and strength that come from being united in Christ.

If there are divisions or tensions in your relationships or community, bring them to God in prayer. Ask Him to bring unity, peace, and healing, knowing that the Holy Spirit can restore what is broken.

Call to Action: Reflect on any areas in your life where unity is needed, whether in your family, church, or community. Pray for God to bring peace and unity, and ask for His guidance in fostering harmony.

Prayer: Father, thank You for the unity of the Spirit. I ask for Your help in maintaining peace and unity in my relationships and within the body of Christ. Soften my heart, help me forgive, and fill me with Your love as I work to build unity. Amen.

May 30
Praying for Boldness

Verse: *"After they prayed, the place where they were meeting was shaken. And they were all filled with the Holy Spirit and spoke the word of God boldly."*

(Acts 4:31, NIV)

Message: Prayer empowers us with boldness. In Acts 4:31, after the early Christians prayed, they were filled with the Holy Spirit and spoke the word of God boldly. Boldness is not about being loud or forceful—it's about having the confidence to speak the truth in love and to stand firm in our faith, even in the face of opposition. Prayer invites the Holy Spirit to fill us with boldness so that we can share the gospel and live out our faith courageously.

The early church faced persecution and threats, but through prayer, they were empowered to continue proclaiming the gospel. When we pray for boldness, we invite the Holy Spirit to give us the courage to live for Christ, even when it's difficult. Boldness comes from knowing that God is with us and that His Spirit is at work in us. Through prayer, we can overcome fear and speak God's truth with confidence and love.

If you are feeling hesitant or fearful in your faith, pray for boldness. Ask the Holy Spirit to fill you with courage and confidence to share the gospel and live out your faith boldly.

Call to Action: Reflect on areas of your life where you need boldness—whether in sharing your faith, standing for truth, or living out your convictions. Pray for the Holy Spirit to fill you with boldness and courage.

Prayer: Lord, thank You for the boldness that comes through the Holy Spirit. I ask that You fill me with courage and confidence to speak Your word and live out my faith. Help me stand firm in the truth, even in the face of opposition, and use me to make an impact for Your kingdom. Amen.

May 31
Praying for God's Will to Be Done

Verse: *"Your kingdom come, Your will be done, on earth as it is in heaven."*

(Matthew 6:10, NIV)

Message: The ultimate goal of prayer is to seek God's will and to align our hearts with His purpose. In the Lord's Prayer, Jesus taught us to pray for God's kingdom to come and His will to be done on earth as it is in heaven. This reminds us that prayer is not just about asking for our desires—it's about seeking God's will above all else. When we pray for His will to be done, we surrender our plans and desires to His perfect wisdom and trust that His ways are higher than ours.

Jesus demonstrated this surrender in the Garden of Gethsemane when He prayed, "Not My will, but Yours be done." Even in the face of suffering, Jesus trusted that the Father's will was best. Through prayer, we can learn to trust God's will for our lives, knowing that He is working all things for good. Praying for God's will to be done is an act of faith and surrender, trusting that His plan is better than anything we could imagine.

If you are struggling to understand God's will in a certain area, bring it to Him in prayer. Surrender your desires and ask for His will to be done, trusting that His plan is perfect.

Call to Action: Reflect on an area of your life where you need to surrender your will to God's. Pray for His will to be done and trust that His plan is greater than your own.

Prayer: Father, thank You for teaching me to pray for Your will to be done. Help me surrender my plans and desires to Your perfect will. I trust that Your ways are higher than mine, and I pray that Your kingdom come and Your will be done in my life and in the world around me. Amen.

June

Finding Peace in God's Presence

June 1
Peace That Surpasses Understanding

Verse: *"And the peace of God, which transcends all understanding, will guard your hearts and your minds in Christ Jesus."*

(Philippians 4:7, NIV)

Message: God's peace is not like the peace the world offers. It is a deep, abiding peace that surpasses all understanding, guarding our hearts and minds no matter what we face. When we turn to God in prayer and trust Him with our worries, He fills us with this supernatural peace that can calm even the most anxious heart. Finding peace in God's presence means trusting that He is in control, even when our circumstances seem chaotic or uncertain.

Paul wrote these words while imprisoned, facing trials and persecution. Yet, even in those difficult circumstances, he experienced the peace of God that guarded his heart and mind. This kind of peace is available to us as well when we choose to trust God and bring our concerns to Him in prayer. We may not always understand why things happen, but we can trust that God's peace will sustain us through every storm. His presence is our refuge, and His peace guards us from fear and anxiety.

If you are feeling overwhelmed, bring your concerns to God in prayer. Trust Him to fill you with peace that surpasses understanding, knowing that He is guarding your heart and mind.

Call to Action: Spend time in prayer, releasing any worries or anxieties to God. Ask Him to fill you with His peace, trusting that He is in control of every situation.

Prayer: Lord, thank You for the peace that surpasses all understanding. I bring my anxieties and concerns to You, trusting that You are in control. Fill my heart and mind with Your peace, and help me rest in Your presence. Amen.

June 2
Peace in the Midst of the Storm

Verse: *"He got up, rebuked the wind and said to the waves, 'Quiet! Be still!' Then the wind died down and it was completely calm."*

(Mark 4:39, NIV)

Message: When storms rage around us, we can find peace in God's presence. In Mark 4:39, Jesus calms the storm with a word, bringing peace and calm to His fearful disciples. This powerful moment shows us that no matter how strong the storms of life may be, Jesus has the authority to bring peace. When we turn to Him, we can experience that same calm and rest, even in the midst of life's most difficult moments.

The disciples were terrified of the storm, but Jesus was with them, asleep in the boat. His presence was a reminder that they had no reason to fear. In the same way, Jesus is with us in every storm, and His presence is our source of peace. We may still face challenges, but when we trust in Jesus and call on Him, He brings calm to our hearts. The winds and waves obey Him, and His peace can quiet our fears.

If you are going through a storm, bring it to Jesus in prayer. Trust Him to speak peace into your situation and calm your heart as you rest in His presence.

Call to Action: Reflect on a storm you are currently facing, whether physical, emotional, or spiritual. Bring it to Jesus in prayer, asking Him to calm your heart and bring peace to your situation.

Prayer: Lord, thank You for being the One who calms the storms in my life. I bring my fears and anxieties to You, trusting that You are in control. Speak peace over my situation, and help me rest in Your presence. Amen.

June 3

The Lord Is My Shepherd

Verse: *"The Lord is my shepherd, I lack nothing.*
He makes me lie down in green pastures, He leads me beside quiet waters,
He refreshes my soul."

(Psalm 23:1-3, NIV)

Message: Psalm 23 paints a beautiful picture of the peace that comes from knowing God as our Shepherd. He leads us beside quiet waters, provides for our needs, and refreshes our souls. Finding peace in God's presence means trusting Him to care for us, just as a shepherd cares for his sheep. When we allow God to lead us, we experience His provision, protection, and peace.

David, the author of Psalm 23, was a shepherd before becoming king, so he knew firsthand the care and attention that sheep require. Just as a shepherd guides and protects his flock, God leads us to places of rest and refreshment. He knows what we need and provides for us, body and soul. When we trust God as our Shepherd, we can rest in His presence, knowing that He is leading us to peace.

If you feel weary or in need of refreshment, turn to God in prayer. Trust Him to lead you beside quiet waters and to restore your soul as you rest in His presence.

Call to Action: Reflect on how God is your Shepherd, providing for your needs and leading you to places of peace. Spend time in prayer, asking Him to refresh your soul and guide you to rest.

Prayer: Father, thank You for being my Shepherd. I trust You to lead me beside quiet waters and to refresh my soul. Help me rest in Your presence and find peace, knowing that You are guiding me every step of the way. Amen.

June 4
Be Still and Know

Verse: *"He says, 'Be still, and know that I am God; I will be exalted among the nations, I will be exalted in the earth.'"*

(Psalm 46:10, NIV)

Message: In the busyness and noise of life, God calls us to be still and recognize His presence. Psalm 46:10 reminds us to pause, reflect, and acknowledge that God is in control. Finding peace in God's presence requires us to stop striving and rest in the knowledge that He is sovereign. When we quiet our hearts and focus on God, we experience His peace, even in the midst of uncertainty or chaos.

In the midst of battles and challenges, the psalmist invites us to be still and know that God is God. This is not about inactivity but about surrendering our need to control and trusting in God's power and presence. Being still before God allows us to hear His voice, receive His peace, and rest in the assurance that He is working all things for our good. When we trust in God's sovereignty, we can let go of anxiety and rest in His peace.

If you feel overwhelmed or anxious, take time to be still before God. Let go of the need to strive, and trust that He is in control.

Call to Action: Spend time in quiet reflection today, being still before God. Focus on His presence, and trust that He is at work, even when you can't see it.

Prayer: Lord, thank You for reminding me to be still and know that You are God. Help me quiet my heart and trust in Your sovereignty. I surrender my worries and concerns to You, knowing that You are in control and that Your peace will guard my heart. Amen.

June 5
God of Peace

Verse: *"Now may the Lord of peace Himself give you peace at all times and in every way. The Lord be with all of you."*

(2 Thessalonians 3:16, NIV)

Message: God is the source of true peace, and He gives us peace at all times and in every way. 2 Thessalonians 3:16 is a beautiful reminder that peace is not something we have to strive for—it is a gift from God. When we turn to Him in prayer and trust in His presence, He fills our hearts with peace that sustains us through every situation. No matter what we are facing, we can find peace in God because He is the God of peace.

Paul wrote this prayer of blessing to the Thessalonian church, encouraging them to trust in God's peace, even in the midst of challenges. This peace is not dependent on circumstances; it is rooted in God's unchanging character. When we trust in the Lord of peace, we experience His peace in every aspect of our lives. Whether we are going through trials or experiencing joy, God's peace is available to us, guarding our hearts and minds in Christ.

If you are seeking peace today, bring your heart before God in prayer. Trust that He is the God of peace and that He will give you peace at all times and in every way.

Call to Action: Reflect on God's role as the Lord of peace in your life. Spend time in prayer, asking Him to fill you with His peace, no matter your circumstances.

Prayer: Father, thank You for being the God of peace. I come before You now, asking for Your peace to fill my heart. Help me trust in You at all times and in every way, knowing that You are with me and that Your peace will sustain me. Amen.

June 6
Cast Your Cares on Him

Verse: *"Cast all your anxiety on Him because He cares for you."*

(1 Peter 5:7, NIV)

Message: God invites us to bring our anxieties and burdens to Him because He cares for us. In 1 Peter 5:7, we are reminded that we don't have to carry our worries alone. God's presence is where we can find peace by surrendering our anxieties to Him. When we choose to cast our cares on Him, we trust that He is big enough to handle every fear, every concern, and every burden we face. His care for us is deep and personal, and He wants us to experience the peace that comes from releasing our worries into His hands.

In the same way that a child trusts a loving parent to handle their fears and worries, we can trust our Heavenly Father. When we pray and give our burdens to God, we are acknowledging that He is in control and that we don't have to carry everything on our own. God's care for us is constant, and He is always ready to give us peace when we come to Him with our concerns. His presence is the place where we can find rest for our troubled hearts.

If you are feeling weighed down by anxiety or fear, bring your cares to God in prayer. Trust that He cares for you and that His presence will bring you peace as you surrender your worries to Him.

Call to Action: Take time to identify the specific worries or anxieties that are weighing on your heart. Bring them to God in prayer, casting them on Him and trusting in His care for you.

Prayer: Father, thank You for Your deep care for me. I cast my anxieties and burdens on You, trusting that You are in control. Help me find peace in Your presence as I release my worries into Your capable hands. Amen.

June 7
God's Presence Is Our Refuge

Verse: *"God is our refuge and strength, an ever-present help in trouble."*

(Psalm 46:1, NIV)

Message: In times of trouble, God's presence is our refuge. Psalm 46:1 reminds us that God is not only our source of strength but also our safe place, our refuge, when life feels overwhelming. When we feel threatened by difficulties, fear, or uncertainty, we can run to God and find shelter in His presence. His peace is available to us, even in the midst of life's most difficult circumstances, because He is always present, ready to help us in times of trouble.

The psalmist paints a picture of God as a fortress—a place of safety and protection. Just as people seek refuge in a stronghold during a storm, we can seek refuge in God's presence when the storms of life come. He is our ever-present help, always near and always available. When we turn to Him in prayer, we find peace, comfort, and strength to face whatever challenges lie ahead. His presence is a constant source of peace, even in the most troubling times.

If you are feeling overwhelmed by troubles or challenges, run to God in prayer. Find refuge in His presence, trusting that He will be your strength and help in times of need.

Call to Action: Reflect on areas of your life where you feel troubled or overwhelmed. Bring them to God in prayer, trusting that He is your refuge and strength, ready to help you.

Prayer: Lord, thank You for being my refuge and strength. I come to You now, seeking peace and comfort in Your presence. Help me trust that You are my ever-present help in times of trouble, and give me the strength to face each day with confidence in Your care. Amen.

June 8
Rest for the Weary

Verse: *"Come to me, all you who are weary and burdened, and I will give you rest."*

(Matthew 11:28, NIV)

Message: Jesus invites us to come to Him when we are weary and burdened, promising to give us rest. In Matthew 11:28, He offers us peace and rest in exchange for our weariness. Life can be exhausting, filled with burdens that weigh on our hearts and minds, but Jesus offers relief and refreshment in His presence. When we come to Him in prayer, we experience the rest that only He can give. His presence is where our souls find rest, and His peace renews our strength.

Jesus understands our weariness and invites us to lay our burdens at His feet. In Him, we find not only physical rest but also rest for our souls. When we are weary from carrying the weight of life's pressures, Jesus is the One who lifts that weight and gives us the peace that we so desperately need. His rest is a gift, and it is available to all who come to Him.

If you are feeling tired or weighed down, accept Jesus' invitation to come to Him in prayer. Lay your burdens at His feet and allow Him to give you the rest and peace that your soul needs.

Call to Action: Reflect on the burdens you are carrying today. Spend time in prayer, laying those burdens before Jesus and trusting Him to give you the rest and peace you need.

Prayer: Lord, thank You for inviting me to come to You when I am weary and burdened. I lay my burdens at Your feet now, trusting that You will give me rest. Help me experience the peace that comes from resting in Your presence. Amen.

June 9
His Peace Guards Our Hearts

Verse: *"And the peace of God, which transcends all understanding, will guard your hearts and your minds in Christ Jesus."*

(Philippians 4:7, NIV)

Message: The peace of God is not only a gift, but it is also a protective force that guards our hearts and minds. In Philippians 4:7, we are reminded that God's peace transcends all understanding, meaning it goes beyond what we can comprehend. This peace doesn't depend on our circumstances; it is rooted in Christ, and it guards us from fear, anxiety, and doubt. When we trust in God and rest in His presence, His peace acts as a shield around our hearts and minds, keeping us grounded in Him.

Paul, who wrote these words, knew what it meant to experience God's peace in the midst of difficult circumstances. From prison to persecution, Paul faced many trials, but through it all, he experienced the peace of God guarding his heart. This same peace is available to us today. When we bring our worries to God in prayer and trust in His care, His peace guards us, protecting our hearts and minds from the storms of life.

If you are struggling with anxiety or worry, turn to God in prayer. Trust that His peace will guard your heart and mind, keeping you safe and secure in Christ.

Call to Action: Spend time in prayer, bringing your worries and concerns to God. Ask Him to fill you with His peace and trust that it will guard your heart and mind from fear and anxiety.

Prayer: Father, thank You for the peace that guards my heart and mind. I bring my worries and concerns to You now, trusting that Your peace will protect me from fear and anxiety. Help me rest in the assurance that You are in control, and let Your peace fill my heart. Amen.

June 10
In His Presence, There Is Fullness of Joy

Verse: "*You make known to me the path of life; You will fill me with joy in Your presence, with eternal pleasures at Your right hand.*"

(Psalm 16:11, NIV)

Message: God's presence is not only a place of peace but also a place of joy. Psalm 16:11 reminds us that in God's presence, there is fullness of joy—joy that transcends our circumstances and fills our hearts with hope and delight. When we seek God's presence, we experience a deep sense of joy that can't be found anywhere else. This joy is a reflection of our relationship with God and the security we have in Him.

David, the author of this psalm, knew what it meant to find joy in God's presence. Despite facing challenges and difficulties, he found his greatest delight in being with God. This joy is not dependent on our external circumstances; it is a deep, abiding joy that comes from knowing we are loved, cared for, and guided by God. When we enter into God's presence, we experience the fullness of joy that comes from being in relationship with Him.

If you are feeling joyless or discouraged, seek God's presence in prayer. Trust that He will fill you with joy as you spend time with Him, and let His presence renew your heart with delight.

Call to Action: Reflect on the joy that comes from being in God's presence. Spend time in prayer, asking God to fill you with the fullness of joy that only He can provide.

Prayer: Lord, thank You for the joy that comes from being in Your presence. Fill my heart with joy as I seek You, and help me find my delight in You, no matter what I'm going through. Let Your presence renew my spirit and fill me with hope and peace. Amen.

June 11
Let the Peace of Christ Rule in Your Hearts

Verse: *"Let the peace of Christ rule in your hearts, since as members of one body you were called to peace. And be thankful."*

(Colossians 3:15, NIV)

Message: God calls us to let the peace of Christ rule in our hearts. This means allowing His peace to govern our thoughts, emotions, and decisions. When Christ's peace rules in our hearts, it shapes how we respond to difficult circumstances and guides us in how we interact with others. Instead of reacting with fear, frustration, or anxiety, we can choose to rest in the peace that comes from knowing Christ is in control. We are called to live in peace, not just for ourselves, but also to promote peace within the body of Christ.

Paul encourages the Colossians to let Christ's peace rule in their hearts, emphasizing that peace should be the defining characteristic of their lives. Just as a ruler governs a kingdom, Christ's peace should have authority over every area of our lives. When we are tempted to let worry or anger take over, we can stop and allow Christ's peace to reign instead. This peace comes from the assurance that God is with us and that He is working all things together for our good.

If you are struggling with unrest in your heart, invite Christ's peace to rule over your emotions and decisions. Trust Him to guide you in every situation and to lead you toward peace.

Call to Action: Reflect on an area of your life where you need Christ's peace to rule. Spend time in prayer, inviting His peace to govern your heart and guide your decisions.

Prayer: Lord, thank You for calling me to live in Your peace. I invite the peace of Christ to rule in my heart and guide my thoughts and actions. Help me trust in You, knowing that Your peace will lead me in the right direction. Amen.

June 12
Abide in His Presence

Verse: *"Remain in me, as I also remain in you. No branch can bear fruit by itself; it must remain in the vine. Neither can you bear fruit unless you remain in me."*

(John 15:4, NIV)

Message: Jesus calls us to abide in Him, to remain connected to His presence as a branch is connected to a vine. This abiding relationship is essential for our spiritual growth and peace. When we stay close to Jesus through prayer, reading His Word, and trusting Him in our daily lives, we experience the peace that comes from knowing we are deeply rooted in Him. We cannot bear spiritual fruit or find lasting peace apart from Him. Abiding in Christ is where we find our strength, our purpose, and our peace.

In John 15, Jesus explains that just as a branch cannot survive without being connected to the vine, we cannot thrive without remaining in Him. When we are disconnected from Christ, we lose the peace that comes from His presence. But when we abide in Him, we experience a sense of peace and purpose that carries us through every season of life. His presence sustains us, and through Him, we bear the fruit of peace, joy, and love.

If you are feeling disconnected or restless, take time to abide in Christ. Spend time in His Word and in prayer, allowing His presence to fill you with peace and strength.

Call to Action: Reflect on how you can remain more closely connected to Christ. Spend time abiding in His presence today, trusting that He will bring peace and fruitfulness to your life.

Prayer: Father, thank You for inviting me to abide in Your presence. Help me stay connected to You in every aspect of my life. Fill me with the peace that comes from remaining in You, and help me bear fruit that reflects Your love and peace to those around me. Amen.

June 13
Peace in God's Timing

Verse: *"He has made everything beautiful in its time."*
(Ecclesiastes 3:11, NIV)

Message: God's timing is perfect, and trusting in His timing brings peace. Ecclesiastes 3:11 reminds us that God makes everything beautiful in its time. This means that even when we don't understand why certain things happen or why we must wait for answers, we can trust that God is working according to His perfect plan. When we trust God's timing, we find peace in the knowledge that He is in control and that everything will happen at the right moment.

In life, it's easy to become anxious when things don't happen as quickly as we'd like, but God's ways and timing are higher than ours. Abraham and Sarah had to wait many years for the fulfillment of God's promise, yet in the end, God made everything beautiful in His time. The same is true for us—God's timing is always for our good, even when it requires patience. When we release our need for control and trust in God's plan, we experience peace in the waiting.

If you are waiting for something in your life, trust in God's perfect timing. Rest in the assurance that He is making everything beautiful, and His peace will guard your heart as you wait.

Call to Action: Reflect on an area where you are waiting for God's timing. Pray for peace and patience as you trust that He is making everything beautiful in His time.

Prayer: Lord, thank You for Your perfect timing. Help me trust in Your plan and find peace in the waiting. I know You are making everything beautiful in Your time, and I ask for patience and faith as I wait for Your promises to unfold. Amen.

June 14
Seeking Peace Through Prayer

Verse: "Do not be anxious about anything, but in every situation, by prayer and petition, with thanksgiving, present your requests to God."

(Philippians 4:6, NIV)

Message: Prayer is the pathway to peace. Philippians 4:6 encourages us to bring every situation before God in prayer, trusting that He hears us and is working on our behalf. When we feel anxious or overwhelmed, prayer is how we release those feelings to God and exchange them for His peace. In every circumstance, whether big or small, God invites us to come to Him in prayer, with thanksgiving, and trust that He will take care of us.

Paul knew what it meant to face difficult circumstances, yet he chose to bring his worries to God in prayer. Through prayer, we align our hearts with God's will and find peace that transcends our understanding. Prayer is not just about asking for things; it's about drawing closer to God, acknowledging our dependence on Him, and trusting that He is in control. When we pray with a heart of thanksgiving, we focus on God's goodness, which brings peace to our hearts.

If you are feeling anxious today, take time to pray and present your requests to God. Trust that He is listening and will fill your heart with peace as you release your worries to Him.

Call to Action: Spend time in prayer today, bringing your worries and concerns to God. Thank Him for His faithfulness, and trust that His peace will guard your heart and mind.

Prayer: Father, thank You for the peace that comes through prayer. I bring my anxieties and concerns before You, trusting that You are in control. Fill my heart with Your peace as I pray, and help me rest in the assurance of Your faithfulness. Amen.

June 15
Peace That Comes From Trusting God

Verse: *"You will keep in perfect peace those whose minds are steadfast, because they trust in You."*

(Isaiah 26:3, NIV)

Message: Perfect peace comes from trusting God completely. Isaiah 26:3 promises that God will keep in perfect peace those who keep their minds steadfastly focused on Him. When we trust God, our hearts are at rest, knowing that He is sovereign and that His plans are for our good. Trusting God means relying on His promises and believing that He is working everything for our good, even when we can't see it. This trust leads to peace that cannot be shaken by life's circumstances.

Isaiah's words remind us that peace is not found in our external circumstances but in the steadfastness of our minds as we focus on God. When we fix our minds on Him, trusting in His character and His Word, we experience a peace that the world cannot offer. This perfect peace guards our hearts from fear and anxiety because we know that God is in control. Trust in Him allows us to walk in peace, no matter what we face.

If you are struggling to find peace, turn your focus to God and trust in His promises. Let His perfect peace fill your heart as you rely on His faithfulness and goodness.

Call to Action: Reflect on areas where you need to trust God more. Pray for steadfastness of mind and ask God to fill you with His perfect peace as you trust in Him.

Prayer: Lord, thank You for the promise of perfect peace. Help me trust in You completely, keeping my mind steadfast and focused on Your faithfulness. Fill my heart with peace that comes from knowing You are in control, and help me walk in that peace each day. Amen.

June 16
Peace from the Good Shepherd

Verse: *"I am the good shepherd. The good shepherd lays down His life for the sheep."*

(John 10:11, NIV)

Message: Jesus is the Good Shepherd who cares for His flock, and in His care, we find peace. In John 10:11, Jesus declares that He is the Good Shepherd who lays down His life for His sheep. This sacrificial love brings us the peace of knowing that we are fully loved, fully known, and fully protected by the One who gave everything for us. When we trust Jesus as our Shepherd, we can rest in the assurance that He is guiding, protecting, and providing for us.

Sheep find peace when they are under the care of a good shepherd, and we find peace when we are under the care of Jesus. He watches over us, leads us to green pastures, and restores our souls. The peace that comes from knowing Jesus as our Shepherd is not just a feeling—it is a deep confidence in His love and care for us. No matter what dangers or difficulties we face, we can trust that our Shepherd is with us, leading us through every valley and protecting us from every harm.

If you are feeling uncertain or anxious, trust in Jesus as your Good Shepherd. Let Him lead you to places of peace, knowing that He is always watching over you.

Call to Action: Reflect on Jesus' role as your Good Shepherd. Spend time in prayer, asking Him to lead you to places of peace and trusting in His care for you.

Prayer: Father, thank You for sending Jesus, my Good Shepherd, to care for me. I trust in His love and protection, knowing that He laid down His life for me. Help me find peace in His presence and follow where He leads, confident in His care. Amen.

June 17
Perfect Peace Through Trust

Verse: "*You will keep in perfect peace those whose minds are steadfast, because they trust in You.*"

(Isaiah 26:3, NIV)

Message: Trusting in God brings perfect peace. Isaiah 26:3 assures us that God keeps those in perfect peace whose minds are steadfast because they trust in Him. Perfect peace is not just the absence of conflict or worry; it is a deep, abiding peace that comes from unwavering trust in God. When we keep our minds focused on Him and trust in His sovereignty, we experience a peace that nothing in this world can take away.

In difficult times, it can be tempting to let our minds wander toward fear, doubt, or worry. But Isaiah calls us to keep our minds steadfastly focused on God. When we trust that He is in control, we find peace, even when circumstances seem uncertain. This peace is not something we have to manufacture on our own—it is a gift from God to those who trust in Him. When we fix our eyes on God and His promises, we find peace that the world cannot give.

If you are struggling to find peace, focus your mind on God and trust in His goodness. Let His perfect peace fill your heart as you rely on His unchanging love and faithfulness.

Call to Action: Reflect on areas where you need to trust God more. Pray for steadfastness of mind and ask God to fill you with His perfect peace as you trust in Him.

Prayer: Lord, thank You for the promise of perfect peace. Help me trust in You completely, keeping my mind steadfast and focused on Your faithfulness. Fill my heart with peace that comes from knowing You are in control, and help me walk in that peace each day. Amen.

June 18
Peace in the Waiting

Verse: *"Wait for the Lord; be strong and take heart and wait for the Lord."*

(Psalm 27:14, NIV)

Message: Waiting on God can be difficult, but it is in the waiting that we often experience His peace. Psalm 27:14 encourages us to be strong, take heart, and wait for the Lord. Waiting requires patience and trust, but when we wait on God, we are reminded that His timing is perfect. We can find peace in knowing that God is working behind the scenes, even when we don't see immediate results. His plans for us are good, and in the waiting, we can rest in His faithfulness.

David, who wrote this psalm, was familiar with waiting. Whether it was waiting to become king after being anointed or waiting for deliverance from his enemies, David learned to trust God's timing. In the same way, when we wait on the Lord, we are reminded that His timing is always better than ours. Waiting strengthens our faith and teaches us to rely on God's wisdom rather than our own understanding. As we wait, we can experience God's peace, knowing that He is working all things together for our good.

If you are in a season of waiting, trust that God is working on your behalf. Take heart and find peace in the knowledge that He is faithful and that His timing is perfect.

Call to Action: Reflect on a situation where you are waiting for God's timing. Pray for peace and patience as you trust that He is working behind the scenes and that His timing is perfect.

Prayer: Lord, thank You for the peace that comes from waiting on You. Help me be strong and take heart as I trust in Your timing. I know that You are working all things for my good, and I rest in the assurance of Your faithfulness. Amen.

June 19
God's Presence Brings Peace

Verse: *"The Lord replied, 'My Presence will go with you, and I will give you rest.'"*

(Exodus 33:14, NIV)

Message: God's presence brings rest and peace. In Exodus 33:14, God assures Moses that His presence will go with him and give him rest. This promise is not just for Moses—it's for all of us. When we are in God's presence, we experience the peace that only He can give. His presence calms our fears, quiets our worries, and fills us with rest, even in the midst of challenges. There is nothing more comforting than knowing that God is with us.

Moses faced a daunting task—leading the Israelites through the wilderness—but he knew that without God's presence, he could not succeed. In the same way, we can face life's challenges with peace when we know that God is with us. His presence is our source of strength, comfort, and rest. When we seek Him in prayer, we are reminded that we are never alone, and His peace surrounds us.

If you are feeling weary or anxious, spend time in God's presence. Trust that He will give you rest and fill you with the peace that comes from knowing He is with you.

Call to Action: Spend time in quiet prayer today, focusing on God's presence. Ask Him to fill you with His peace and rest as you trust in His promise to be with you.

Prayer: Father, thank You for the peace that comes from Your presence. I trust in Your promise to be with me and give me rest. Help me experience the fullness of Your peace as I seek You and rest in Your presence. Amen.

June 20
Peace in Times of Trouble

Verse: *"I have told you these things, so that in me you may have peace. In this world you will have trouble. But take heart! I have overcome the world."*

(John 16:33, NIV)

Message: Jesus promised us that even though we will face trouble in this world, we can have peace in Him. John 16:33 reminds us that our peace is not dependent on our circumstances but on our relationship with Jesus. He has already overcome the world, and because of that, we can have confidence and peace no matter what challenges we face. This peace is a deep assurance that comes from knowing that Jesus has already secured victory over every trial.

The disciples faced persecution and hardships after Jesus left them, yet He gave them this assurance before He departed. Jesus didn't promise a life free of trouble, but He promised His peace through every situation. In the same way, we can find peace in God's presence, knowing that He has already overcome whatever we face. We are not promised a life without problems, but we are promised peace in the midst of them because Jesus walks with us through it all.

If you are going through a difficult time, take heart and remember that Jesus has overcome the world. Find peace in His presence, trusting that He is with you in every trial.

Call to Action: Reflect on a current challenge you are facing. Bring it to Jesus in prayer, trusting that He has already overcome the world and that He will give you His peace.

Prayer: Lord, thank You for the peace You offer me, even in times of trouble. I trust in Your victory and rest in Your presence, knowing that You have overcome the world. Help me find peace in You, no matter what challenges I face. Amen.

June 21
God's Peace Guards Our Minds

Verse: *"You will keep in perfect peace those whose minds are steadfast, because they trust in You."*

(Isaiah 26:3, NIV)

Message: God promises to keep us in perfect peace when we trust in Him and keep our minds steadfastly focused on Him. In Isaiah 26:3, we are reminded that peace is a product of trust. When we fix our thoughts on God and place our full trust in His sovereignty and goodness, peace follows. This peace guards our minds, keeping us from being overwhelmed by fear, anxiety, or doubt.

In times of uncertainty, it's easy for our minds to wander toward worry or fear. But Isaiah encourages us to keep our minds steadfastly focused on God. Trusting in Him allows us to experience His perfect peace, even in the midst of turmoil. This peace isn't based on our circumstances—it comes from knowing that God is in control and that His plans are good. Keeping our minds focused on God through prayer, meditation on His Word, and trusting in His promises brings us the peace that only He can provide.

If you are struggling with anxious thoughts, focus your mind on God's promises. Trust that He will keep you in perfect peace as you keep your mind fixed on Him.

Call to Action: Take time to meditate on God's promises today. Reflect on Isaiah 26:3 and pray for steadfastness of mind as you trust in God's peace.

Prayer: Lord, thank You for the promise of perfect peace. Help me keep my mind steadfastly focused on You, trusting in Your faithfulness and goodness. Let Your peace guard my mind and heart from fear and anxiety. Amen.

June 22
The Prince of Peace

Verse: "*For to us a child is born, to us a son is given, and the government will be on His shoulders. And He will be called Wonderful Counselor, Mighty God, Everlasting Father, Prince of Peace.*"

(Isaiah 9:6, NIV)

Message: Jesus is the Prince of Peace, and He came to bring peace to a world filled with conflict, chaos, and brokenness. Isaiah 9:6 prophesies about the coming Messiah, who would be called the Prince of Peace. Jesus fulfilled this prophecy through His life, death, and resurrection, making peace between us and God possible. Through Jesus, we have access to true, lasting peace—peace that surpasses understanding and transforms our hearts.

As the Prince of Peace, Jesus brings peace into every area of our lives. He reconciles us to God, giving us peace in our relationship with Him. He calms our troubled hearts, bringing peace in the midst of fear and anxiety. And He empowers us to be peacemakers in a broken world, extending His peace to others. The peace that Jesus gives is not like the world's peace—it is deeper, stronger, and more enduring. When we turn to Jesus, we find the peace that our hearts long for.

If you are seeking peace, come to the Prince of Peace. Let Jesus fill your heart with His peace, and trust Him to guide you through every challenge.

Call to Action: Reflect on how Jesus, the Prince of Peace, brings peace into your life. Spend time in prayer, thanking Him for His peace and asking Him to fill your heart with it today.

Prayer: Lord Jesus, thank You for being the Prince of Peace. I come to You now, asking for Your peace to fill my heart and mind. Help me rest in Your presence and share Your peace with others. Amen.

June 23
Peace with God Through Jesus

Verse: *"Therefore, since we have been justified through faith, we have peace with God through our Lord Jesus Christ."*

(Romans 5:1, NIV)

Message: One of the greatest gifts of salvation is the peace we have with God through Jesus Christ. Romans 5:1 reminds us that because we have been justified by faith, we are no longer separated from God. Through Jesus' sacrifice, we are reconciled to God, and this reconciliation brings us peace. This peace is not just a feeling—it is a restored relationship with our Creator. We are no longer enemies of God, but we are His beloved children, and we can rest in the peace of knowing that we are fully accepted and loved by Him.

Before we knew Christ, we were separated from God by our sin. But through Jesus, we are brought near, and our relationship with God is restored. This peace with God is the foundation for all other peace in our lives. When we know that we are at peace with our Creator, we can face life's challenges with confidence, knowing that we are secure in His love. The peace of God transforms us, giving us hope, joy, and assurance of eternal life.

If you have been struggling with guilt, shame, or fear, remember that through Jesus, you have peace with God. Rest in the assurance that you are fully forgiven, loved, and accepted by Him.

Call to Action: Reflect on the peace you have with God through Jesus. Spend time in prayer, thanking Him for the gift of salvation and the peace that comes from being reconciled to God.

Prayer: Father, thank You for the peace I have with You through Jesus. I thank You for the gift of salvation and for reconciling me to Yourself. Help me live in the peace that comes from knowing I am fully loved and accepted by You. Amen.

June 24
Peace as a Fruit of the Spirit

Verse: *"But the fruit of the Spirit is love, joy, peace, forbearance, kindness, goodness, faithfulness, gentleness, and self-control."*

(Galatians 5:22-23, NIV)

Message: Peace is a fruit of the Holy Spirit, and as we walk by the Spirit, we will experience peace in our hearts and lives. Galatians 5:22-23 lists peace as one of the nine fruits of the Spirit, showing that peace is not something we produce on our own—it is a result of the Holy Spirit working in us. When we are led by the Spirit, we experience His peace, even in difficult circumstances. This peace is not dependent on external factors; it is the supernatural peace that comes from being in a right relationship with God.

The peace of the Spirit is different from the peace the world offers. It is not a fleeting feeling of calm but a deep, abiding peace that sustains us through every trial. As we grow in our relationship with God and allow the Holy Spirit to work in us, we bear the fruit of peace in our hearts and lives. This peace affects how we respond to stress, conflict, and challenges, and it also enables us to be peacemakers, spreading God's peace to those around us.

If you desire more peace in your life, ask the Holy Spirit to fill you and produce His peace in your heart. Trust that as you walk by the Spirit, His peace will overflow in your life.

Call to Action: Reflect on the fruit of peace in your life. Spend time in prayer, asking the Holy Spirit to produce His peace in you and to help you live as a peacemaker in the world.

Prayer: Lord, thank You for the peace that comes from Your Spirit. Fill me with Your Holy Spirit and produce the fruit of peace in my heart and life. Help me walk by the Spirit, trusting in Your peace no matter what I face, and use me to bring Your peace to others. Amen.

June 25
God's Peace, Our Strength

Verse: *"The Lord gives strength to His people; the Lord blesses His people with peace."*

(Psalm 29:11, NIV)

Message: God's peace is not only a source of comfort but also a source of strength. In Psalm 29:11, we are reminded that the Lord gives strength to His people and blesses them with peace. This peace is not passive—it empowers us to face life's challenges with confidence and resilience. When we are anchored in the peace of God, we find the strength to persevere through trials, knowing that His presence sustains us. God's peace is not the absence of difficulty, but His empowering presence in the midst of it.

In the Bible, we see many examples of how God's peace strengthened His people. When the Israelites faced overwhelming obstacles, it was God's presence and peace that enabled them to stand firm. The same is true for us today. God's peace doesn't just calm our hearts; it gives us the strength we need to keep going when life gets tough. His peace empowers us to trust in His promises, to stand strong in our faith, and to endure whatever comes our way.

If you are feeling weak or discouraged, ask God for His peace and strength. Trust that His peace will not only calm your heart but also give you the power to face each day with courage and faith.

Call to Action: Reflect on how God's peace strengthens you in times of difficulty. Spend time in prayer, asking God to fill you with His peace and give you the strength to persevere through any challenges you are facing.

Prayer: Lord, thank You for the peace that strengthens me. I ask for Your peace to fill my heart and give me the strength I need to face the challenges ahead. Help me trust in Your presence and rest in the assurance that You are with me every step of the way. Amen.

June 26
Peace in Knowing God's Plan

Verse: *"'For I know the plans I have for you,' declares the Lord, 'plans to prosper you and not to harm you, plans to give you hope and a future.'"*

(Jeremiah 29:11, NIV)

Message: One of the greatest sources of peace is knowing that God has a plan for our lives. Jeremiah 29:11 reassures us that God's plans are good—plans to prosper us, not to harm us, plans to give us hope and a future. When we trust in God's plan, we find peace in the midst of uncertainty. Even when we don't understand what is happening, we can rest in the knowledge that God is in control and that His plans for us are filled with hope.

The people of Israel received this promise while they were in exile, facing difficult circumstances. Yet God reminded them that He had not forgotten them and that His plans for them were good. In the same way, God's plans for our lives are filled with purpose, even when we face hardships or delays. Trusting in God's plan brings peace because we know that He is working all things for our good, and His purposes for us are filled with hope and a future.

If you are feeling uncertain about the future, trust in God's plan. Bring your hopes and fears to Him in prayer, and rest in the peace that comes from knowing His plans are good.

Call to Action: Reflect on the plans God has for your life. Spend time in prayer, thanking Him for His good plans and trusting that He is working for your future, even when you can't see it.

Prayer: Father, thank You for the good plans You have for my life. Help me trust in Your purpose and rest in the peace that comes from knowing You are in control. Fill me with hope for the future, and help me walk in faith as I trust in Your plan. Amen.

June 27
Peace in Times of Transition

Verse: *"The Lord Himself goes before you and will be with you; He will never leave you nor forsake you. Do not be afraid; do not be discouraged."*

(Deuteronomy 31:8, NIV)

Message: Transitions can be unsettling, but God's presence brings peace, even in times of change. Deuteronomy 31:8 reminds us that the Lord goes before us and is always with us. He will never leave us or forsake us. When we face new seasons, new challenges, or unexpected changes, we can trust that God is already ahead of us, preparing the way. His presence brings us peace and assurance that we are not alone.

The Israelites were about to enter the Promised Land, a major transition after years of wandering in the wilderness. God's promise to go before them and be with them gave them the courage and peace to step into the unknown. In the same way, God is with us in every transition, whether it's a new job, a move, a change in relationships, or a new season in life. His presence calms our fears and gives us the peace we need to move forward with confidence.

If you are facing a transition, trust that God is going before you. Bring your worries to Him in prayer, and rest in the peace of knowing He will never leave you or forsake you.

Call to Action: Reflect on any transitions or changes you are facing. Spend time in prayer, asking God to go before you and give you peace as you step into the future with confidence in His presence.

Prayer: Lord, thank You for going before me and being with me in every transition. I trust that You are preparing the way and that You will never leave me. Help me find peace in Your presence as I move forward in faith, knowing that You are always with me. Amen.

June 28
The Peace of Surrender

Verse: "Trust in the Lord with all your heart and lean not on your own understanding; in all your ways submit to Him, and He will make your paths straight."

(Proverbs 3:5-6, NIV)

Message: Peace comes when we surrender our own understanding and trust fully in God. Proverbs 3:5-6 calls us to trust in the Lord with all our hearts and to submit to Him in all our ways. When we stop relying on our own wisdom and surrender to God's direction, we find peace. Trusting God means letting go of our need to control outcomes and believing that He knows what's best for us. In surrender, we find the peace that comes from knowing we are in God's hands.

Solomon, the author of Proverbs, understood the importance of trusting in God's wisdom rather than our own. Life's uncertainties often tempt us to try and figure things out on our own, but true peace comes when we release our need to understand everything and simply trust that God is in control. When we submit our plans, desires, and worries to God, He promises to direct our paths and lead us into peace. Surrender is not a sign of weakness—it's a pathway to peace.

If you are struggling with uncertainty or control, surrender your worries to God. Trust Him with all your heart, and let His peace guide you as you follow His ways.

Call to Action: Reflect on areas of your life where you are holding onto control. Spend time in prayer, surrendering those areas to God and asking Him to lead you on the right path.

Prayer: Father, thank You for the peace that comes from surrendering to You. Help me trust You with all my heart and lean not on my own understanding. I surrender my plans, worries, and desires to You, and I trust You to make my paths straight. Amen.

June 29
Eternal Peace in Christ

Verse: *"The God of peace will soon crush Satan under your feet. The grace of our Lord Jesus be with you."*

(Romans 16:20, NIV)

Message: God promises us eternal peace through Jesus Christ, and one day, all evil and suffering will be completely overcome. Romans 16:20 reminds us that the God of peace will soon crush Satan under our feet. This is the ultimate promise of peace—peace that is eternal and lasting. While we experience God's peace now in His presence, we also look forward to the day when all things will be made new, and peace will reign forever.

Paul's words to the Romans were a reminder that, despite the challenges they faced, victory was assured. Jesus' death and resurrection secured victory over sin, death, and Satan, and one day, that victory will be fully realized. Until then, we live in the peace that comes from knowing the battle is already won. No matter what we face in this life, we have the assurance of eternal peace through Jesus Christ, and this hope gives us strength to endure.

If you are feeling discouraged or overwhelmed, remember the promise of eternal peace. Trust that God is with you now and that His final victory will bring everlasting peace.

Call to Action: Reflect on the hope of eternal peace in Christ. Spend time in prayer, thanking God for the victory He has already won and for the peace that comes from knowing His promises are true.

Prayer: Lord, thank You for the promise of eternal peace. I trust in Your victory over sin, death, and Satan, and I look forward to the day when Your peace will reign forever. Help me live in the hope of Your promises and rest in the peace that only You can give. Amen.

July

Living in Freedom through Christ

July 1
Freedom in Christ

Verse: *"It is for freedom that Christ has set us free. Stand firm, then, and do not let yourselves be burdened again by a yoke of slavery."*

(Galatians 5:1, NIV)

Message: Christ has set us free so that we may live in freedom. Galatians 5:1 reminds us that Jesus died to free us from the power of sin and the bondage of the law. This freedom is not just a future hope—it's a present reality that we can live in daily. However, Paul urges us to stand firm in that freedom, because there is always the temptation to return to old ways of thinking or living. To live in Christ's freedom means to walk in the new life He has given us, unburdened by the weight of sin and guilt.

In the Bible, we see how the Israelites, after being freed from slavery in Egypt, often longed to return to their old ways, even though they had been liberated. Similarly, as believers, we are sometimes tempted to fall back into the habits or mindsets that enslaved us before we knew Christ. But Jesus has set us free, and He calls us to walk in that freedom every day. This freedom is not about doing whatever we want, but about living in the fullness of life that Christ offers—free from fear, shame, and condemnation.

If you find yourself slipping back into old patterns or feeling weighed down by guilt, remember that Christ has set you free. Stand firm in that freedom and live the life He has called you to live.

Call to Action: Reflect on any areas where you may still feel burdened or trapped. Bring them to Christ in prayer, asking Him to help you stand firm in the freedom He has given you.

Prayer: Lord, thank You for setting me free through Christ. Help me stand firm in that freedom and not return to the things that once enslaved me. Fill my heart with the joy and peace that come from living in the freedom You have given me. Amen.

July 2
Free from Condemnation

Verse: "Therefore, there is now no condemnation for those who are in Christ Jesus."

(Romans 8:1, NIV)

Message: One of the most beautiful aspects of living in freedom through Christ is knowing that there is no condemnation for those who are in Him. Romans 8:1 assures us that because of Jesus' sacrifice, we are no longer condemned by our past sins or failures. We are forgiven, redeemed, and set free. This freedom from condemnation means that we don't have to live in guilt or shame anymore. In Christ, we are made new, and our sins are wiped clean.

In the story of the woman caught in adultery (John 8), Jesus told her, "Neither do I condemn you. Go now and leave your life of sin." Jesus didn't come to condemn, but to save, and He offers the same grace and freedom to us. We no longer have to be defined by our past mistakes. Instead, we can live in the freedom of knowing that we are fully forgiven. This freedom empowers us to move forward with confidence, living out our new identity in Christ.

If you are struggling with feelings of guilt or shame, remember that in Christ, there is no condemnation. Embrace the freedom He offers and live in the knowledge that you are fully forgiven.

Call to Action: Spend time in prayer, thanking God for the freedom from condemnation that you have in Christ. Release any guilt or shame you may be holding onto, and accept His grace and forgiveness.

Prayer: Father, thank You for freeing me from condemnation through Christ. I am grateful for Your grace and forgiveness. Help me to live in the freedom of knowing that my past does not define me, and that I am made new in You. Amen.

July 3
Freedom from Fear

Verse: *"For the Spirit God gave us does not make us timid, but gives us power, love and self-discipline."*

(2 Timothy 1:7, NIV)

Message: Fear is a form of bondage that can hold us back from fully living in the freedom Christ has given us. But 2 Timothy 1:7 reminds us that God has given us His Spirit, which is not one of fear, but of power, love, and self-discipline. Living in the Spirit means we are no longer enslaved by fear—we are empowered to live boldly, to love others fully, and to walk in the confidence of who we are in Christ.

In the Bible, we see how fear gripped the hearts of the Israelites when they stood at the edge of the Promised Land. Despite God's promises, fear of the giants kept them from stepping into their inheritance. Like them, we may face "giants" in our lives—challenges, uncertainties, or fears that make us hesitate. But God calls us to step out in faith, trusting in His strength. The Spirit that lives within us is powerful, and when we rely on Him, we can overcome fear and walk in freedom.

If fear is holding you back from fully living the life God has called you to, ask Him to fill you with His Spirit of power and love. Step out in faith, knowing that He has already overcome your fears.

Call to Action: Reflect on any areas of your life where fear is holding you back. Pray for God's Spirit to fill you with courage, power, and love, and take a step of faith today.

Prayer: Lord, thank You for the Spirit of power, love, and self-discipline that You have given me. Help me to walk in freedom from fear, trusting in Your strength and love. I ask for Your courage to overcome the fears that try to hold me back. Amen.

July 4
Freedom to Love Others

Verse: "You, my brothers and sisters, were called to be free. But do not use your freedom to indulge the flesh; rather, serve one another humbly in love."

(Galatians 5:13, NIV)

Message: The freedom we have in Christ is not just for our own benefit—it is also an opportunity to serve others in love. Galatians 5:13 reminds us that our freedom is not a license to indulge in selfish desires, but a call to humbly love and serve others. In Christ, we are free from the self-centeredness that once controlled us. Now, we are empowered by His love to care for others, to serve them, and to build them up in the Lord.

Jesus demonstrated this freedom through His life of service. Though He was God, He humbled Himself and served others, even to the point of laying down His life. As His followers, we are called to do the same. Living in freedom means loving others selflessly and using our freedom to advance God's kingdom, not our own desires. When we serve others in love, we reflect the heart of Christ and experience the true joy and freedom that comes from living for God and others.

If you've been focusing solely on your own needs, ask God to help you see how you can use your freedom to serve others. Let love be the motivation behind all that you do.

Call to Action: Reflect on how you can use the freedom you have in Christ to serve others. Spend time in prayer, asking God to show you ways you can humbly love and care for those around you.

Prayer: Father, thank You for the freedom I have in Christ. Help me use that freedom to love and serve others as Jesus did. Fill my heart with compassion, and show me how I can use my freedom to bless those around me. Amen.

July 5
Free from the Power of Sin

Verse: *"For we know that our old self was crucified with Him so that the body ruled by sin might be done away with, that we should no longer be slaves to sin."*

(Romans 6:6, NIV)

Message: One of the greatest freedoms we have in Christ is freedom from the power of sin. Romans 6:6 reminds us that our old self, which was ruled by sin, has been crucified with Christ. We are no longer slaves to sin—Jesus has broken the chains that once held us captive. This means that sin no longer has control over us, and we are free to live righteous, holy lives through the power of the Holy Spirit.

Before we knew Christ, sin controlled our thoughts, actions, and desires. But now, because of Jesus' death and resurrection, we are no longer under the power of sin. The battle has been won, and we are free to live in victory. This doesn't mean we'll never struggle with temptation, but it does mean that sin no longer has the final say in our lives. Through Christ, we have the power to resist temptation and live in the freedom that comes from being children of God.

If you find yourself struggling with sin, remember that in Christ, you are no longer a slave to sin. Ask God for strength and walk in the freedom He has given you through the Holy Spirit.

Call to Action: Reflect on any areas where you feel bound by sin. Spend time in prayer, asking God for His strength and guidance to live in the freedom from sin that Christ has given you.

Prayer: Lord, thank You for setting me free from the power of sin through Christ. Help me live in that freedom, resisting temptation and walking in the new life You have given me. Fill me with Your Spirit and guide me in righteousness. Amen.

July 6
Freedom to Walk in the Spirit

Verse*: "So I say, walk by the Spirit, and you will not gratify the desires of the flesh."*

(Galatians 5:16, NIV)

Message: Living in freedom through Christ means walking by the Spirit. Galatians 5:16 teaches us that when we walk by the Spirit, we won't fulfill the desires of the flesh. The freedom Christ gives is not just about being freed from sin, but about being empowered to live a life led by the Holy Spirit. Walking in the Spirit allows us to overcome temptation, live in purity, and follow God's will for our lives. It is the Spirit that guides us daily, enabling us to live in the fullness of the freedom Christ provides.

In the early church, Paul reminded believers that freedom in Christ wasn't an excuse to follow sinful desires, but rather an invitation to live a life transformed by the Spirit. As we rely on the Holy Spirit to guide us, we find that we no longer have to battle our flesh alone. The Spirit gives us the strength and wisdom to make choices that honor God and reflect His character. Walking in the Spirit leads to a life of true freedom—free from the desires that once enslaved us.

If you want to live in the fullness of your freedom in Christ, ask the Holy Spirit to guide you in your daily life. Trust Him to help you overcome the desires of the flesh and walk in God's will.

Call to Action: Spend time in prayer, asking the Holy Spirit to guide your steps. Reflect on areas where you need His help to resist the desires of the flesh and walk in the freedom Christ provides.

Prayer: Lord, thank You for the gift of the Holy Spirit who guides me daily. Help me walk by the Spirit and resist the desires of the flesh. Lead me in Your will and give me the strength to live in the freedom You've given me. Amen.

July 7
Free to Be a New Creation

Verse: *"Therefore, if anyone is in Christ, the new creation has come: The old has gone, the new is here!"*

(2 Corinthians 5:17, NIV)

Message: In Christ, we are not just forgiven; we are made new. 2 Corinthians 5:17 declares that anyone who is in Christ is a new creation—the old is gone, and the new has come. This freedom means we are no longer defined by our past sins, mistakes, or failures. We are given a fresh start, a new identity, and the freedom to live as God intended us to live. Being a new creation in Christ means embracing the life He offers and letting go of the old self that was once bound by sin.

The Bible is full of stories of transformation—people whose lives were radically changed after encountering Jesus. Paul, once a persecutor of Christians, became one of the greatest apostles after his conversion. Zacchaeus, a corrupt tax collector, was transformed after meeting Jesus and immediately repented of his dishonest ways. These stories remind us that in Christ, we are not bound by who we used to be. Instead, we are free to live as new creations, walking in the freedom and purpose God has given us.

If you are holding onto your past, remember that in Christ, you are a new creation. Embrace the freedom to live as the person God has made you to be.

Call to Action: Reflect on how being a new creation in Christ has changed your life. Spend time in prayer, thanking God for the transformation He has brought and asking Him to help you live in the newness of life He has given.

Prayer: Lord, thank You for making me a new creation in Christ. Help me live in the freedom of my new identity, leaving behind the old self and embracing the new life You have given me. Thank You for the transformation You are working in my heart each day. Amen.

July 8
Freedom from Legalism

> *Verse:* "*For in Christ Jesus neither circumcision nor uncircumcision has any value. The only thing that counts is faith expressing itself through love.*"
>
> **(Galatians 5:6, NIV)**

Message: Living in freedom through Christ means we are no longer bound by legalism. Galatians 5:6 reminds us that it is not about external rituals or religious rules, but about faith expressing itself through love. Legalism focuses on outward appearances and rule-following, but Christ sets us free from this mindset. We are not saved by our works or religious observances, but by faith in Jesus. This freedom allows us to focus on loving God and loving others, rather than trying to earn our salvation through human effort.

Jesus often confronted the Pharisees, who were known for their strict adherence to the law. While they prided themselves on keeping religious rules, their hearts were far from God. Jesus showed that true righteousness is not about following rules for the sake of appearances, but about loving God with all our hearts and loving others as ourselves. Living in Christ's freedom means we no longer have to strive to earn God's love—we are already loved, and our faith is expressed through love for others.

If you've been striving to follow religious rules to earn God's favor, remember that in Christ, you are free. Focus on loving God and others, and let your faith be expressed through love.

Call to Action: Reflect on whether you've been relying on rules or rituals rather than faith in Christ. Spend time in prayer, asking God to help you live in the freedom of His love and to express your faith through love for others.

Prayer: Father, thank You for setting me free from the burden of legalism. Help me live by faith, expressing my love for You and others. I thank You that I don't have to earn Your love but can live in the freedom of Your grace. Amen.

July 9
Freedom to Forgive

Verse: *"Be kind and compassionate to one another, forgiving each other, just as in Christ God forgave you."*

(Ephesians 4:32, NIV)

Message: One of the most powerful aspects of living in freedom through Christ is the freedom to forgive. Ephesians 4:32 reminds us that we are called to forgive others just as God has forgiven us in Christ. Holding onto grudges, bitterness, or unforgiveness keeps us in bondage, but forgiveness sets us free. When we forgive, we let go of the pain and hurt, allowing God's peace to fill our hearts. Just as we have been freely forgiven, we are empowered to forgive others.

In the Bible, we see many examples of forgiveness, including Jesus forgiving those who crucified Him. One powerful story is that of Joseph, who forgave his brothers even after they sold him into slavery. Despite the pain they caused him, Joseph chose to forgive, and his forgiveness led to reconciliation and restoration. In the same way, when we forgive others, we experience the freedom of living without bitterness, and we open the door for God's healing and restoration in our relationships.

If you are holding onto unforgiveness, ask God to help you forgive. Remember that in Christ, you have been freely forgiven, and that same grace empowers you to forgive others.

Call to Action: Reflect on anyone you may need to forgive. Spend time in prayer, asking God for the strength to forgive, and release any bitterness or pain to Him.

Prayer: Lord, thank You for the freedom to forgive. I ask for Your strength to forgive those who have hurt me, just as You have forgiven me. Help me release any bitterness or pain and live in the peace of Your grace. Amen.

July 10
Freedom from Worry

Verse: "Cast all your anxiety on Him because He cares for you."

(1 Peter 5:7, NIV)

Message: Worry and anxiety can be burdens that weigh us down, but in Christ, we are free to cast our cares on Him. 1 Peter 5:7 encourages us to bring all of our anxieties to God because He cares for us. We don't have to carry the weight of our worries on our own. Jesus invites us to give them to Him and trust that He will provide, guide, and protect us. This freedom from worry allows us to live in peace, knowing that God is in control and that He cares deeply for us.

In Matthew 6, Jesus tells His followers not to worry about their lives, reminding them that if God takes care of the birds and the flowers, how much more will He care for us? Worry accomplishes nothing, but trust in God brings peace. When we choose to cast our anxieties on God, we acknowledge that He is bigger than our problems and that He is faithful to meet all of our needs. Living in this freedom means walking in trust rather than fear, knowing that God is always with us.

If worry has been consuming your thoughts, take time to cast your cares on God in prayer. Trust that He cares for you and that He is able to handle every worry you bring to Him.

Call to Action: Reflect on any anxieties or worries you have been carrying. Spend time in prayer, giving those worries to God and trusting Him to care for you.

Prayer: Lord, thank You for caring for me. I cast my anxieties on You, trusting that You will take care of every need and every concern. Help me live in the freedom of knowing that You are in control and that I am safe in Your care. Amen.

July 11
Freedom to Live in Peace

Verse: *"And the peace of God, which transcends all understanding, will guard your hearts and your minds in Christ Jesus."*

(Philippians 4:7, NIV)

Message: In Christ, we are free to live in peace, no matter our circumstances. Philippians 4:7 reminds us that the peace of God transcends all understanding and guards our hearts and minds in Christ. This peace is not based on the absence of problems but on the presence of God in our lives. When we trust God with our worries and fears, His peace fills our hearts, protecting us from anxiety and stress. Living in Christ's freedom means walking in the peace that comes from knowing we are loved, cared for, and secure in Him.

Jesus modeled this peace throughout His ministry, even when faced with opposition, storms, and ultimately, the cross. His peace came from His relationship with the Father, and He invites us to experience that same peace. Through prayer and trust in God, we can live in the freedom of peace, knowing that nothing in this world can separate us from God's love. When we walk in God's peace, we are free from fear, worry, and the need to control everything. His peace guards our hearts and minds, giving us rest and joy in all situations.

If you're feeling overwhelmed or stressed, turn to God in prayer. Ask Him to fill you with His peace that surpasses understanding, and trust that He will guard your heart and mind.

Call to Action: Spend time in prayer, bringing your worries to God. Trust Him to fill you with His peace and guard your heart and mind from anxiety.

Prayer: Father, thank You for the peace that transcends all understanding. I bring my worries and concerns to You, trusting that You will guard my heart and mind in Christ Jesus. Help me walk in the freedom of Your peace each day. Amen.

July 12
Free to Serve with Joy

Verse: "Each of you should use whatever gift you have received to serve others, as faithful stewards of God's grace in its various forms."

(1 Peter 4:10, NIV)

Message: One of the greatest freedoms we experience in Christ is the freedom to serve others with joy. 1 Peter 4:10 encourages us to use the gifts we have received to serve others as faithful stewards of God's grace. Serving others is not a burden; it's a privilege and a joy. When we live in the freedom of Christ, we are no longer focused solely on our own needs and desires—we are empowered to serve others out of the overflow of God's love and grace in our lives.

Jesus, the ultimate example of a servant, washed His disciples' feet and called them to do the same for others. He demonstrated that true greatness comes through serving. When we serve others, we reflect Christ's love and character. This kind of service is not done out of obligation but out of the joy and freedom we experience in Christ. As we use our gifts to bless others, we find fulfillment and joy in knowing that we are part of God's work in the world.

If you're looking for ways to experience more joy in your walk with Christ, consider how you can serve others. Use your gifts to bless those around you, and watch as God fills your heart with joy and freedom.

Call to Action: Reflect on the gifts God has given you and how you can use them to serve others. Spend time in prayer, asking God to help you serve with joy and be a faithful steward of His grace.

Prayer: Lord, thank You for the freedom to serve others with joy. Help me use the gifts You've given me to bless those around me and to be a faithful steward of Your grace. Fill my heart with joy as I serve, knowing that I am reflecting Your love to the world. Amen.

July 13
Free from the Power of Darkness

Verse: *"For He has rescued us from the dominion of darkness and brought us into the kingdom of the Son He loves, in whom we have redemption, the forgiveness of sins."*

(Colossians 1:13-14, NIV)

Message: In Christ, we are free from the power of darkness. Colossians 1:13-14 declares that God has rescued us from the dominion of darkness and brought us into the kingdom of His Son, Jesus. Through Jesus, we have redemption and the forgiveness of sins, which means we no longer live under the control of sin, shame, or fear. The power of darkness has been broken, and we are free to live as children of light, walking in the freedom Christ has given us.

The Bible tells many stories of how Jesus brought people out of darkness and into the light. Whether it was healing the sick, casting out demons, or forgiving sins, Jesus freed people from the chains of darkness. Today, we experience that same freedom. Whatever struggles, sins, or fears we face, we can trust that Christ has already won the victory. We are no longer slaves to the power of darkness but are free to live in the light of God's kingdom, where redemption, love, and forgiveness reign.

If you feel weighed down by darkness, whether it's sin, fear, or shame, bring it to Jesus in prayer. Trust that He has rescued you from the power of darkness and brought you into the freedom of His light.

Call to Action: Reflect on any areas of your life where you feel bound by darkness. Bring those areas to God in prayer, and trust in the freedom and redemption you have through Christ.

Prayer: Father, thank You for rescuing me from the dominion of darkness and bringing me into the kingdom of Your Son. I trust in the freedom I have in Christ, and I ask You to help me walk in the light of Your redemption and love. Amen.

July 14
Freedom to Live by Faith

Verse: *"For we live by faith, not by sight."*

(2 Corinthians 5:7, NIV)

Message: Living in freedom through Christ means living by faith, not by sight. 2 Corinthians 5:7 reminds us that our lives as believers are not governed by what we can see with our physical eyes but by faith in God's promises. Walking by faith means trusting God even when we don't have all the answers, even when the path ahead is unclear. It's about relying on God's Word and His character rather than on our circumstances. Faith sets us free from fear and doubt because we trust that God is in control and His plans for us are good.

Throughout the Bible, we see examples of people who lived by faith: Abraham left his homeland without knowing where he was going, trusting God to lead him. Moses led the Israelites through the Red Sea, trusting that God would deliver them. These men and women of faith walked in the freedom of trusting God's promises, even when they couldn't see the outcome. When we live by faith, we experience the freedom that comes from knowing we don't have to have everything figured out—God is guiding us, and His plans are perfect.

If you are struggling to trust God in an area of your life, bring it to Him in prayer. Ask Him to strengthen your faith and help you live in the freedom of trusting Him fully.

Call to Action: Reflect on an area of your life where you need to live by faith rather than sight. Spend time in prayer, asking God to strengthen your faith and help you trust in His promises.

Prayer: Lord, thank You for the freedom to live by faith. Help me trust in Your promises and rely on Your guidance, even when I can't see the whole picture. Strengthen my faith, and help me walk in the freedom that comes from trusting You completely. Amen.

July 15
Freedom to Live in Holiness

Verse: *"But just as He who called you is holy, so be holy in all you do; for it is written: 'Be holy, because I am holy.'"*

(1 Peter 1:15-16, NIV)

Message: In Christ, we are free to live in holiness. 1 Peter 1:15-16 calls us to be holy in all we do because God is holy. Holiness is not about perfection but about being set apart for God's purposes. When we live in the freedom Christ gives us, we are no longer bound by the sinful patterns of the world. Instead, we are empowered by the Holy Spirit to live lives that reflect God's holiness and righteousness. Living in holiness means choosing to honor God with our thoughts, actions, and words, walking in the freedom that comes from living according to His will.

In the Bible, we see that God's people were called to be set apart from the surrounding nations. They were to live differently, reflecting God's character to the world around them. As believers, we are called to do the same. Living in holiness is not a burden—it's a privilege. Through Christ, we are free from the power of sin and are empowered to live lives that please God. Holiness brings freedom because it aligns us with God's perfect will for our lives, leading us into the fullness of joy, peace, and purpose.

If you desire to live a life of holiness, ask God to help you walk in His ways. Trust that through His Spirit, you are free to live a life that honors Him in all you do.

Call to Action: Reflect on what it means to live a life of holiness. Spend time in prayer, asking God to help you live in the freedom of holiness, honoring Him in every area of your life.

Prayer: Father, thank You for the freedom to live in holiness. Help me walk in Your ways, reflecting Your holiness in everything I do. Empower me by Your Spirit to live a life that honors You, and lead me into the freedom that comes from living according to Your will. Amen.

July 16
Freedom from Guilt

Verse: *"In Him we have redemption through His blood, the forgiveness of sins, in accordance with the riches of God's grace."*

(Ephesians 1:7, NIV)

Message: Guilt can be a heavy burden, but in Christ, we are free from guilt because we have been forgiven. Ephesians 1:7 reminds us that we have redemption and forgiveness through the blood of Jesus, and this forgiveness is given according to God's abundant grace. Christ's sacrifice on the cross paid the price for our sins, and because of His grace, we are free from the guilt and shame that once weighed us down. This freedom allows us to walk confidently in our new identity as forgiven children of God.

The Bible tells the story of the prodigal son, who squandered his inheritance and returned home feeling guilty and ashamed. Yet, his father welcomed him back with open arms and celebrated his return. In the same way, God's forgiveness erases our guilt. No matter how far we've strayed or what mistakes we've made, God's grace is greater. Through Christ's redemption, we can live in the freedom that comes from knowing we are forgiven and loved by our Heavenly Father.

If you are carrying the weight of guilt, bring it to God in prayer. Trust that through Christ, you are forgiven, and live in the freedom of His grace.

Call to Action: Reflect on any guilt or shame you may be holding onto. Spend time in prayer, thanking God for His forgiveness and grace, and release your guilt into His hands.

Prayer: Father, thank You for the freedom from guilt that comes through Your forgiveness. I am grateful for the redemption I have in Christ. Help me to live in the freedom of Your grace, leaving behind guilt and shame, and embracing my identity as Your forgiven child. Amen.

July 17
Freedom to Stand Firm

Verse: *"Stand firm, then, and do not let yourselves be burdened again by a yoke of slavery."*

(Galatians 5:1, NIV)

Message: Christ has set us free, and now we are called to stand firm in that freedom. Galatians 5:1 encourages us not to fall back into the old patterns of sin, guilt, or fear that once enslaved us. Jesus paid the ultimate price to liberate us from the power of sin, and we must hold on to that freedom with boldness and faith. The enemy will try to deceive us into believing that we are still under the yoke of our past mistakes, but the truth is that in Christ, we are free, forgiven, and empowered to live for Him.

In the Bible, the Israelites were freed from slavery in Egypt, but many times in the wilderness, they looked back with longing for the past, forgetting the hardships they endured. They had to be reminded to stand firm in the freedom God had given them. In the same way, we may sometimes be tempted to return to old habits, but God calls us to live in the fullness of the freedom He has given us. Standing firm means trusting in the work of Christ and walking forward in the new life He offers us, not letting the past enslave us once again.

If you find yourself struggling with old patterns or temptations, ask God to strengthen you. Stand firm in the freedom Christ has given you and live in the victory He has won.

Call to Action: Reflect on any areas where you may be tempted to return to old habits. Pray for God's strength to stand firm in the freedom Christ has given you, trusting in His victory over sin.

Prayer: Lord, thank You for the freedom I have in Christ. Help me stand firm and not return to the old ways of living that once enslaved me. Strengthen me to live in the freedom You've given me and to walk confidently in Your victory. Amen.

July 18
Freedom from Comparison

Verse: *"Each one should test their own actions. Then they can take pride in themselves alone, without comparing themselves to someone else."*

(Galatians 6:4, NIV)

Message: Comparison can be a subtle trap that steals our joy and undermines our sense of worth, but in Christ, we are free from the need to compare ourselves to others. Galatians 6:4 reminds us to focus on our own walk with God, testing our actions and finding our identity in Him, not in how we measure up to others. Christ has set us free to live fully as the individuals He created us to be, each with unique gifts, callings, and purposes. Comparison can distract us from our own journey and diminish the work God is doing in our lives.

In the parable of the talents, Jesus illustrated the importance of using the gifts God has given us without comparing ourselves to others. Each servant was given different amounts to manage, but they were judged on how faithfully they used what they had been given, not on how they compared to one another. God calls us to be faithful with what He has entrusted to us, and to live in the freedom of our unique calling, free from the burden of comparison.

If you find yourself caught in the trap of comparing yourself to others, ask God to help you see yourself through His eyes. Embrace the freedom to live out your own unique calling, knowing that you are valued and loved by God.

Call to Action: Reflect on areas where you may be comparing yourself to others. Spend time in prayer, asking God to help you focus on His purpose for your life and live in the freedom of your unique identity in Christ.

Prayer: Father, thank You for freeing me from the need to compare myself to others. Help me to focus on the unique calling You have for me and to live confidently in the gifts You have given me. I trust that my identity is secure in You, and I ask for the strength to live out that identity fully. Amen.

July 19
Freedom to Love Without Fear

Verse: *"There is no fear in love. But perfect love drives out fear, because fear has to do with punishment. The one who fears is not made perfect in love."*

(1 John 4:18, NIV)

Message: In Christ, we are free to love others without fear. 1 John 4:18 teaches us that perfect love drives out fear. This means that when we are rooted in God's perfect love, we no longer have to fear rejection, failure, or judgment. God's love sets us free to love others unconditionally and boldly, knowing that we are fully accepted and loved by Him. Fear often holds us back from loving others as we should, but in Christ, we are empowered to love without reservation.

Jesus modeled this fearless love throughout His ministry. He loved those whom society rejected, He healed those whom others avoided, and He reached out to those who had been cast aside. His love was fearless because it flowed from His perfect relationship with the Father. As His followers, we are called to love others with that same fearless love. When we are secure in God's love for us, we are free to love others without worrying about the outcome. We can love freely because we are fully loved by God.

If fear has been holding you back from loving others, bring it to God in prayer. Ask Him to fill your heart with His perfect love and to help you live in the freedom to love boldly and without fear.

Call to Action: Reflect on any fears that may be hindering you from loving others fully. Spend time in prayer, asking God to fill you with His perfect love and drive out fear, so you can love others as He loves you.

Prayer: Lord, thank You for the freedom to love without fear. Fill my heart with Your perfect love, and help me love others boldly and unconditionally. Drive out any fear that holds me back, and let Your love flow through me to those around me. Amen.

July 20
Freedom in God's Rest

Verse: *"Come to me, all you who are weary and burdened, and I will give you rest."*

(Matthew 11:28, NIV)

Message: One of the most beautiful freedoms we have in Christ is the freedom to rest in Him. In Matthew 11:28, Jesus invites all who are weary and burdened to come to Him, promising to give them rest. In a world that constantly demands more from us, Jesus offers us the gift of rest—not just physical rest, but spiritual and emotional rest. In Christ, we are free from striving and performance, and we are invited to find peace and refreshment in His presence.

The story of Mary and Martha in Luke 10 illustrates the importance of resting in Jesus. While Martha was busy with all the preparations, Mary chose to sit at Jesus' feet and listen to His words. Jesus commended Mary for choosing "what is better," reminding us that in our busyness, we often neglect the need to simply be in His presence. Living in freedom means that we don't have to earn God's approval through our work—we are already loved, and we can rest in that truth.

If you are feeling weary or burdened, take time to rest in Jesus. Come to Him in prayer, and allow Him to refresh your soul with His peace and love.

Call to Action: Reflect on areas of your life where you may be striving or carrying burdens that you were not meant to bear. Spend time resting in Jesus' presence and trusting in His invitation to give you rest.

Prayer: Father, thank You for the freedom to rest in You. I come to You with my burdens and my weariness, trusting that You will give me rest. Help me to let go of the need to strive and to rest in Your love and grace. Amen.

July 21
Freedom from Shame

Verse: *"Those who look to Him are radiant; their faces are never covered with shame."*

(Psalm 34:5, NIV)

Message: In Christ, we are free from the weight of shame. Psalm 34:5 assures us that when we look to God, our faces will be radiant, and we will never be covered with shame. Shame is a heavy burden that can distort our view of ourselves and keep us from experiencing the fullness of God's grace. But Jesus bore our shame on the cross so that we can walk in the freedom of knowing that we are loved, accepted, and forgiven by God. When we focus on Him, our identity is shaped by His love, not by our past mistakes.

The woman caught in adultery, described in John 8, stood condemned by others and filled with shame. But Jesus didn't condemn her; instead, He offered her forgiveness and a new start. "Neither do I condemn you," He said. "Go now and leave your life of sin." Jesus offers that same freedom from shame to us. When we turn to Him, our shame is replaced by His grace, and we are free to live in the light of His love and forgiveness.

If you are struggling with feelings of shame, bring them to Jesus in prayer. Trust that He has already removed your shame, and walk in the freedom of knowing you are fully forgiven and loved by Him.

Call to Action: Reflect on any areas where shame may be holding you back. Spend time in prayer, asking God to replace your shame with His grace and to help you live in the freedom of His love.

Prayer: Lord, thank You for freeing me from the burden of shame. I turn to You, knowing that You have forgiven me and removed my shame. Help me live in the light of Your grace, confident in Your love and acceptance. Amen.

July 22
Freedom to Trust God's Plans

Verse: *"For I know the plans I have for you," declares the Lord, "plans to prosper you and not to harm you, plans to give you hope and a future."*

(Jeremiah 29:11, NIV)

Message: Living in freedom through Christ means trusting in God's plans for our lives. Jeremiah 29:11 reminds us that God has good plans for us—plans to prosper us and give us hope and a future. We are free from the fear and anxiety that come with trying to control our own lives. Instead, we can trust that God's plans are always better than our own, and He is leading us toward a future filled with hope. This freedom allows us to live with peace and confidence, knowing that God is in control.

In the Bible, we see how God's plans often unfolded differently than people expected, yet they were always for the best. Joseph's journey from slavery to becoming a ruler in Egypt was full of unexpected twists, but each step was part of God's plan to save His people. In the same way, we may not always understand the path God leads us on, but we can trust that He is working all things together for our good. His plans are filled with hope and purpose, and as we trust Him, we experience the freedom that comes from surrendering to His will.

If you're struggling to trust God's plans for your life, bring your fears to Him in prayer. Ask Him to help you live in the freedom of trusting His good and perfect plan for your future.

Call to Action: Reflect on areas where you may be trying to control your own future. Spend time in prayer, surrendering your plans to God and asking Him to help you trust His purpose for your life.

Prayer: Father, thank You for the freedom to trust in Your plans for my life. I surrender my own desires and fears to You, knowing that Your plans are for my good. Help me live in the peace and freedom that come from trusting in Your perfect will. Amen.

July 23
Freedom from Temptation

Verse: *"No temptation has overtaken you except what is common to mankind. And God is faithful; He will not let you be tempted beyond what you can bear. But when you are tempted, He will also provide a way out so that you can endure it."*

(1 Corinthians 10:13, NIV)

Message: In Christ, we are free from the power of temptation. 1 Corinthians 10:13 reminds us that no temptation is too strong for us to overcome, because God is faithful and provides a way out. Temptation is a reality we all face, but through Christ, we are not slaves to it. We have the power, through the Holy Spirit, to resist temptation and choose the path of righteousness. God's faithfulness ensures that we are never left alone in our struggles—He always provides a way for us to escape temptation and remain strong in our faith.

In the wilderness, Jesus Himself faced temptation, but He responded with the Word of God, standing firm in His identity and His mission. His victory over temptation reminds us that we too can overcome through the power of God's Word and the strength of the Holy Spirit. We don't have to fall into the traps of sin; we are free to live in victory. God's faithfulness is our assurance that we are never left without a way to overcome temptation.

If you are facing temptation, turn to God in prayer. Ask for His strength and guidance, trusting that He will provide the way out and empower you to stand firm in your faith.

Call to Action: Reflect on any temptations you may be facing and how you can rely on God's strength to overcome them. Spend time in prayer, asking God to provide the way out and to strengthen your resolve to resist temptation.

Prayer: Lord, thank You for the freedom to overcome temptation through Your strength. I trust in Your faithfulness to provide a way out when I am tempted, and I ask for the power of Your Holy Spirit to help me stand firm. Lead me in the path of righteousness, and help me walk in victory over temptation. Amen.

July 24
Freedom to Live in Joy

Verse: *"The joy of the Lord is your strength."*

(Nehemiah 8:10, NIV)

Message: Living in freedom through Christ means living in joy. Nehemiah 8:10 reminds us that the joy of the Lord is our strength. This joy is not dependent on our circumstances, but on our relationship with God. In Christ, we are free to experience deep and lasting joy, even in the midst of trials. His presence fills us with joy, and this joy gives us the strength to face whatever challenges come our way. When we live in the freedom of Christ, we can embrace each day with joy, knowing that our future is secure in Him.

The apostle Paul wrote many of his letters from prison, yet they are filled with expressions of joy and thanksgiving. Paul's joy was not based on his external circumstances but on his relationship with Christ. He knew that no matter what he faced, his joy was secure in the Lord. We can experience that same joy when we focus on God's presence in our lives. This joy is our strength, giving us the endurance and hope to keep going, no matter what we encounter.

If you're struggling to find joy, ask God to fill you with His presence and to help you live in the freedom of His joy. Let His joy strengthen you for each day.

Call to Action: Reflect on the joy of the Lord as your strength. Spend time in prayer, asking God to fill you with His joy and to help you live in the freedom of that joy, no matter your circumstances.

Prayer: Father, thank You for the joy that is my strength. Fill my heart with Your joy, and help me live each day in the freedom of that joy, trusting in Your presence and Your promises. Strengthen me through Your joy, and help me embrace each day with hope and gratitude. Amen.

July 25
Freedom in God's Love

Verse: *"For I am convinced that neither death nor life, neither angels nor demons, neither the present nor the future, nor any powers, neither height nor depth, nor anything else in all creation, will be able to separate us from the love of God that is in Christ Jesus our Lord."*

(Romans 8:38-39, NIV)

Message: In Christ, we experience the profound freedom that comes from being fully loved by God. Romans 8:38-39 offers a powerful assurance that nothing—absolutely nothing—can separate us from God's love in Christ Jesus. This truth frees us from fear, anxiety, and insecurity because we know that God's love is unshakable and eternal. It means we don't have to strive for approval or fear abandonment. We are rooted in God's unconditional love, which is stronger than any circumstance or force in life.

Paul, the author of Romans, experienced many trials—imprisonment, persecution, and suffering for the Gospel—yet he was confident that God's love would never fail him. He understood that this love was not based on his performance but was secured in Christ. Like Paul, we can live confidently, knowing that even when life feels uncertain, God's love remains constant. This love frees us from the need to earn God's approval or be perfect; instead, we can rest in the truth that we are already fully loved and accepted.

If you are struggling with feelings of unworthiness or fear, remember that nothing can separate you from God's love. Live in the freedom that comes from knowing you are deeply loved and that His love will never fail.

Call to Action: Reflect on God's unshakable love for you. Spend time in prayer, thanking Him for His unconditional love, and ask Him to help you live in the freedom that comes from being secure in His love.

Prayer: Father, thank You for Your unchanging love. I am so grateful that nothing can separate me from the love You have for me in Christ Jesus. Help me live in the freedom of knowing I am fully loved and accepted by You, and let Your love cast out all fear and insecurity in my heart. Amen.

July 26
Freedom from Worry

Verse: *"Therefore I tell you, do not worry about your life, what you will eat or drink; or about your body, what you will wear. Is not life more than food, and the body more than clothes?"*

(Matthew 6:25, NIV)

Message: Jesus calls us to live free from worry, knowing that God will provide for all our needs. In Matthew 6:25, He encourages us not to worry about the basic necessities of life. Worry often stems from fear and a lack of trust in God's provision, but Jesus reminds us that life is about more than just material things. When we trust in God as our provider, we are free from the anxiety and fear that often accompany worrying about the future. God knows our needs, and He is faithful to meet them.

Jesus uses the example of the birds of the air and the flowers of the field, pointing out that God cares for them, and how much more will He care for us, His children. We don't need to be consumed with worry, because our Heavenly Father is in control. Living in this freedom allows us to focus on what truly matters—our relationship with God and the calling He has for our lives. When we trust in His provision, we experience peace and contentment, free from the burden of worry.

If worry has been weighing you down, bring your concerns to God in prayer. Trust that He is faithful to provide for your needs, and live in the freedom of His care.

Call to Action: Reflect on the areas of your life where worry has been consuming your thoughts. Spend time in prayer, releasing those worries to God, and trust in His faithful provision.

Prayer: Father, thank You for freeing me from the burden of worry. I trust in Your provision and care for my life. Help me release my concerns to You, knowing that You will provide for all my needs. Let me live in the peace and freedom of trusting in Your faithfulness. Amen.

July 27
Freedom to Seek First God's Kingdom

Verse: *"But seek first His kingdom and His righteousness, and all these things will be given to you as well."*

(Matthew 6:33, NIV)

Message: Jesus invites us to live in the freedom of seeking God's kingdom first. In Matthew 6:33, He tells us that when we prioritize God's kingdom and His righteousness, everything else will fall into place. Living in freedom means aligning our hearts with God's purposes rather than being consumed with worldly pursuits. When we seek God's kingdom first, we are free from the pressure to chase after material success or validation from others. Instead, we live with purpose and peace, knowing that God will provide for our needs as we focus on Him.

In the Bible, we see how Jesus' disciples left everything behind to follow Him, seeking first His kingdom. They found freedom in letting go of their old lives and embracing the mission of spreading the Gospel. In the same way, when we seek God's kingdom above all else, we experience the joy and fulfillment that comes from living in alignment with His will. We are free to pursue His purposes, knowing that He will take care of everything we need.

If you've been focused on earthly concerns, ask God to help you realign your priorities. Seek first His kingdom, and trust that everything else will fall into place.

Call to Action: Reflect on how you can seek God's kingdom first in your life. Spend time in prayer, asking God to help you prioritize His purposes and trust that He will take care of your needs.

Prayer: Lord, thank You for the freedom to seek first Your kingdom. Help me realign my heart and priorities with Your will. I trust that as I seek You first, You will provide for all my needs and lead me into the life You've called me to live. Amen.

July 28
Freedom in God's Protection

Verse: *"The Lord is my light and my salvation—whom shall I fear? The Lord is the stronghold of my life—of whom shall I be afraid?"*

(Psalm 27:1, NIV)

Message: In Christ, we are free from fear because we live under God's protection. Psalm 27:1 reminds us that the Lord is our light and our salvation, and because of this, we have no reason to fear. Fear can be paralyzing, but when we trust in God's protection, we are free to live boldly and courageously. The Lord is the stronghold of our lives, and nothing can come against us without passing through His hands. This freedom from fear allows us to walk confidently, knowing that God is with us and will guard and protect us.

David, who wrote this psalm, faced many dangerous situations in his life, yet he was confident in God's protection. Whether he was fighting Goliath, fleeing from King Saul, or leading Israel into battle, David knew that the Lord was his protector and deliverer. In the same way, we can live in the freedom of God's protection, knowing that He is our stronghold. When we trust in His care, fear loses its grip on our hearts, and we are free to live with boldness and faith.

If fear has been holding you back, bring it to God in prayer. Trust in His protection, and live in the freedom that comes from knowing He is your stronghold.

Call to Action: Reflect on any fears that have been keeping you from living fully in God's freedom. Spend time in prayer, asking God to remind you of His protection and help you walk confidently in His care.

Prayer: Father, thank You for being my protector and my stronghold. I trust in Your protection and ask You to help me live free from fear. Remind me that You are always with me, and help me walk in the boldness and freedom that come from knowing You are my light and salvation. Amen.

July 29
Freedom to Share the Gospel

Verse: *"But you will receive power when the Holy Spirit comes on you; and you will be My witnesses in Jerusalem, and in all Judea and Samaria, and to the ends of the earth."*

(Acts 1:8, NIV)

Message: Living in freedom through Christ means having the boldness and power to share the Gospel with others. Acts 1:8 reminds us that we have received power through the Holy Spirit to be witnesses of Christ to the ends of the earth. This freedom allows us to speak boldly about our faith, knowing that God's Spirit is with us and empowers us to fulfill His mission. We are not bound by fear, doubt, or insecurity when it comes to sharing our faith—Christ has given us the freedom and authority to proclaim His name.

In the early church, the disciples were filled with the Holy Spirit and boldly shared the message of Jesus, even in the face of persecution. They didn't shrink back in fear; instead, they trusted in the power of the Spirit to guide them and give them the words to speak. As followers of Christ, we too are called to be His witnesses. We have the freedom to share the Gospel, knowing that God is working through us. When we step out in faith, He will provide the words and the opportunities to share His love with others.

If you've been hesitant to share your faith, ask God for boldness. Trust that the Holy Spirit will empower you to be a witness for Christ, and embrace the freedom to share His love with the world.

Call to Action: Reflect on opportunities where you can share the Gospel. Spend time in prayer, asking God for boldness and guidance from the Holy Spirit as you step out in faith to share your testimony.

Prayer: Lord, thank You for the freedom to share the Gospel. Empower me with Your Holy Spirit to be a bold witness for You. Help me trust in Your guidance, and give me the words to share Your love and truth with those around me. Amen.

July 30
Freedom to Be Who God Made You to Be

Verse: "For we are God's handiwork, created in Christ Jesus to do good works, which God prepared in advance for us to do."

(Ephesians 2:10, NIV)

Message: In Christ, we are free to embrace our identity as God's masterpiece. Ephesians 2:10 tells us that we are God's handiwork, created in Christ to do good works that He has prepared for us. This means that each of us has a unique purpose and calling, and we are free to live out that purpose with confidence and joy. We don't need to compare ourselves to others or try to be someone we're not—we are free to be who God made us to be.

God has designed each of us with specific gifts, talents, and passions. When we embrace our identity in Christ, we are free to walk in the good works He has prepared for us. Whether it's serving in ministry, raising a family, creating art, or building a business, we are called to reflect God's love and character in all that we do. Living in this freedom means trusting that God has a plan for our lives and that we are uniquely equipped to fulfill that plan.

If you've been struggling with your sense of purpose or identity, bring it to God in prayer. Ask Him to remind you of who He has created you to be, and trust that He has prepared good works for you to walk in.

Call to Action: Reflect on your unique gifts and calling. Spend time in prayer, asking God to help you embrace your identity as His handiwork and to guide you into the good works He has prepared for you.

Prayer: Father, thank You for creating me with a purpose. Help me embrace my identity as Your masterpiece and live in the freedom of being who You made me to be. Guide me into the good works You have prepared for me, and help me reflect Your love and character in all I do. Amen.

July 31
Freedom to Walk in Victory

Verse: *"But thanks be to God! He gives us the victory through our Lord Jesus Christ."*

(1 Corinthians 15:57, NIV)

Message: As believers in Christ, we are called to walk in the victory that has already been won for us through Jesus. 1 Corinthians 15:57 reminds us that God has given us victory through our Lord Jesus Christ. This victory isn't something we have to earn—it's a gift of grace that comes from Christ's triumph over sin, death, and the grave. Because of Jesus' sacrifice and resurrection, we are no longer bound by the chains of sin, fear, or death. We are free to live in victory every day, knowing that the ultimate battle has been won on our behalf.

In the Bible, we see examples of people who walked in victory because of their faith in God. David defeated Goliath, not because of his strength, but because of his trust in God's power. The Israelites crossed the Red Sea because they believed in God's promise of deliverance. In the same way, we are called to live in the victory that Christ has secured for us. We may face challenges, but we can stand firm in the knowledge that Jesus has already overcome the world. This victory gives us the freedom to live boldly, with hope and confidence, no matter what we face.

If you feel defeated by your circumstances, remember that in Christ, you are already victorious. Walk in the freedom of that victory, trusting that God has given you the strength to overcome every challenge.

Call to Action: Reflect on areas where you need to claim Christ's victory. Spend time in prayer, thanking God for the victory He has given you through Jesus, and ask Him to help you live in that victory daily.

Prayer: Lord, thank You for the victory I have in Christ. I am grateful that through Jesus, I am free from sin, fear, and death. Help me walk in the freedom of Your victory each day, trusting in Your strength and living boldly for You. Amen.

August

Growing in Spiritual Maturity

August 1
Growing in Grace

Verse: *"But grow in the grace and knowledge of our Lord and Savior Jesus Christ. To Him be glory both now and forever! Amen."*
(2 Peter 3:18, NIV)

Message: Spiritual maturity begins with growth in grace and knowledge. 2 Peter 3:18 encourages us to grow in both our understanding of God's grace and our knowledge of Jesus. Maturity in faith isn't about being perfect but about continually seeking to understand God's love more deeply and letting that understanding transform how we live. As we grow in grace, we become more patient, forgiving, and compassionate, reflecting Christ's character in our lives.

The apostle Peter, who once denied Jesus, learned firsthand about the power of grace. Through his failures, Peter grew in his understanding of God's mercy and love, and he became a bold leader of the early church. In the same way, spiritual growth comes through our experiences of God's grace, especially in moments of failure or difficulty. As we experience God's grace, we are empowered to extend that grace to others and to walk in a deeper relationship with Jesus.

If you're seeking to grow in your faith, ask God to help you understand His grace more fully. Let that grace shape how you treat others and deepen your walk with Christ.

Call to Action: Reflect on how you've experienced God's grace in your life. Spend time in prayer, asking God to help you grow in grace and in the knowledge of Jesus, allowing His love to transform your heart.

Prayer: Lord, thank You for Your grace that transforms my life. Help me grow in both grace and knowledge of You, so I can reflect Your love more fully. Teach me to extend grace to others, and lead me into deeper spiritual maturity. Amen.

August 2
Maturing in Wisdom

Verse: *"The fear of the Lord is the beginning of wisdom, and knowledge of the Holy One is understanding."*

(Proverbs 9:10, NIV)

Message: True spiritual maturity involves growing in wisdom, and Proverbs 9:10 teaches us that the fear of the Lord is the beginning of wisdom. This fear is not a terrified fear but a reverence and deep respect for God's holiness and power. As we mature spiritually, we begin to see life through the lens of God's wisdom rather than our own limited understanding. This wisdom shapes how we make decisions, how we treat others, and how we respond to challenges.

Solomon, known as the wisest king, prayed for wisdom instead of riches or power. God granted him extraordinary insight because he sought to lead with wisdom rather than selfish ambition. Spiritual maturity comes when we seek God's wisdom in every aspect of our lives—when we prioritize His ways above our own. By revering God and seeking His guidance, we develop the discernment and understanding needed to navigate life's complexities.

If you desire to grow in wisdom, ask God to reveal His heart and will to you. Lean into the wisdom found in His Word, and trust Him to guide your steps with divine understanding.

Call to Action: Reflect on areas where you need God's wisdom. Spend time in prayer, asking God to grant you wisdom and understanding, and commit to seeking His guidance in all you do.

Prayer: Father, thank You for the wisdom that comes from knowing You. Help me to grow in wisdom as I seek to honor You with my life. Teach me to revere You and to trust Your guidance, so I can walk in maturity and discernment. Amen.

August 3
Bearing Fruit in Every Season

Verse: *"That person is like a tree planted by streams of water, which yields its fruit in season and whose leaf does not wither —whatever they do prospers."*

(Psalm 1:3, NIV)

Message: Spiritual maturity means bearing fruit in every season of life, just like a tree planted by streams of water. Psalm 1:3 paints a beautiful picture of a person rooted in God's Word, constantly nourished and flourishing. This kind of maturity is not about outward success but about inner growth that remains steadfast through every season, whether times of blessing or challenge. A spiritually mature person draws strength from God's Word, allowing it to shape their life and decisions.

In the Gospels, Jesus often spoke of the importance of bearing fruit. He used the analogy of vines and branches, teaching that those who remain in Him will bear much fruit. The fruit of spiritual maturity includes qualities like love, joy, peace, patience, and kindness. These fruits are not dependent on our circumstances but are the natural result of a life rooted in Christ. As we grow in maturity, we learn to bear fruit in every season, trusting that God is working in us even during difficult times.

If you're longing to see more spiritual fruit in your life, focus on deepening your relationship with Christ. Let His Word nourish you, and trust that He will help you bear fruit in every season.

Call to Action: Reflect on the spiritual fruit in your life. Are there areas where you want to see more growth? Spend time in prayer, asking God to help you stay rooted in His Word so you can bear fruit in every season.

Prayer: Lord, thank You for the promise that I can bear fruit in every season as I stay rooted in You. Help me to deepen my relationship with You and to trust in Your Word. Let my life be fruitful for Your kingdom, reflecting Your love and character. Amen.

August 4
Learning to Trust God More

Verse: *"Trust in the Lord with all your heart and lean not on your own understanding; in all your ways submit to Him, and He will make your paths straight."*

(Proverbs 3:5-6, NIV)

Message: Trusting God is a hallmark of spiritual maturity. Proverbs 3:5-6 teaches us to trust in the Lord with all our hearts and to avoid relying on our own understanding. As we grow spiritually, we learn to place our full confidence in God, even when we don't understand His ways or timing. Trusting God means surrendering our own plans and desires to His will, knowing that He is working all things for our good.

In the Bible, we see countless examples of people who trusted God even when it didn't make sense. Abraham trusted God's promise of a son even in his old age. Joseph trusted God's plan for his life, even when he was sold into slavery. This kind of trust grows through experience and relationship with God. The more we see His faithfulness in our lives, the more we learn to trust Him with everything. Spiritual maturity means learning to trust God not only in the good times but also in the difficult moments, believing that He will make our paths straight.

If you're struggling to trust God in a certain area of your life, bring it to Him in prayer. Ask Him to help you release your own understanding and trust in His perfect plan.

Call to Action: Reflect on areas where you may be leaning on your own understanding rather than trusting in God. Spend time in prayer, asking Him to help you trust Him more deeply and submit to His guidance.

Prayer: Father, thank You for Your faithfulness. Help me to trust You with all my heart and to submit my plans and desires to You. Teach me to lean on Your understanding rather than my own, and guide me as I follow Your path for my life. Amen.

August 5
Growing in Humility

Verse: *"Humble yourselves before the Lord, and He will lift you up."*

(James 4:10, NIV)

Message: Humility is a key aspect of spiritual maturity. James 4:10 encourages us to humble ourselves before the Lord, with the promise that He will lift us up in due time. Growing in humility means recognizing our dependence on God and being willing to submit to His will above our own. It means choosing to serve others rather than seeking our own recognition. Spiritual maturity is marked by a heart that seeks to honor God and lift others up rather than exalting ourselves.

Jesus, the perfect example of humility, humbled Himself by becoming obedient to death on a cross (Philippians 2:8). Though He was God, He did not seek to exalt Himself but chose to serve and give His life for others. As we grow in spiritual maturity, we are called to follow His example, putting others before ourselves and relying on God's strength rather than our own. Humility allows us to experience God's grace more fully, as we acknowledge our need for Him in every area of our lives.

If you're seeking to grow in spiritual maturity, ask God to help you develop a heart of humility. Trust that as you humble yourself before Him, He will lift you up in His perfect time.

Call to Action: Reflect on areas where you may be struggling with pride. Spend time in prayer, asking God to help you grow in humility and to serve others as Christ did.

Prayer: Lord, thank You for the example of humility that Jesus gave. Help me to grow in humility and to rely on Your strength rather than my own. Teach me to serve others with a humble heart, and let my life reflect Your love and grace. Amen.

August 6
Maturing Through Perseverance

Verse: "Consider it pure joy, my brothers and sisters, whenever you face trials of many kinds, because you know that the testing of your faith produces perseverance. Let perseverance finish its work so that you may be mature and complete, not lacking anything."

(James 1:2-4, NIV)

Message: Spiritual maturity is often shaped through perseverance. James 1:2-4 encourages us to consider it pure joy when we face trials, knowing that these difficulties test our faith and help us develop perseverance. As we persevere through challenges, we grow stronger in our faith and more mature in our walk with Christ. Trials are not something to be feared or avoided, but opportunities for God to refine our character and deepen our trust in Him.

The Bible is filled with examples of people who grew through perseverance. Job endured immense suffering but held onto his faith, and in the end, God restored him and blessed him abundantly. Paul faced persecution and hardship throughout his ministry, yet he continued to preach the Gospel with boldness. These trials were not wasted—they became part of their spiritual growth. When we persevere through difficulties, we become more complete, more dependent on God, and more capable of reflecting His love and grace in the world.

If you're facing trials today, ask God to help you see them as opportunities for growth. Trust that He is using these challenges to mature you and complete His work in your life.

Call to Action: Reflect on any challenges you're currently facing. Spend time in prayer, asking God to help you persevere and to use these trials to mature your faith.

Prayer: Lord, thank You for the trials that help me grow. Help me to persevere through challenges and to trust that You are using them to shape me into the person You've called me to be. Let these difficulties refine my character and deepen my faith in You. Amen.

August 7
Growing in Love

Verse: *"And this is my prayer: that your love may abound more and more in knowledge and depth of insight, so that you may be able to discern what is best and may be pure and blameless for the day of Christ."*

(Philippians 1:9-10, NIV)

Message: Spiritual maturity is marked by a deepening love for others. In Philippians 1:9-10, Paul prays that love would abound more and more in knowledge and insight, leading to greater discernment and purity. As we grow in love, we also grow in wisdom and understanding. This kind of love isn't just emotional—it's a love that is grounded in truth, wisdom, and an increasing understanding of God's heart. When we grow in love, we reflect Christ more fully, and our relationships become a testimony to His grace.

Jesus said that the greatest commandments are to love God and to love others. As we mature in our faith, our capacity to love grows. We begin to love more selflessly, seeking the good of others over our own desires. This kind of love requires humility, patience, and a deep connection with God. The more we understand His love for us, the more we are able to extend that love to others. Growing in love is a lifelong journey, but it is one that leads us closer to the heart of God and helps us reflect His character to the world.

If you're seeking to grow in spiritual maturity, ask God to help you grow in love. Let His love fill your heart and guide your actions, so that you may reflect His grace and truth in all your relationships.

Call to Action: Reflect on how you can grow in love in your relationships. Spend time in prayer, asking God to deepen your love for others and to give you insight into how you can show His love more fully.

Prayer: Father, thank You for the love You have shown me through Christ. Help my love to abound more and more in knowledge and insight, so that I may grow in wisdom and purity. Teach me to love others as You have loved me, and help me reflect Your grace in all that I do. Amen.

August 8
Growing in Patience

Verse: *"Be completely humble and gentle; be patient, bearing with one another in love."*

(Ephesians 4:2, NIV)

Message: Patience is a fruit of spiritual maturity, and Ephesians 4:2 calls us to be humble, gentle, and patient, bearing with one another in love. Growing in patience means learning to wait on God's timing and extend grace to others, even when it's difficult. Patience allows us to remain peaceful in the face of frustration, trusting that God is at work even when we can't see the results. As we mature, our ability to practice patience with others and ourselves deepens, reflecting the character of Christ.

The Bible offers many examples of patience. Abraham waited many years for the promise of a son to be fulfilled. Joseph endured years of slavery and imprisonment before he saw God's plan unfold. Their patience was rooted in trust that God's timing was perfect. Spiritual maturity involves trusting God's process, even when we don't understand the delays or challenges. As we grow in patience, we also grow in faith, knowing that God's plans are good and His timing is perfect.

If you are struggling with impatience, ask God to help you grow in this area. Trust that He is at work, even in the waiting, and that His timing is always perfect.

Call to Action: Reflect on areas of your life where you need to grow in patience. Spend time in prayer, asking God to help you trust His timing and to extend grace to others as you wait.

Prayer: Lord, thank You for Your patience with me. Help me grow in patience as I wait on Your timing and extend grace to others. Teach me to trust in Your perfect plan, and help me reflect Your peace and love in all situations. Amen.

August 9
Maturing in Prayer

Verse: *"Devote yourselves to prayer, being watchful and thankful."*
(Colossians 4:2, NIV)

Message: A mature believer understands the power and necessity of prayer. Colossians 4:2 calls us to be devoted to prayer, watching for God's work in our lives and giving thanks for His faithfulness. Prayer is not just about asking God for things—it is about developing a deeper relationship with Him. As we grow in spiritual maturity, our prayers become more focused on aligning our hearts with God's will and seeking His presence in every area of our lives.

Jesus often withdrew to quiet places to pray, demonstrating the importance of constant communication with the Father. His life was marked by a deep devotion to prayer, and as His followers, we are called to develop that same devotion. Spiritual maturity involves a prayer life that goes beyond requests; it becomes a conversation with God where we listen as much as we speak. As we mature in prayer, we become more attuned to God's voice and more sensitive to His leading in our lives.

If you desire to grow in your spiritual maturity, ask God to deepen your prayer life. Commit to spending regular time in prayer, not just asking for things but listening for His voice and thanking Him for His faithfulness.

Call to Action: Reflect on your current prayer life. Spend time in prayer today, asking God to help you grow in your devotion to prayer and to seek His presence more consistently.

Prayer: Father, thank You for the gift of prayer. Help me grow in my devotion to prayer, seeking Your will and Your presence in all areas of my life. Teach me to be watchful and thankful, and guide me as I learn to listen for Your voice. Amen.

August 10
Growing in Faith

Verse: *"Now faith is confidence in what we hope for and assurance about what we do not see."*

(Hebrews 11:1, NIV)

Message: Spiritual maturity requires a growing and deepening faith. Hebrews 11:1 defines faith as confidence in what we hope for and assurance about what we do not see. Faith is not based on our circumstances but on our trust in God's promises. As we mature in our faith, we learn to rely more fully on God, even when we don't understand His plans or see the outcome. Faith helps us navigate the uncertainties of life with confidence and hope, knowing that God is always faithful.

The Bible's "hall of faith" in Hebrews 11 highlights many heroes of the faith who trusted God in the midst of uncertainty. Abraham left his homeland, not knowing where God would lead him. Noah built an ark, trusting in God's warning about the coming flood. These examples remind us that faith often requires stepping out in obedience before we see the full picture. As we grow in spiritual maturity, we develop the kind of faith that holds onto God's promises, even in the face of doubt or difficulty.

If you're struggling with doubt or uncertainty, ask God to strengthen your faith. Trust that He is faithful, and hold onto the hope that comes from His promises.

Call to Action: Reflect on any areas of your life where you need to trust God more fully. Spend time in prayer, asking God to increase your faith and give you confidence in His promises.

Prayer: Lord, thank You for the gift of faith. Help me grow in my confidence in Your promises, even when I can't see the outcome. Strengthen my faith, and help me trust in Your goodness and faithfulness in every area of my life. Amen.

August 11
Growing in Obedience

Verse: *"Blessed rather are those who hear the word of God and obey it."* (Luke 11:28, NIV)

Message: Spiritual maturity is demonstrated through our obedience to God's Word. In Luke 11:28, Jesus reminds us that true blessing comes from hearing the Word of God and obeying it. It's not enough to simply know what the Bible says; we must live it out. Obedience is a key sign of spiritual growth, as it reflects our trust in God's wisdom and His direction for our lives. As we grow spiritually, our desire to follow God's commands becomes stronger, and we experience the blessing that comes from living according to His will.

Abraham's life is a powerful example of obedience. When God called him to leave his home and go to a land he didn't know, Abraham obeyed, even though the path was uncertain. Later, when God asked Abraham to sacrifice his son Isaac, Abraham's obedience was unwavering. This kind of obedience flows from a deep trust in God, knowing that His plans are always good. As we grow in maturity, our obedience to God's commands becomes more natural, and we experience the joy that comes from following His will.

If you are seeking to grow in obedience, ask God to help you hear His Word clearly and to give you the strength to live it out in your daily life.

Call to Action: Reflect on areas of your life where you may be struggling to obey God's Word. Spend time in prayer, asking for His help to trust His commands and live in obedience to His will.

Prayer: Father, thank You for Your Word and the guidance it gives me. Help me to grow in obedience, trusting that Your commands are for my good. Give me the strength to follow Your will, even when it's difficult, and let my life reflect the blessing that comes from obeying You. Amen.

August 12
Maturing Through Forgiveness

Verse: "Bear with each other and forgive one another if any of you has a grievance against someone. Forgive as the Lord forgave you."

(Colossians 3:13, NIV)

Message: Forgiveness is an essential aspect of spiritual maturity. In Colossians 3:13, we are called to forgive others as the Lord has forgiven us. Growing in spiritual maturity means learning to let go of bitterness, resentment, and anger, and instead choosing forgiveness. When we forgive, we reflect God's grace in our lives and allow healing to take place in our hearts. Forgiveness frees us from the burden of carrying past hurts and helps us to grow in love and compassion toward others.

Jesus modeled forgiveness on the cross when He prayed for those who crucified Him, saying, "Father, forgive them, for they do not know what they are doing." As followers of Christ, we are called to extend that same grace to others. This is not always easy, but it is a sign of spiritual maturity. Forgiving others doesn't mean excusing their actions, but it means releasing the hurt and trusting God to bring justice and healing. When we forgive, we experience freedom and peace, and we grow in our ability to love others as God loves us.

If you are struggling to forgive someone, bring that hurt to God in prayer. Ask Him to help you release it and to fill your heart with His grace and love.

Call to Action: Reflect on any grudges or unforgiveness you may be holding onto. Spend time in prayer, asking God to help you forgive as He has forgiven you.

Prayer: Lord, thank You for the forgiveness You have given me through Jesus. Help me to grow in forgiveness and to release any bitterness or anger I'm holding onto. Fill my heart with Your grace and help me extend that grace to others, as You have forgiven me. Amen.

August 13
Growing in Holiness

Verse: "But just as He who called you is holy, so be holy in all you do; for it is written: 'Be holy, because I am holy.'"

(1 Peter 1:15-16, NIV)

Message: Holiness is a key mark of spiritual maturity. In 1 Peter 1:15-16, we are called to be holy in all that we do, because God Himself is holy. Holiness means being set apart for God's purposes, living in a way that honors Him, and reflecting His character in every area of our lives. As we grow in spiritual maturity, our lives should increasingly reflect the holiness of God. This includes how we think, speak, and act, as well as how we treat others.

In the Old Testament, God called the Israelites to be a holy nation, set apart from the surrounding cultures. They were to reflect God's holiness through their obedience and worship. Similarly, as followers of Christ, we are called to live in a way that sets us apart from the world. Holiness is not about perfection but about living in alignment with God's will, seeking His righteousness, and allowing His Spirit to transform us from the inside out. As we grow in holiness, we draw closer to God and become more like Jesus.

If you desire to grow in holiness, ask God to help you live a life that reflects His character. Trust in His grace to transform you and guide you into a life that honors Him.

Call to Action: Reflect on areas of your life where you can grow in holiness. Spend time in prayer, asking God to help you live in alignment with His will and to reflect His holiness in all that you do.

Prayer: Father, thank You for calling me to be holy, as You are holy. Help me to grow in holiness and to live in a way that honors You. Transform my heart and mind, and guide me in Your ways so that my life reflects Your righteousness and love. Amen.

August 14
Maturing in the Word of God

Verse: *"All Scripture is God-breathed and is useful for teaching, rebuking, correcting and training in righteousness, so that the servant of God may be thoroughly equipped for every good work."*

(2 Timothy 3:16-17, NIV)

Message: Spiritual maturity is closely tied to our relationship with God's Word. 2 Timothy 3:16-17 teaches us that all Scripture is God-breathed and useful for our growth in righteousness. As we grow in spiritual maturity, we must also grow in our understanding and application of the Bible. The Word of God is our guide, our source of wisdom, and the foundation for how we live as followers of Christ. The more we immerse ourselves in Scripture, the more equipped we become to live out God's will in every area of our lives.

Jesus used Scripture to teach, to confront religious leaders, and even to resist temptation in the wilderness. His life was deeply rooted in the Word of God, and as His followers, we are called to do the same. Growing in spiritual maturity means allowing the Word to shape our thoughts, our decisions, and our actions. The Bible is not just a book to be read—it is a living and active guide that transforms us as we apply it to our lives.

If you want to grow in spiritual maturity, make time each day to study and reflect on God's Word. Ask Him to teach you through Scripture and to help you live according to His truth.

Call to Action: Reflect on how often you engage with God's Word. Spend time in prayer, asking God to deepen your understanding of Scripture and to help you apply it to your daily life.

Prayer: Lord, thank You for the gift of Your Word. Help me grow in my understanding of Scripture and to apply it to every area of my life. Equip me through Your Word to live out Your will, and guide me in righteousness as I seek to follow You. Amen.

August 15
Growing in Faithfulness

Verse: *"Now it is required that those who have been given a trust must prove faithful."*

(1 Corinthians 4:2, NIV)

Message: Faithfulness is a mark of spiritual maturity. 1 Corinthians 4:2 reminds us that those who have been given a trust must prove faithful. As followers of Christ, we have been entrusted with the Gospel, with gifts, and with the opportunity to serve God and others. Growing in spiritual maturity means being faithful with what God has given us, whether it's our time, talents, or resources. Faithfulness is not about perfection but about consistently choosing to honor God with our lives.

In the parable of the talents, Jesus taught about the importance of faithfulness. The servants who were faithful with the resources entrusted to them were rewarded, while the one who buried his talent out of fear missed out on the blessing of serving his master. Spiritual maturity involves taking responsibility for what God has entrusted to us and using it to glorify Him. This includes being faithful in small things, knowing that God sees our efforts and rewards those who serve Him with a faithful heart.

If you want to grow in faithfulness, ask God to help you steward what He has given you with diligence and integrity. Trust that as you are faithful in the little things, He will entrust you with more.

Call to Action: Reflect on areas of your life where you can be more faithful. Spend time in prayer, asking God to help you use your time, talents, and resources to honor Him and serve others.

Prayer: Father, thank You for the opportunities You've given me to serve You. Help me to grow in faithfulness and to steward what You've entrusted to me with integrity and diligence. Let my life be marked by faithfulness to You and to the work You've called me to. Amen.

August 16
Growing in Gentleness

Verse*: "Let your gentleness be evident to all. The Lord is near."*

(Philippians 4:5, NIV)

Message: Spiritual maturity involves cultivating a spirit of gentleness. Philippians 4:5 reminds us that our gentleness should be evident to all, because the Lord is near. Gentleness is not weakness; it is strength under control. It reflects the heart of Christ, who was gentle and humble, even when He had the power to act differently. As we grow in spiritual maturity, we learn to respond to others with gentleness, even in difficult situations. This gentleness draws people closer to God, as they experience His love and grace through our actions.

Jesus' interactions with others were marked by gentleness, especially with those who were marginalized or hurting. He invited the weary and burdened to come to Him, promising rest for their souls. This gentleness didn't mean that He ignored sin, but He corrected with compassion and love. When we grow in gentleness, we reflect this same spirit of Christ. We can be firm in truth while still showing kindness and respect, knowing that gentleness can often disarm hostility and open hearts to the Gospel.

If you struggle with responding gently in challenging situations, ask God to cultivate a spirit of gentleness in you. Let His love and peace guide your interactions with others.

Call to Action: Reflect on how you can demonstrate more gentleness in your relationships. Spend time in prayer, asking God to help you respond with gentleness, especially in moments of tension or frustration.

Prayer: Lord, thank You for the example of gentleness You've given me through Jesus. Help me grow in this area and to respond to others with kindness, even in difficult situations. Let my gentleness reflect Your love and grace, drawing others closer to You. Amen.

August 17
Maturing in Peace

Verse: *"Let the peace of Christ rule in your hearts, since as members of one body you were called to peace. And be thankful."*

(Colossians 3:15, NIV)

Message: A mark of spiritual maturity is allowing the peace of Christ to rule in our hearts. Colossians 3:15 encourages us to let this peace guide us, especially within the body of Christ. As we grow spiritually, we learn to let go of anxiety and worry, trusting in God's sovereignty. His peace becomes the anchor of our lives, enabling us to remain calm in the midst of life's storms. This peace not only benefits us, but it also fosters unity and harmony within the community of believers.

Jesus promised His followers peace, saying, "Peace I leave with you; my peace I give you" (John 14:27). This peace is different from what the world offers—it's a deep, abiding peace that comes from knowing that God is in control. As we grow in spiritual maturity, we learn to rely on this peace, allowing it to rule in our hearts and govern our actions. This peace becomes a testimony to others, showing that our hope and trust are rooted in Christ, not in our circumstances.

If you are struggling to find peace, ask God to help you let go of your worries and allow His peace to rule in your heart. Trust in His plan and rest in His presence.

Call to Action: Reflect on any areas of your life where anxiety or worry has taken hold. Spend time in prayer, asking God to fill you with His peace and to help you trust Him more deeply.

Prayer: Father, thank You for the peace that surpasses understanding. Help me let go of my anxieties and allow Your peace to rule in my heart. Teach me to trust in Your plan and rest in Your presence, so that my life may reflect the peace You give. Amen.

August 18
Growing in Self-Control

Verse: *"Like a city whose walls are broken through is a person who lacks self-control."*

(Proverbs 25:28, NIV)

Message: Self-control is a crucial aspect of spiritual maturity. Proverbs 25:28 warns us that without self-control, we are like a city with broken walls—vulnerable to attacks and unable to protect ourselves. Growing in self-control means learning to manage our desires, emotions, and impulses in a way that honors God. This kind of discipline doesn't come from our own strength but from the work of the Holy Spirit within us. As we grow spiritually, we develop the ability to say no to sinful desires and yes to the things that lead to righteousness.

Paul often wrote about the importance of self-control, especially in his letters to the churches. In 1 Corinthians 9:25, he compared the Christian life to a race, where self-discipline is necessary to run well. Just as an athlete trains their body to perform at its best, we must train ourselves spiritually to grow in self-control. This growth is essential for overcoming temptation, resisting sin, and living a life that honors God. Self-control allows us to remain steady, focused, and aligned with God's will, even when temptations arise.

If you are struggling with self-control in any area of your life, ask God to help you grow in this fruit of the Spirit. Trust that He will give you the strength to overcome temptation and live a life of discipline and integrity.

Call to Action: Reflect on areas where you need to grow in self-control. Spend time in prayer, asking God to help you develop discipline and to rely on the Holy Spirit to guide your thoughts and actions.

Prayer: Lord, thank You for the gift of self-control through the Holy Spirit. Help me grow in this area and to live a life that honors You. Teach me to resist temptation and to manage my desires in a way that reflects Your righteousness and love. Amen.

August 19
Maturing in Joy

Verse: *"The fruit of the Spirit is love, joy, peace, forbearance, kindness, goodness, faithfulness, gentleness and self-control."*

(Galatians 5:22-23, NIV)

Message: Joy is one of the fruits of the Spirit and a sign of spiritual maturity. Galatians 5:22-23 lists joy as one of the characteristics that should naturally flow from a believer who is walking in the Spirit. This joy is not based on circumstances but on the unchanging nature of God's love and faithfulness. As we grow spiritually, our joy becomes rooted in our relationship with Christ, allowing us to experience deep, abiding joy even in difficult times.

In the book of Acts, we see how the early Christians, despite facing persecution, were filled with joy. Their joy came from knowing Christ and the power of His resurrection. This joy wasn't dependent on their circumstances—it flowed from their connection with Jesus. Similarly, as we mature in our faith, we learn to experience joy in all seasons of life. This joy gives us strength and sustains us through trials, reminding us that our hope is in Christ, not in the temporary things of this world.

If you're struggling to find joy, ask God to help you shift your focus from your circumstances to His presence. Let His Spirit fill you with joy that transcends your situation.

Call to Action: Reflect on what is robbing you of joy and how you can reconnect with God's presence. Spend time in prayer, asking God to fill you with His Spirit and restore your joy.

Prayer: Father, thank You for the joy that comes from Your Spirit. Help me to live in that joy, even when life is difficult. Remind me that my joy is found in You, and teach me to rejoice in all circumstances, knowing that You are always with me. Amen.

August 20
Growing in Boldness

Verse: "For the Spirit God gave us does not make us timid, but gives us power, love and self-discipline."

(2 Timothy 1:7, NIV)

Message: Spiritual maturity involves growing in boldness for Christ. 2 Timothy 1:7 reminds us that God has given us a spirit of power, love, and self-discipline, not a spirit of fear. As we grow in our relationship with God, we become more confident in our identity as His children and more bold in living out our faith. This boldness is not about being aggressive or forceful, but about living with courage and confidence, knowing that God is with us and that His power is at work in us.

The early apostles, after receiving the Holy Spirit, were filled with boldness to preach the Gospel, even in the face of persecution. They were unafraid because they knew that God's power was at work in them. As we mature in our faith, we too are called to live boldly, sharing the truth of the Gospel and standing firm in our convictions. This boldness comes from the Holy Spirit, who empowers us to live courageously for Christ, no matter the circumstances.

If you've been hesitant to step out in boldness for Christ, ask God to fill you with His Spirit and give you the courage to live boldly for Him.

Call to Action: Reflect on areas where you need to be more bold in your faith. Spend time in prayer, asking God to fill you with His Spirit and give you the courage to live boldly and confidently for Him.

Prayer: Lord, thank You for the spirit of power, love, and self-discipline that You have given me. Help me to grow in boldness and to live courageously for You. Fill me with Your Spirit, and empower me to stand firm in my faith and share Your love with the world. Amen.

August 21
Maturing in Patience with Others

Verse: *"Be completely humble and gentle; be patient, bearing with one another in love."*

(Ephesians 4:2, NIV)

Message: Spiritual maturity involves learning to be patient with others, just as God is patient with us. Ephesians 4:2 calls us to be humble, gentle, and patient, bearing with one another in love. Patience is not just about waiting for things to happen; it's also about how we treat others, especially when they disappoint or frustrate us. Growing in patience with others is a reflection of our understanding of God's grace. As we mature spiritually, we develop the ability to extend grace and patience to those around us, even in challenging circumstances.

The Bible is filled with examples of God's patience with His people. Despite Israel's repeated disobedience, God continually showed mercy and patience, giving them opportunities to turn back to Him. Jesus demonstrated patience with His disciples, even when they failed to understand His teachings or doubted His power. As followers of Christ, we are called to extend this same patience to others, recognizing that we too are recipients of God's grace.

If you are struggling to be patient with someone, ask God to help you grow in patience and love. Trust that He is at work in both your heart and theirs.

Call to Action: Reflect on any relationships where you may be struggling to show patience. Spend time in prayer, asking God to help you grow in patience and to bear with others in love.

Prayer: Lord, thank You for Your patience with me. Help me to grow in patience with others and to bear with them in love. Teach me to extend grace and understanding, reflecting Your love and gentleness in all my relationships. Amen.

August 22
Growing in Trust

Verse: "Trust in the Lord with all your heart and lean not on your own understanding; in all your ways submit to Him, and He will make your paths straight."

(Proverbs 3:5-6, NIV)

Message: Trusting God fully is a sign of spiritual maturity. Proverbs 3:5-6 encourages us to trust in the Lord with all our hearts and to not rely on our own understanding. Spiritual growth involves learning to trust God even when we don't have all the answers or when life doesn't make sense. Trusting God means submitting our plans, fears, and desires to Him, believing that He is in control and that He will guide us on the right path. As we grow in maturity, we learn to rest in God's sovereignty, trusting that His plans are good and that He is faithful to lead us.

In the Bible, Abraham's journey with God was a powerful example of trust. God called him to leave his home and go to a land he did not know, and Abraham obeyed without knowing the full plan. His faith and trust in God led to the fulfillment of God's promises. Spiritual maturity comes when we learn to trust God in every area of our lives, even when the path is uncertain.

If you're struggling to trust God, bring your doubts and fears to Him in prayer. Ask Him to help you trust in His wisdom and to guide your steps with confidence.

Call to Action: Reflect on any areas of your life where you are struggling to trust God. Spend time in prayer, asking Him to help you trust in His plan and to lean on His understanding, not your own.

Prayer: Father, thank You for Your faithfulness. Help me to trust in You with all my heart and to submit my plans and desires to Your will. Teach me to rely on Your wisdom and not my own understanding, and guide me on the path You have for me. Amen.

August 23
Growing in Contentment

Verse: *"I have learned to be content whatever the circumstances."* *(Philippians 4:11, NIV)*

Message: Spiritual maturity involves learning to be content in all circumstances. In Philippians 4:11, Paul shares that he has learned the secret of being content, whether in times of plenty or in times of need. Contentment comes from trusting God's provision and being grateful for what we have, rather than constantly longing for more. As we grow spiritually, we develop the ability to find peace and satisfaction in Christ, regardless of our external circumstances. Contentment allows us to live with gratitude and joy, knowing that God is enough.

Paul's life was marked by hardship—imprisonment, persecution, and suffering—yet he learned to be content because his hope was in Christ. He didn't rely on material wealth or comfort for his peace; instead, he trusted that God would provide everything he needed. As we grow in spiritual maturity, we too learn to rely on God for our contentment, trusting that He is our provider and that He will supply all our needs according to His will.

If you struggle with discontentment, ask God to help you find peace in Him. Trust that He is enough, and let Him fill your heart with gratitude for His provision.

Call to Action: Reflect on areas where you may be struggling with contentment. Spend time in prayer, asking God to help you find peace and satisfaction in Him, regardless of your circumstances.

Prayer: Lord, thank You for being my provider. Help me to find contentment in You, no matter my circumstances. Teach me to trust in Your provision and to live with gratitude for all that You have given me. Let my heart be satisfied in You alone. Amen.

August 24
Maturing Through Serving Others

Verse: *"For even the Son of Man did not come to be served, but to serve, and to give His life as a ransom for many."*

(Mark 10:45, NIV)

Message: Spiritual maturity is demonstrated through serving others. Jesus, the Son of God, came not to be served but to serve and give His life for us. As we grow spiritually, we are called to follow His example by serving others with humility and love. Serving others is not just a task we perform—it is a reflection of Christ's heart. When we serve, we demonstrate the love of Christ to those around us, and we grow in our understanding of what it means to live a life of selflessness and compassion.

In the Gospels, we see how Jesus served others by healing the sick, feeding the hungry, and even washing His disciples' feet. His life was marked by acts of service and compassion. As we mature in our faith, we are called to develop this same attitude of serving others, putting their needs before our own. Serving others helps us grow in humility, love, and grace, as we reflect Christ's character in our actions.

If you're looking for ways to grow spiritually, consider how you can serve others in your community, church, or family. Ask God to give you a heart that desires to serve, just as Christ served.

Call to Action: Reflect on how you can serve others in your daily life. Spend time in prayer, asking God to help you develop a heart of service and to use your gifts and resources to bless others.

Prayer: Father, thank You for the example of service that Jesus gave. Help me to grow in my desire to serve others and to reflect Your love through my actions. Teach me to put others before myself, and use me to be a blessing to those around me. Amen.

August 25

Growing in Humility

Verse: *"Do nothing out of selfish ambition or vain conceit. Rather, in humility value others above yourselves."*

(Philippians 2:3, NIV)

Message: Humility is a key sign of spiritual maturity. In Philippians 2:3, we are called to do nothing out of selfish ambition but to value others above ourselves. True humility means recognizing that we are all equal before God and that our worth does not come from our achievements but from our identity in Christ. As we grow spiritually, we learn to let go of pride and to put others first, serving them with love and grace. Humility allows us to see others as God sees them, and it helps us build stronger, more loving relationships.

Jesus was the ultimate example of humility. Though He was God, He humbled Himself by becoming human and even submitting to death on a cross. His life teaches us that true greatness comes from humility and service. As we grow in spiritual maturity, we are called to follow His example, choosing to humble ourselves and lift others up. This kind of humility leads to peace, unity, and a deeper relationship with God and others.

If you struggle with pride or selfishness, ask God to help you grow in humility. Trust that as you humble yourself before Him, He will lift you up in due time.

Call to Action: Reflect on areas of your life where you need to grow in humility. Spend time in prayer, asking God to help you value others above yourself and to serve with a humble heart.

Prayer: Lord, thank You for the example of humility that Jesus set. Help me to grow in humility and to value others above myself. Teach me to serve with love and grace, and help me reflect Your character in all that I do. Amen.

August 26
Maturing in Faithfulness

Verse: *"Whoever can be trusted with very little can also be trusted with much, and whoever is dishonest with very little will also be dishonest with much."*

(Luke 16:10, NIV)

Message: Spiritual maturity involves growing in faithfulness, both in the small and big things in life. Luke 16:10 teaches us that if we are faithful in the little things, God will trust us with more. Faithfulness is about consistently doing what is right, even when no one is watching. It's about honoring God in the everyday moments, knowing that He sees and rewards our faithfulness. As we grow spiritually, we become more committed to being reliable and trustworthy, both in our relationship with God and in our relationships with others.

In the parable of the talents, Jesus praised the servants who were faithful with what their master entrusted to them. They didn't let fear or laziness stop them from being productive and responsible. In the same way, God calls us to be faithful with the opportunities, gifts, and resources He has given us. Spiritual maturity means being good stewards of all that God has entrusted to us, knowing that faithfulness in small things leads to greater responsibility and blessing.

If you desire to grow in faithfulness, ask God to help you be diligent and trustworthy in every area of your life. Trust that as you are faithful with the little, God will entrust you with more.

Call to Action: Reflect on areas of your life where you can be more faithful. Spend time in prayer, asking God to help you be diligent and trustworthy in all that He has entrusted to you.

Prayer: Father, thank You for calling me to be faithful in all things. Help me to grow in faithfulness, both in the small and big things in my life. Teach me to honor You with everything You've entrusted to me, and help me be trustworthy in all that I do. Amen.

August 27
Growing in Dependence on God

Verse: *"I am the vine; you are the branches. If you remain in me and I in you, you will bear much fruit; apart from me you can do nothing."*

(John 15:5, NIV)

Message: Spiritual maturity means growing in our dependence on God. In John 15:5, Jesus reminds us that He is the vine and we are the branches. Apart from Him, we can do nothing, but when we remain connected to Him, we bear much fruit. This teaches us that spiritual growth is not about self-reliance but about abiding in Christ. The more we depend on Him, the more we are empowered to live fruitful lives that reflect His character and love.

Throughout His ministry, Jesus modeled dependence on the Father. He frequently withdrew to pray, seeking God's guidance and strength for everything He did. As we grow spiritually, we learn to rely less on our own abilities and more on God's power. This dependence leads to a deeper relationship with Him and greater fruitfulness in our lives. Remaining connected to Christ is the key to spiritual growth and maturity.

If you're feeling overwhelmed or relying too much on your own strength, take time to reconnect with God. Ask Him to help you depend on Him in every area of your life.

Call to Action: Reflect on areas where you may be relying too much on yourself. Spend time in prayer, asking God to help you depend on Him more fully and to remain connected to Christ in all that you do.

Prayer: Lord, thank You for being the vine and for giving me life and strength. Help me to depend on You in every area of my life and to remain connected to You so that I can bear much fruit. Teach me to trust in Your power, not my own. Amen.

August 28
Maturing Through Trials

Verse: *"Consider it pure joy, my brothers and sisters, whenever you face trials of many kinds, because you know that the testing of your faith produces perseverance."*

(James 1:2-3, NIV)

Message: Spiritual maturity is often developed through trials. James 1:2-3 encourages us to consider it pure joy when we face trials, because they test our faith and produce perseverance. Trials refine our character, deepen our trust in God, and help us grow in spiritual strength. Though difficulties are never easy, they have a purpose—they shape us into the people God has called us to be. As we mature spiritually, we learn to embrace trials as opportunities for growth and trust in God's faithfulness through every challenge.

Throughout Scripture, we see people who grew through trials—Joseph, David, Paul, and others. Their faith was tested, but through perseverance, they became stronger and more grounded in their relationship with God. In the same way, trials in our lives are meant to produce perseverance and maturity. Spiritual growth doesn't happen in comfort; it happens when we walk through difficult seasons, relying on God's strength and trusting that He is working all things together for good.

If you're facing trials today, ask God to give you strength and perseverance. Trust that He is using these challenges to refine you and make you more like Christ.

Call to Action: Reflect on any trials you are currently facing and how God may be using them to help you grow. Spend time in prayer, asking God for strength and perseverance as you navigate these challenges.

Prayer: Father, thank You for using trials to help me grow. Help me to see the challenges I face as opportunities to develop perseverance and deepen my trust in You. Strengthen me in the midst of trials, and help me grow into the person You've called me to be. Amen.

August 29
Growing in Gratitude

Verse: *"Give thanks in all circumstances; for this is God's will for you in Christ Jesus."*

(1 Thessalonians 5:18, NIV)

Message: A sign of spiritual maturity is the ability to give thanks in all circumstances. 1 Thessalonians 5:18 calls us to have a heart of gratitude, regardless of our situation. Gratitude shifts our focus from what we lack to the blessings we already have. As we grow in spiritual maturity, we learn to recognize God's goodness in every season, even in times of difficulty. Giving thanks helps us cultivate a heart of joy and contentment, trusting that God is always working for our good.

The apostle Paul, who wrote this letter, knew what it meant to give thanks in difficult circumstances. He faced imprisonment, persecution, and hardship, yet he continually thanked God for His provision and grace. Gratitude is a choice that allows us to see the hand of God in all things. When we give thanks, we open our hearts to receive more of His peace and joy, knowing that He is always with us.

If you're struggling to find things to be thankful for, ask God to help you see His blessings in your life. Practice giving thanks in all circumstances, trusting that God is working for your good.

Call to Action: Reflect on areas of your life where you can cultivate more gratitude. Spend time in prayer, thanking God for His blessings, even in difficult seasons.

Prayer: Lord, thank You for Your goodness and faithfulness in my life. Help me to give thanks in all circumstances, recognizing Your hand at work in every season. Cultivate a heart of gratitude in me, and help me trust that You are always working for my good. Amen.

August 30
Maturing in Hope

Verse: "But those who hope in the Lord will renew their strength. They will soar on wings like eagles; they will run and not grow weary, they will walk and not be faint."

(Isaiah 40:31, NIV)

Message: Spiritual maturity is marked by a hope that is anchored in the Lord. Isaiah 40:31 reminds us that those who hope in the Lord will renew their strength and rise above life's challenges. Hope is not just wishful thinking—it is a confident expectation in God's promises. As we grow in maturity, our hope becomes more rooted in God's character and His faithfulness. This hope gives us strength to endure hardships, knowing that God will fulfill His promises in His perfect timing.

In the Bible, we see examples of people whose hope sustained them through difficult times. Abraham hoped in God's promise of a son, even when it seemed impossible. The Israelites hoped for deliverance, even after years of wandering in the wilderness. Spiritual maturity involves placing our hope in God's unfailing love and trusting that He will renew our strength, no matter what we face. This hope sustains us and allows us to keep going, even when the journey is long and hard.

If you're feeling weary or discouraged, ask God to renew your hope in Him. Trust that He will give you the strength to rise above your circumstances and continue walking in faith.

Call to Action: Reflect on areas of your life where you may have lost hope. Spend time in prayer, asking God to renew your hope in His promises and to give you strength for the journey.

Prayer: Father, thank You for the hope I have in You. Help me to place my hope in Your promises, knowing that You are faithful. Renew my strength and help me rise above the challenges I face, trusting that You will fulfill Your Word in my life. Amen.

August 31
Growing in God's Love

Verse: *"And so we know and rely on the love God has for us. God is love. Whoever lives in love lives in God, and God in them."*

(1 John 4:16, NIV)

Message: The greatest sign of spiritual maturity is growing in God's love. 1 John 4:16 tells us that God is love, and when we live in love, we live in God. Spiritual growth is not just about knowledge or service—it's about allowing God's love to fill our hearts and transform our lives. As we grow in love, we reflect God's character to the world, and we experience the fullness of His presence in our lives. Love is the foundation of our faith, and it is the greatest commandment we are called to follow.

Jesus taught that the greatest commandments are to love God with all our heart and to love our neighbor as ourselves. As we mature spiritually, we learn to love more deeply, more selflessly, and more sacrificially. This love is not something we can manufacture on our own—it comes from God, who fills us with His Spirit and teaches us how to love. Growing in God's love transforms our relationships, our attitudes, and our purpose in life.

If you desire to grow in spiritual maturity, ask God to fill your heart with His love. Let His love guide your actions, your words, and your relationships, so that you may reflect His love to the world.

Call to Action: Reflect on how you can grow in love for God and others. Spend time in prayer, asking God to fill you with His love and to help you live a life that reflects His love to those around you.

Prayer: Lord, thank You for Your perfect love. Help me to grow in that love and to live in a way that reflects Your character. Fill my heart with Your love, and teach me to love You with all my heart and to love others as You have loved me. Amen.

September

Serving Others with Joy

September 1
The Joy of Serving Others

Verse: *"Serve wholeheartedly, as if you were serving the Lord, not people."*

(Ephesians 6:7, NIV)

Message: Serving others is a central part of our calling as followers of Christ, and Ephesians 6:7 reminds us that we are to serve wholeheartedly, as if we were serving the Lord. When we serve with joy, our actions become an offering to God, and we bring Him glory. Joyful service doesn't come from seeking recognition or praise from people, but from knowing that we are serving God. As we mature in our faith, we learn to embrace the privilege of serving others, reflecting Christ's love in our actions.

Jesus, the ultimate servant, came to serve, not to be served. He washed His disciples' feet and instructed them to do the same for others. This joyful attitude of serving was central to His ministry, and it is what we are called to imitate. When we serve others with joy, we experience the fulfillment that comes from living out our purpose in Christ. True joy in service comes when we focus on the eternal impact our actions have and the honor of partnering with God in His work.

If you want to serve with joy, ask God to shift your perspective and remind you that every act of service is an opportunity to honor Him.

Call to Action: Reflect on your attitude toward serving others. Spend time in prayer, asking God to help you serve with joy and wholeheartedly, knowing that you are ultimately serving Him.

Prayer: Father, thank You for the privilege of serving others. Help me to serve with joy and a heart that honors You. Let my actions reflect Your love, and remind me that when I serve others, I am serving You. Amen.

September 2
Using Your Gifts to Serve

Verse: "Each of you should use whatever gift you have received to serve others, as faithful stewards of God's grace in its various forms."

(1 Peter 4:10, NIV)

Message: Every believer has been given unique gifts by God, and 1 Peter 4:10 encourages us to use those gifts to serve others. Whether it's teaching, encouragement, hospitality, or another gift, God has entrusted us with abilities to bless others and advance His kingdom. When we use our gifts to serve others, we are being faithful stewards of the grace God has given us. As we grow in our understanding of our gifts, we also grow in our joy in serving, knowing that we are contributing to God's work in the world.

In the parable of the talents, Jesus emphasized the importance of using what God has given us. The servant who multiplied his talents was praised for his faithfulness, while the one who buried his talent out of fear missed out on the blessing of service. God has equipped each of us with unique talents and gifts, and He calls us to use them joyfully to serve others. When we serve in our areas of gifting, we experience fulfillment and purpose, knowing that we are partnering with God in His mission.

If you're unsure of what gifts you have, ask God to reveal them to you and guide you in how to use them to serve others.

Call to Action: Reflect on the gifts God has given you. Spend time in prayer, asking Him to show you how to use your gifts to serve others and bring glory to His name.

Prayer: Lord, thank You for the gifts You have given me. Help me to use them faithfully to serve others and to be a good steward of Your grace. Show me where I can serve and give me joy in knowing that I am using my gifts for Your kingdom. Amen.

September 3
Serving in Humility

Verse: "Do nothing out of selfish ambition or vain conceit. Rather, in humility value others above yourselves."

(Philippians 2:3, NIV)

Message: True service comes from a heart of humility. Philippians 2:3 teaches us to value others above ourselves, serving with humility rather than seeking recognition or personal gain. Humility means putting others' needs before our own and serving them with a genuine desire to help and bless them. As we serve with humility, we reflect the heart of Christ, who, though He was God, humbled Himself to serve humanity and ultimately give His life for us.

Jesus modeled humble service when He washed His disciples' feet, a task usually reserved for the lowest servant. By doing this, He demonstrated that greatness in the kingdom of God is found in humble service to others. Serving others with humility is not about being noticed or praised; it's about loving others and meeting their needs, just as Jesus did. When we serve with humility, we find joy in knowing that we are following the example of our Savior and honoring God with our actions.

If you find yourself seeking recognition in your service, ask God to cultivate a heart of humility in you, so you can serve others joyfully without seeking praise.

Call to Action: Reflect on your motives for serving. Spend time in prayer, asking God to help you serve with humility and to value others above yourself, following Christ's example.

Prayer: Father, thank You for the example of humility that Jesus gave. Help me to serve others with humility, not seeking recognition but seeking to love and bless them. Teach me to value others above myself and to find joy in serving as Jesus did. Amen.

September 4
Serving with Compassion

Verse: "*When He saw the crowds, He had compassion on them, because they were harassed and helpless, like sheep without a shepherd.*"

(Matthew 9:36, NIV)

Message: Serving others with joy also means serving with compassion. In Matthew 9:36, we see Jesus moved with compassion for the crowds, who were harassed and helpless. Jesus' heart was full of compassion for those in need, and His service to others flowed from this deep sense of care and love. Compassion is what drives us to serve others, not out of obligation, but out of a genuine desire to help and uplift those who are struggling.

Throughout the Gospels, Jesus' compassion led Him to heal the sick, feed the hungry, and teach the lost. His acts of service were always motivated by love for those who were suffering or in need. As we grow in spiritual maturity, we are called to serve with the same compassion that Jesus showed. When we allow God's love to fill our hearts, we are moved to serve others with joy, knowing that we are reflecting His compassion to the world.

If you want to grow in compassion, ask God to open your heart to the needs of those around you. Let His love flow through you as you serve others.

Call to Action: Reflect on how you can serve others with compassion. Spend time in prayer, asking God to help you see the needs of those around you and to serve with a heart full of compassion.

Prayer: Lord, thank You for Your compassion toward me. Help me to serve others with the same compassion that You showed, caring for those who are hurting and in need. Let my heart be moved by love, and let my service reflect Your grace and kindness. Amen.

SEPTEMBER 5
JOY IN SERVING WITHOUT EXPECTATION

Verse: *"Freely you have received; freely give."*

(Matthew 10:8, NIV)

Message: Serving others with joy means serving without expecting anything in return. In Matthew 10:8, Jesus told His disciples to freely give, just as they had freely received from Him. When we serve with no expectation of reward or recognition, we are reflecting the heart of Christ, who gave everything for us without expecting anything in return. Joyful service is about giving generously from the grace we have received, knowing that our reward comes from God, not from people.

Jesus freely gave His time, His love, and ultimately His life for us. His acts of service were not motivated by a desire for recognition but by His love for humanity. As His followers, we are called to serve others with the same generosity. When we serve without expecting anything in return, we experience the joy that comes from giving freely. This joy is not dependent on how others respond but is rooted in the satisfaction of knowing that we are honoring God with our actions.

If you find yourself seeking recognition or reward for your service, ask God to help you serve with a heart that gives freely, as Christ did.

Call to Action: Reflect on your motivations for serving. Spend time in prayer, asking God to help you serve others freely, without expecting anything in return, and to experience the joy of giving as Christ gave.

Prayer: Father, thank You for the grace and love I have freely received from You. Help me to serve others with the same generosity, giving freely without expecting anything in return. Let my service be an offering of love to You, and fill my heart with the joy of serving in Your name. Amen.

September 6
Serving Through Love

Verse: "*You, my brothers and sisters, were called to be free. But do not use your freedom to indulge the flesh; rather, serve one another humbly in love.*"

(Galatians 5:13, NIV)

Message: We are called to use our freedom in Christ to serve one another humbly in love. Galatians 5:13 reminds us that the freedom we have in Christ is not for selfish purposes but to serve others. True service flows from love—love for God and love for others. When we serve out of love, we are fulfilling the law of Christ and reflecting His heart. This kind of service brings joy because it aligns us with God's purposes and allows us to be His hands and feet in the world.

Jesus constantly demonstrated serving through love. Whether He was feeding the hungry, healing the sick, or teaching the multitudes, His actions were always motivated by love. As we follow His example, we are called to serve others, not out of obligation, but because we love them as Christ loves us. This love compels us to put others' needs before our own and to serve with humility and joy.

If you want to serve with joy, ask God to fill your heart with love for others. Let His love be the motivation behind every act of service.

Call to Action: Reflect on how you can serve others through love in your daily life. Spend time in prayer, asking God to fill you with His love so that you may serve others humbly and joyfully.

Prayer: Father, thank You for the love You've shown me through Jesus. Help me to serve others humbly and in love, reflecting the heart of Christ in all that I do. Let my service be motivated by love, and bring joy to those I serve. Amen.

September 7
Serving Without Complaining

Verse: *"Do everything without grumbling or arguing, so that you may become blameless and pure, 'children of God without fault in a warped and crooked generation.'"*

(Philippians 2:14-15, NIV)

Message: Serving others with joy means serving without complaining or arguing. Philippians 2:14-15 encourages us to do everything without grumbling, so that we may shine as children of God. It's easy to serve when it's convenient, but true joy in service comes when we choose to serve, even in difficult or inconvenient situations, without complaint. This kind of service sets us apart and reflects the heart of God, who calls us to be blameless and pure in a world that often focuses on self-interest.

Jesus served others without complaining, even when He was tired or when the people He served were ungrateful. His focus was on fulfilling the Father's will, and He found joy in serving, knowing that it brought glory to God. As we grow in spiritual maturity, we are called to serve with the same attitude—choosing to serve with a joyful heart, even when it's challenging. When we serve without grumbling, we reflect God's character and bring light to a world that often focuses on what's easiest or most comfortable.

If you find yourself complaining when it comes to serving, ask God to help you serve with a heart of gratitude and joy, even in difficult moments.

Call to Action: Reflect on how you can serve without complaining, even in challenging situations. Spend time in prayer, asking God to help you have a joyful and grateful heart as you serve others.

Prayer: Lord, thank You for the example of Jesus, who served others without complaining. Help me to serve with a joyful heart, even when it's difficult or inconvenient. Teach me to serve without grumbling, so that I may reflect Your love and grace to those around me. Amen.

September 8
Finding Strength in Serving

Verse*: "The Lord is my strength and my shield; my heart trusts in Him, and He helps me. My heart leaps for joy, and with my song I praise Him."*

(Psalm 28:7, NIV)

Message: When we serve others, we can find strength in the Lord. Psalm 28:7 reminds us that God is our strength and shield, and as we trust in Him, He helps us. Serving others can sometimes feel overwhelming, especially when we face challenges or feel weary. But when we rely on God's strength rather than our own, we find the joy and energy we need to continue serving with gladness. God promises to strengthen and sustain us as we pour out our lives in service to others.

Throughout His ministry, Jesus often withdrew to pray and be with the Father. He found strength and renewal in His relationship with God, which enabled Him to continue serving and teaching others. In the same way, we must learn to depend on God's strength as we serve. When we trust in Him, He refreshes our hearts and fills us with joy, giving us the energy and desire to continue serving with love.

If you're feeling weary in your service, turn to God for strength. Ask Him to renew your heart and give you the energy to serve others with joy.

Call to Action: Reflect on where you may be feeling weary in your service. Spend time in prayer, asking God to strengthen you and to fill your heart with renewed joy as you serve.

Prayer: Father, thank You for being my strength and shield. When I feel weary, help me to trust in You for the strength I need to continue serving others with joy. Renew my heart and give me the energy to serve with gladness, knowing that You are with me. Amen.

September 9
Serving Others with Kindness

Verse: *"Be kind and compassionate to one another, forgiving each other, just as in Christ God forgave you."*

(Ephesians 4:32, NIV)

Message: Serving others with joy means serving with kindness and compassion. Ephesians 4:32 encourages us to be kind and compassionate to one another, forgiving others just as God forgave us through Christ. Kindness is a powerful expression of love, and it can make a significant impact on those we serve. When we choose to serve with kindness, we reflect the heart of God and demonstrate His love to a world that is often harsh and unforgiving.

Jesus served others with kindness, even when He was misunderstood or rejected. His kindness extended to everyone—whether it was healing the sick, feeding the hungry, or comforting the brokenhearted. As His followers, we are called to show that same kindness in our service. When we serve others with compassion and understanding, we bring joy to those around us and glorify God through our actions. Kindness is contagious, and it has the power to transform hearts and lives.

If you struggle with showing kindness in your service, ask God to fill your heart with His love and compassion. Let His kindness overflow in your actions toward others.

Call to Action: Reflect on how you can serve others with more kindness and compassion. Spend time in prayer, asking God to help you show kindness in all your interactions, especially as you serve.

Prayer: Lord, thank You for the kindness and compassion You've shown me through Christ. Help me to serve others with that same kindness, reflecting Your love in everything I do. Teach me to be compassionate and forgiving, and let my service bring joy to those around me. Amen.

September 10
Joy in Serving Together

Verse: "And let us consider how we may spur one another on toward love and good deeds, not giving up meeting together, as some are in the habit of doing, but encouraging one another."

(Hebrews 10:24-25, NIV)

Message: There is great joy in serving others as part of a community. Hebrews 10:24-25 reminds us to encourage one another and to spur each other on toward love and good deeds. Serving together strengthens our relationships, builds unity, and allows us to make a greater impact for the kingdom of God. When we serve alongside others, we experience the joy of fellowship and the blessing of working together for a common purpose.

The early church in the book of Acts demonstrated this beautifully. They were united in heart and mind, sharing everything they had and serving one another in love. This sense of community brought great joy, and their service to one another was a powerful testimony to the world around them. As we serve with others, we are encouraged and strengthened, knowing that we are not alone in our efforts. Together, we can accomplish more for God's kingdom and experience the joy that comes from serving in unity.

If you feel isolated in your service, consider joining with others in your church or community. Ask God to lead you to opportunities where you can serve together with fellow believers.

Call to Action: Reflect on how you can serve alongside others in your community. Spend time in prayer, asking God to help you build relationships with those you can serve with, and to bring joy and unity through your collective service.

Prayer: Father, thank You for the joy of serving alongside others. Help me to build strong relationships with those in my community and to serve together in love and unity. Let our service be a testimony to Your love and bring joy to all who are involved. Amen.

September 11

Serving as an Expression of Faith

Verse: "In the same way, faith by itself, if it is not accompanied by action, is dead."

(James 2:17, NIV)

Message: True faith is shown through action, and serving others is one of the clearest expressions of our faith. James 2:17 teaches us that faith without action is dead. When we serve others, we put our faith into practice, demonstrating that we believe in the teachings of Jesus and are committed to living them out. Service becomes a living testimony of our faith in God and His love for humanity. It is through these actions that people can see the love of Christ reflected in us.

The story of the Good Samaritan in Luke 10 illustrates this principle. While others passed by a man in need, the Samaritan acted on his compassion and helped the injured man, even though they were from different backgrounds. His faith was made evident through his actions. Serving others with joy, regardless of the circumstances, allows us to share the love of Christ in a tangible way. When we serve, we show the world that our faith is alive and active.

If you want to grow in your faith, ask God to give you opportunities to serve and to show His love through your actions.

Call to Action: Reflect on how your faith is expressed through your actions. Spend time in prayer, asking God to show you ways you can serve others as an expression of your faith.

Prayer: Lord, thank You for the opportunity to put my faith into action through serving others. Help me to live out my faith by showing Your love to those around me. Let my actions be a testimony to Your grace and goodness. Amen.

September 12
Serving with a Willing Heart

Verse: *"Each of you should give what you have decided in your heart to give, not reluctantly or under compulsion, for God loves a cheerful giver."*

(2 Corinthians 9:7, NIV)

Message: God calls us to serve with a willing and joyful heart. 2 Corinthians 9:7 encourages us to give and serve cheerfully, not out of obligation or reluctance. When we serve with a willing heart, our actions become an expression of love and gratitude toward God. Serving should never feel like a burden or something we do out of compulsion. Instead, it is an opportunity to bless others and glorify God. A willing heart brings joy not only to those we serve but also to ourselves, as we experience the fulfillment that comes from giving freely.

Jesus willingly laid down His life for us, showing the ultimate example of selfless service. He didn't serve out of obligation but out of love. When we serve with that same willing heart, we reflect His character. Whether it's giving our time, talents, or resources, serving with joy is an act of worship. It shows that we trust God's provision and want to use what He's given us to bless others.

If you've been serving reluctantly or out of obligation, ask God to give you a willing heart. Trust that as you give freely, He will bless both you and those you serve.

Call to Action: Reflect on your attitude toward serving. Spend time in prayer, asking God to give you a willing and cheerful heart as you serve others, knowing that He loves a cheerful giver.

Prayer: Father, thank You for the example of willing service that Jesus gave. Help me to serve with a cheerful heart, not out of obligation but out of love. Teach me to give freely and joyfully, trusting that You will use my service for Your glory. Amen.

September 13

Serving the Least of These

Verse: *"Truly I tell you, whatever you did for one of the least of these brothers and sisters of mine, you did for Me."*

(Matthew 25:40, NIV)

Message: When we serve others, especially those in need, we are serving Jesus Himself. In Matthew 25:40, Jesus teaches us that whatever we do for the "least of these," we do for Him. This means that when we serve the poor, the hungry, the sick, and the marginalized, we are honoring Christ. True service doesn't seek recognition or reward but seeks to meet the needs of those who are often overlooked by society. Serving others with joy means recognizing the inherent worth of every person, no matter their situation, and showing them the love of Christ through our actions.

Jesus spent much of His time with those who were considered "least" in society—the poor, the outcasts, and the sinners. He didn't shy away from serving those who were forgotten or rejected by others. In the same way, we are called to serve those who are often overlooked. When we serve them, we are serving Jesus Himself. This kind of service brings deep joy, as we experience the privilege of being the hands and feet of Christ to those who need it most.

If you want to serve with joy, ask God to open your eyes to the needs of those around you, especially those who are marginalized or in need.

Call to Action: Reflect on how you can serve "the least of these" in your community. Spend time in prayer, asking God to help you see those in need and to give you the heart to serve them as if you were serving Christ Himself.

Prayer: Lord, thank You for the opportunity to serve You by serving others. Help me to see the needs of those around me, especially those who are often overlooked. Let my service be a reflection of Your love, and help me to serve with joy, knowing that when I serve others, I am serving You. Amen.

September 14
The Blessing of Serving Others

Verse: "*Give, and it will be given to you. A good measure, pressed down, shaken together and running over, will be poured into your lap. For with the measure you use, it will be measured to you.*"

(Luke 6:38, NIV)

Message: There is a blessing in serving others that extends beyond what we give. Luke 6:38 teaches us that when we give, it will be given back to us in abundance. This doesn't necessarily mean material blessings, but it does mean that when we serve with generosity and love, we are blessed in return with joy, fulfillment, and deeper relationships with God and others. Serving others allows us to experience the blessing of being part of God's work and seeing His love in action.

Jesus taught that it is more blessed to give than to receive (Acts 20:35). When we serve with a generous heart, we open ourselves up to the blessings of God's grace and provision. Serving others connects us with God's heart, deepens our relationships with those we serve, and brings joy that surpasses what we could ever gain by focusing on ourselves. The more we give, the more we receive in terms of spiritual blessings, joy, and contentment.

If you want to experience the blessing of serving, ask God to help you give generously of your time, talents, and resources. Trust that He will pour out His blessings in ways you may not expect.

Call to Action: Reflect on how you can give and serve more generously in your life. Spend time in prayer, asking God to help you serve with a generous heart and to trust in the blessings that come from serving others.

Prayer: Father, thank You for the blessings that come from serving others. Help me to give generously and joyfully, knowing that You will pour out Your blessings in return. Let my service be an act of worship, and let me experience the joy and fulfillment that come from serving others in Your name. Amen.

September 15
Serving Through Encouragement

Verse: *"Therefore encourage one another and build each other up, just as in fact you are doing."*

(1 Thessalonians 5:11, NIV)

Message: One of the simplest and most powerful ways to serve others is through encouragement. 1 Thessalonians 5:11 calls us to encourage one another and build each other up. Encouragement is a gift that can lift someone's spirit, give them hope, and remind them of God's love. When we take the time to encourage others, we are serving them in a way that reflects the heart of Christ. Encouragement can come through words, actions, or even a simple act of kindness, and it has the power to make a significant difference in someone's life.

In the New Testament, Barnabas was known as the "son of encouragement" because he consistently lifted others up and supported them in their faith journeys. His encouragement helped the early church grow and strengthened the faith of those around him. As we serve through encouragement, we build up the body of Christ and reflect God's love to those who need it most. Encouraging others brings joy to both the giver and the receiver, as we experience the power of God's grace in action.

If you want to serve through encouragement, ask God to open your eyes to those who need a kind word or act of encouragement today.

Call to Action: Reflect on how you can encourage someone today. Spend time in prayer, asking God to lead you to someone who needs encouragement, and commit to building them up in love.

Prayer: Lord, thank You for the power of encouragement. Help me to serve others by building them up and offering words of hope and kindness. Let my encouragement reflect Your love and grace, and use me to lift up those who are struggling. Amen.

September 16
Serving with a Pure Heart

Verse: *"Create in me a pure heart, O God, and renew a steadfast spirit within me."*

(Psalm 51:10, NIV)

Message: True service flows from a pure heart, and Psalm 51:10 reminds us of the importance of having a heart that is right before God. When we serve others, it's important that our motives are pure—that we serve out of love and a desire to glorify God, rather than for personal gain or recognition. A pure heart focuses on others' needs and God's glory, rather than seeking selfish ambitions. As we grow in spiritual maturity, God refines our hearts, helping us to serve with sincerity and joy.

David's prayer in Psalm 51 came after he realized the depth of his sin and sought God's forgiveness. He knew that true service to God could only come from a heart that was cleansed and renewed. Similarly, when we ask God to purify our hearts, we become more aligned with His will, and our service becomes an act of worship. Serving with a pure heart brings joy because it's not about us—it's about loving others and bringing glory to God.

If you find yourself struggling with selfish motives in your service, ask God to purify your heart and renew your spirit so that your service may be joyful and sincere.

Call to Action: Reflect on the motives behind your service. Spend time in prayer, asking God to cleanse your heart and help you serve with purity and love, seeking only to glorify Him.

Prayer: Father, thank You for the opportunity to serve others. Create in me a pure heart, and renew a steadfast spirit within me. Help me to serve with sincerity and love, focusing on glorifying You and blessing those around me. Amen.

September 17
Serving Without Seeking Praise

Verse: *"Be careful not to practice your righteousness in front of others to be seen by them. If you do, you will have no reward from your Father in heaven."*

(Matthew 6:1, NIV)

Message: Serving others with joy means serving without seeking the praise of people. Matthew 6:1 reminds us that our acts of righteousness should not be done to gain the approval of others, but to honor God. When we serve for the applause of people, our reward is temporary and shallow. But when we serve for God's glory, He sees our hearts and rewards us in ways far greater than human praise. True joy in service comes when we are focused on pleasing God, not on receiving recognition.

Jesus taught His disciples to serve in humility, warning against doing good deeds for the sake of attention. The Pharisees often served to be seen, seeking approval and admiration from others. But Jesus calls us to a different standard—to serve quietly, humbly, and without seeking recognition. When we serve with this attitude, we find joy in knowing that God sees our hearts and is pleased with our efforts, even if no one else notices.

If you've been serving to seek the approval of others, ask God to help you shift your focus to serving for His glory alone.

Call to Action: Reflect on how you can serve without seeking recognition or praise from others. Spend time in prayer, asking God to help you serve with humility and joy, knowing that He sees your heart.

Prayer: Lord, thank You for the privilege of serving You. Help me to serve without seeking praise or recognition from others, focusing only on bringing glory to Your name. Teach me to serve with a humble heart, finding joy in knowing that You see my efforts. Amen.

September 18
Serving the Body of Christ

Verse: *"Now you are the body of Christ, and each one of you is a part of it."*

(1 Corinthians 12:27, NIV)

Message: As members of the body of Christ, we are called to serve one another. 1 Corinthians 12:27 reminds us that we each have a role to play in the body of Christ, and when we serve one another, we strengthen the body as a whole. Serving others within the church is a vital part of spiritual growth and unity. Each of us has been given different gifts and talents, and when we use them to serve the body, we help build up the church and reflect the love of Christ.

The early church in Acts demonstrated the power of serving one another. They shared their resources, cared for the poor, and encouraged each other in their faith. This kind of service brought great joy and strengthened the church, allowing it to grow and thrive. When we serve within the body of Christ, we not only bless others, but we also grow in our relationship with God and experience the joy of being part of His family.

If you're looking for ways to serve, ask God to show you how you can use your gifts to serve others within the body of Christ.

Call to Action: Reflect on how you can serve the body of Christ. Spend time in prayer, asking God to guide you in using your gifts and talents to bless others and strengthen the church.

Prayer: Father, thank You for placing me in the body of Christ. Help me to serve others within the church, using the gifts You have given me to build up the body. Let my service be a reflection of Your love and grace, and let it bring joy to those I serve. Amen.

September 19
Serving with Perseverance

Verse: *"Let us not become weary in doing good,
for at the proper time we will reap a harvest if we do not give up."*

(Galatians 6:9, NIV)

Message: Serving others can sometimes be exhausting, but Galatians 6:9 encourages us not to grow weary in doing good. Serving with perseverance means continuing to serve, even when it's difficult or when we don't see immediate results. God promises that we will reap a harvest if we do not give up. This means that our efforts to serve others, whether big or small, are never in vain. God sees every act of kindness, and in His perfect timing, He will bring fruit from our service.

Jesus served faithfully throughout His ministry, even when He was tired, misunderstood, or rejected. He continued to heal, teach, and love, knowing that His mission was to glorify the Father and serve others. As we serve, we may face challenges or discouragement, but God calls us to persevere, trusting that He will bring about His purposes through our efforts. Serving with perseverance leads to spiritual growth and allows us to experience the joy of seeing God work through us.

If you're feeling weary in your service, ask God to renew your strength and give you the perseverance to continue serving with joy.

Call to Action: Reflect on any areas of your life where you may be growing weary in serving. Spend time in prayer, asking God to give you the strength and perseverance to keep serving, trusting that He will bring a harvest in His time.

Prayer: Lord, thank You for the promise that my efforts to serve are never in vain. Help me to persevere in doing good, even when it's difficult or when I feel weary. Renew my strength, and let me serve with joy, trusting that You will bring about a harvest in Your perfect time. Amen.

September 20
Serving with a Heart of Gratitude

Verse: *"And whatever you do, whether in word or deed, do it all in the name of the Lord Jesus, giving thanks to God the Father through Him."*

(Colossians 3:17, NIV)

Message: Serving with joy comes from having a heart of gratitude. Colossians 3:17 encourages us to do everything in the name of Jesus, giving thanks to God. Gratitude transforms our perspective on serving, turning it from a duty into a privilege. When we serve with a thankful heart, we recognize that everything we do is for God's glory and that He has given us the opportunity to bless others. Gratitude brings joy to our service because we are focused on the goodness of God and the blessing of being part of His work.

The apostle Paul often wrote about giving thanks, even in difficult circumstances. He understood that a heart of gratitude leads to joy and contentment, regardless of the situation. When we serve with gratitude, we are able to focus on the blessings God has given us and the privilege of serving Him by serving others. This attitude brings joy, peace, and fulfillment to our service, and it allows us to experience the blessing of giving thanks in all things.

If you want to serve with joy, ask God to fill your heart with gratitude. Focus on His goodness, and let thanksgiving overflow in your service.

Call to Action: Reflect on the blessings in your life, and how you can serve others with a heart of gratitude. Spend time in prayer, thanking God for the opportunity to serve and asking Him to fill you with joy and thankfulness as you do.

Prayer: Father, thank You for the opportunity to serve others in Your name. Help me to serve with a heart of gratitude, giving thanks to You in everything I do. Let my service be an expression of my thankfulness for all that You have done, and fill my heart with joy as I serve. Amen.

September 21
Serving with Compassion

Verse: *"Be kind and compassionate to one another, forgiving each other, just as in Christ God forgave you."*

(Ephesians 4:32, NIV)

Message: Serving others requires a heart of compassion. Ephesians 4:32 reminds us to be kind and compassionate, showing the same love and forgiveness that Christ has shown to us. Compassion is more than just feeling sympathy for someone; it moves us to act. It drives us to serve others in a way that meets their needs and reflects God's love. When we serve with compassion, we honor God by reflecting His heart for the hurting, the broken, and the lost.

Jesus modeled compassion throughout His ministry. When He saw the crowds, He had compassion on them because they were like sheep without a shepherd (Matthew 9:36). His compassion led Him to heal the sick, feed the hungry, and teach those who were spiritually lost. As we grow in our relationship with Christ, we are called to develop this same compassion for others. Compassionate service brings joy, not only to those we serve but also to us as we experience the privilege of reflecting God's love in tangible ways.

If you struggle with serving others compassionately, ask God to soften your heart and fill you with His love for those in need.

Call to Action: Reflect on areas where you can serve with more compassion. Spend time in prayer, asking God to help you see others through His eyes and to serve them with kindness and grace.

Prayer: Lord, thank You for Your compassion toward me. Help me to show that same compassion to others as I serve. Let my heart be moved with kindness, and let my actions reflect Your love and grace in every situation. Amen.

September 22
Serving in Unity

Verse: *"How good and pleasant it is when God's people live together in unity!"*

(Psalm 133:1, NIV)

Message: There is great joy in serving together in unity. Psalm 133:1 highlights the beauty of God's people living and serving in harmony. Unity strengthens the body of Christ, allowing us to work together for God's kingdom with one heart and mind. When we serve in unity, we reflect the love and oneness of God, and we can accomplish far more together than we ever could on our own. Serving in unity brings joy because it fosters strong relationships and builds up the church.

In the early church, believers were united in heart and mind, sharing their possessions and serving one another with gladness (Acts 4:32). This unity allowed the church to grow and thrive, and it was a powerful testimony to the world around them. Serving together in unity allows us to encourage one another, bear each other's burdens, and celebrate the victories we achieve for God's kingdom. When we serve in unity, we experience the joy of fellowship and the strength that comes from working together for a common purpose.

If you've been serving alone or struggling with disunity, ask God to help you build relationships and serve in unity with others in the body of Christ.

Call to Action: Reflect on how you can promote unity in your church or community as you serve. Spend time in prayer, asking God to help you serve together with others in unity, working toward a common goal.

Prayer: Father, thank You for the beauty of unity in the body of Christ. Help me to serve in unity with others, working together for Your kingdom. Teach me to promote peace, harmony, and love as I serve, and let our service be a testimony of Your love to the world. Amen.

September 23
Serving the Needy

Verse: *"Whoever is kind to the poor lends to the Lord, and He will reward them for what they have done."*

(Proverbs 19:17, NIV)

Message: Serving those in need is an act of kindness that honors God. Proverbs 19:17 reminds us that when we are kind to the poor, we are lending to the Lord, and He will reward us for our compassion. Serving the needy is close to God's heart, as He cares deeply for the vulnerable and the marginalized. When we serve those who are struggling, we are partnering with God in His mission to bring hope and restoration to the world. Serving the poor brings joy because it allows us to be the hands and feet of Jesus, meeting practical needs while sharing His love.

Jesus often ministered to the poor and the outcast, showing us that serving those in need is central to His mission. In Matthew 25, He taught that when we care for the hungry, the thirsty, the stranger, the sick, and the imprisoned, we are doing it for Him. This means that our acts of service to the needy are not only a blessing to them but also an offering to God. When we serve with a heart of compassion, we reflect God's love and mercy to those who need it most.

If you're unsure of how to serve the needy in your community, ask God to open your eyes to the needs around you and to give you opportunities to make a difference.

Call to Action: Reflect on how you can serve the poor and needy in your community. Spend time in prayer, asking God to show you practical ways to bless and serve those who are struggling.

Prayer: Lord, thank You for Your heart for the poor and the needy. Help me to serve those who are struggling with kindness and compassion, knowing that when I serve them, I am serving You. Let my service reflect Your love and bring hope to those in need. Amen.

September 24
Serving Through Hospitality

Verse: *"Offer hospitality to one another without grumbling."*

(1 Peter 4:9, NIV)

Message: Hospitality is a powerful way to serve others, and 1 Peter 4:9 encourages us to offer hospitality without grumbling. Opening our homes and hearts to others is a way to show God's love in practical, tangible ways. Hospitality creates a welcoming environment where people can feel valued, loved, and cared for. When we offer hospitality with joy, we reflect God's heart of generosity and kindness. It's not about having a perfect home or elaborate meals, but about creating a space where people can experience love and fellowship.

Jesus often practiced hospitality, sharing meals with His disciples and even with sinners and tax collectors. These moments of fellowship were opportunities for Him to teach, encourage, and show love. As we open our homes and lives to others, we create opportunities for connection, encouragement, and ministry. Hospitality is a form of service that fosters relationships and allows people to experience the love of Christ through our actions.

If you find it difficult to offer hospitality, ask God to help you see it as an opportunity to serve others with joy and love, creating spaces where people can feel welcomed and cared for.

Call to Action: Reflect on how you can practice hospitality in your life. Spend time in prayer, asking God to give you a heart that welcomes others and to help you serve through hospitality with joy.

Prayer: Father, thank You for the opportunity to serve others through hospitality. Help me to open my home and heart to others, offering a place of love and fellowship. Let my hospitality be a reflection of Your kindness, and help me serve with joy and generosity. Amen.

September 25
Serving with Joy in Every Task

Verse: *"Whatever you do, work at it with all your heart, as working for the Lord, not for human masters."*

(Colossians 3:23, NIV)

Message: Serving with joy means approaching every task, big or small, as if we are doing it for the Lord. Colossians 3:23 reminds us to work with all our hearts, not for human recognition, but as an offering to God. Whether we are serving in ministry, at work, or in our daily responsibilities, when we serve with joy and dedication, we bring glory to God. Every task becomes an act of worship when we do it with the right attitude and focus. Joy in service comes from knowing that we are serving the Lord, not just people, and that He sees and values our efforts.

Jesus Himself modeled this when He washed His disciples' feet, a humble and lowly task. He showed that no act of service is too small when it is done in love and humility. As we serve with joy in every task, we reflect Christ's servant heart and bring honor to God. This attitude transforms mundane tasks into opportunities to glorify God and bless others.

If you've been struggling to find joy in your daily tasks, ask God to help you see them as opportunities to serve Him and others with a heart of joy and gratitude.

Call to Action: Reflect on your attitude toward the tasks you do each day. Spend time in prayer, asking God to help you serve with joy in everything, knowing that you are ultimately working for Him.

Prayer: Lord, thank You for the opportunity to serve You in every area of my life. Help me to serve with joy and dedication, knowing that I am working for You, not for human recognition. Let every task I do be an offering of love to You, and fill my heart with joy as I serve. Amen.

SEPTEMBER 26
THE JOY OF SERVING IN SMALL WAYS

Verse: "*And if anyone gives even a cup of cold water to one of these little ones who is my disciple, truly I tell you, that person will certainly not lose their reward.*"

(Matthew 10:42, NIV)

Message: Serving others doesn't always have to involve grand gestures or major sacrifices. Jesus teaches in Matthew 10:42 that even giving a cup of cold water in His name is significant. No act of service is too small in God's eyes. When we serve with joy in the little things, we are still honoring God and reflecting His love to others. Sometimes, the simplest acts of kindness—like a word of encouragement, a listening ear, or helping with a small task—can have the greatest impact.

Jesus often noticed and praised the small acts of faith and service, like the widow who gave her last coins or the child who shared his lunch to feed the multitude. These small offerings were significant because they were given with a willing heart and a desire to serve. When we serve in small ways, we are participating in God's work and making a difference in people's lives. These moments of service, though they may seem insignificant, are precious in God's sight and bring Him joy.

If you feel that your contributions are too small to matter, remember that God values every act of service, no matter how small. Serve with joy, knowing that your efforts are seen and cherished by God.

Call to Action: Reflect on the small ways you can serve others in your daily life. Spend time in prayer, asking God to help you find joy in serving through simple acts of kindness and love.

Prayer: Lord, thank You for valuing even the smallest acts of service. Help me to serve with joy in the little things, knowing that You see and cherish every effort. Let my life be filled with small acts of love that bring glory to You and bless others. Amen.

September 27
Serving with a Sacrificial Heart

Verse: *"Greater love has no one than this: to lay down one's life for one's friends."*

(John 15:13, NIV)

Message: True service often requires sacrifice. John 15:13 reminds us that there is no greater love than to lay down one's life for others. While most of us are not called to literally lay down our lives, serving others sacrificially means putting their needs before our own and giving of our time, energy, and resources without expecting anything in return. Sacrificial service reflects the heart of Jesus, who gave everything for us out of love.

Jesus modeled sacrificial service throughout His ministry, culminating in His ultimate sacrifice on the cross. He laid down His life to save us, demonstrating the depth of His love. As His followers, we are called to serve others in the same spirit of love and sacrifice. This doesn't always mean grand gestures; it can be as simple as giving up our comfort, time, or preferences to serve someone else. When we serve with a sacrificial heart, we experience the joy of knowing that we are walking in the footsteps of Jesus and showing His love to the world.

If you've been hesitant to serve because of the cost, ask God to help you serve with a sacrificial heart, trusting that He will bless your efforts and fill you with joy.

Call to Action: Reflect on areas where you can serve more sacrificially. Spend time in prayer, asking God to help you put others' needs before your own and to serve with a heart full of love and sacrifice.

Prayer: Father, thank You for the example of sacrificial love that Jesus gave. Help me to serve others with a heart of sacrifice, putting their needs before my own. Teach me to love as Jesus loved, and fill my heart with joy as I serve in His name. Amen.

September 28
Serving with Integrity

Verse: *"The integrity of the upright guides them, but the unfaithful are destroyed by their duplicity."*

(Proverbs 11:3, NIV)

Message: Serving with joy requires integrity. Proverbs 11:3 teaches us that the integrity of the upright guides them. Integrity means being honest, trustworthy, and consistent in our words and actions. When we serve others with integrity, we reflect the character of God, who is faithful and true. Serving with integrity means doing the right thing, even when no one is watching and when it might be difficult. It's about being faithful in both the big and small tasks, knowing that God values our integrity.

Jesus lived a life of perfect integrity, always doing the will of the Father and remaining true to His mission. As we seek to serve others, we are called to follow Jesus' example, serving with honesty, faithfulness, and consistency. Integrity in service builds trust and allows us to represent Christ in a way that honors Him. When we serve with integrity, we experience the joy of knowing that we are honoring God and serving others in a way that reflects His truth and love.

If you struggle with maintaining integrity in your service, ask God to help you remain faithful and true, even when it's difficult or unnoticed by others.

Call to Action: Reflect on how you can serve with greater integrity. Spend time in prayer, asking God to help you be honest, trustworthy, and faithful in every area of your service.

Prayer: Lord, thank You for Your faithfulness and truth. Help me to serve with integrity, always doing what is right and honoring You in everything I do. Teach me to be faithful in both the big and small tasks, knowing that You value my integrity. Amen.

September 29
Serving with Joy Despite Challenges

Verse: *"Consider it pure joy, my brothers and sisters, whenever you face trials of many kinds, because you know that the testing of your faith produces perseverance."*

(James 1:2-3, NIV)

Message: Serving others with joy doesn't always come easily, especially when we face challenges. James 1:2-3 encourages us to consider it pure joy when we face trials, knowing that these difficulties strengthen our faith and produce perseverance. Serving with joy during difficult times shows the depth of our trust in God. It demonstrates that our joy doesn't come from our circumstances but from our relationship with Christ. As we persevere in service, even when it's hard, we grow in our faith and experience the joy of knowing that God is with us, strengthening and sustaining us.

The apostle Paul often faced challenges in his ministry—imprisonment, persecution, and hardship—but he continued to serve with joy, trusting that God was working through him. Paul's joy wasn't dependent on his circumstances; it came from knowing that he was serving the Lord and advancing the Gospel. When we serve with this same attitude, we find joy even in the midst of trials, knowing that God is using our efforts to bring about His purposes.

If you're facing challenges in your service, ask God to give you the strength to persevere and the joy to continue serving, knowing that He is with you.

Call to Action: Reflect on any challenges you may be facing in your service. Spend time in prayer, asking God to help you persevere and to fill you with joy as you continue to serve, even in difficult times.

Prayer: Father, thank You for the promise that You are with me in the midst of trials. Help me to serve with joy, even when it's difficult, and to trust that You are using my service for Your glory. Strengthen my faith, and help me persevere with a joyful heart. Amen.

September 30
Serving with Eternity in Mind

Verse: *"For we are God's handiwork, created in Christ Jesus to do good works, which God prepared in advance for us to do."*

(Ephesians 2:10, NIV)

Message: As we serve others, it's important to keep eternity in mind. Ephesians 2:10 reminds us that we are God's handiwork, created to do good works that He has prepared for us. The acts of service we perform now have an eternal impact. When we serve others, we are participating in God's eternal plan, and the good we do has lasting significance. Serving with eternity in mind gives us a greater sense of purpose and joy, knowing that our efforts are part of something much bigger than ourselves.

Jesus always had eternity in mind as He served others. His acts of healing, teaching, and loving pointed people to the eternal kingdom of God. As we serve, we should also have this perspective, knowing that our service can point people to Christ and make an eternal difference in their lives. This gives us joy and motivation to serve faithfully, knowing that our efforts, though they may seem small, are part of God's greater plan for His kingdom.

If you struggle to see the eternal significance of your service, ask God to help you keep eternity in mind as you serve, trusting that He is using your efforts for His eternal purposes.

Call to Action: Reflect on how your acts of service can have an eternal impact. Spend time in prayer, asking God to give you a greater sense of purpose and joy as you serve with eternity in mind.

Prayer: Lord, thank You for the good works You have prepared for me to do. Help me to serve with eternity in mind, knowing that my efforts are part of Your eternal plan. Give me joy and purpose as I serve, trusting that You are using my life for Your kingdom. Amen.

October

God is With You in Your Trials

October 1
God's Presence in Every Trial

Verse: "The Lord is close to the brokenhearted and saves those who are crushed in spirit."

(Psalm 34:18, NIV)

Message: When life feels overwhelming and our hearts are broken, Psalm 34:18 offers the comforting promise that God is near. He isn't distant in our trials; rather, He draws close to those who are hurting. In the middle of our pain and struggles, God's presence is a source of strength, comfort, and hope. He walks with us through every challenge, reminding us that we are not alone. This reassurance allows us to endure trials with the knowledge that God is by our side, caring for us deeply.

David, the author of this psalm, experienced numerous trials, including persecution, betrayal, and hardship. Yet he found comfort in knowing that God was near, even in his darkest moments. The same is true for us—when we feel crushed by the weight of life's struggles, God is with us, offering His comfort and saving grace. His presence is not just a fleeting moment of comfort but a steadfast assurance that we can hold on to, no matter the severity of our trials.

In times of trial, turn to God and rest in His presence. Know that even when you feel brokenhearted, He is near, and His love will carry you through.

Call to Action: Reflect on times when you've felt God's presence during difficult seasons. Spend time in prayer, asking God to draw near to you and give you peace in the midst of your trials.

Prayer: Lord, thank You for being close to me, especially when I am brokenhearted. Help me to remember that You are always near, even in my darkest moments. Fill me with Your comfort and peace as I walk through trials, and remind me that You will never leave me. Amen.

October 2
Strength in Weakness

Verse: *"But He said to me, 'My grace is sufficient for you, for my power is made perfect in weakness.' Therefore I will boast all the more gladly about my weaknesses, so that Christ's power may rest on me."*

(2 Corinthians 12:9, NIV)

Message: In the face of trials, it's natural to feel weak and overwhelmed, but 2 Corinthians 12:9 reminds us that God's grace is sufficient for us. His power is made perfect in our weakness. When we acknowledge our limitations and depend on God, He steps in with His strength and sustains us. Our trials become opportunities for God's power to be revealed in our lives, and we experience His grace in ways we never could if we relied solely on our own strength.

The apostle Paul wrote this verse after pleading with God to remove a "thorn" in his life—a persistent struggle or challenge. Instead of taking it away, God reminded Paul that His grace was enough. Paul learned to rejoice in his weakness because it was in those moments that Christ's power rested on him. This perspective shift can change how we approach our own trials. Instead of resenting our weaknesses, we can embrace them, knowing that they are opportunities for God's strength to shine through.

If you're feeling weak in the midst of your trials, trust that God's grace is sufficient. His power will carry you through, even when you feel like you can't go on.

Call to Action: Reflect on any areas where you feel weak or inadequate. Spend time in prayer, asking God to show His strength through your weakness and to help you rely on His grace.

Prayer: Father, thank You for Your sufficient grace. When I am weak, help me to trust in Your strength. Let Your power be made perfect in my weakness, and teach me to lean on You for everything I need during my trials. Amen.

October 3
God is Our Refuge

Verse: *"God is our refuge and strength, an ever-present help in trouble."*

(Psalm 46:1, NIV)

Message: In times of trouble, we can run to God as our refuge and strength. Psalm 46:1 reassures us that God is an ever-present help, not just in moments of calm, but in the midst of the storm. When life's trials seem overwhelming, God offers a safe place where we can find peace and protection. He is our fortress, and no trouble is too great for Him to handle. As we face challenges, we can draw near to Him, trusting that He will provide the strength we need to endure.

Throughout the Bible, we see examples of God being a refuge for His people. Whether it was the Israelites seeking protection during battles or David fleeing from his enemies, God was always there as a stronghold and defender. Today, we can find the same comfort in knowing that God is our refuge. He isn't distant or indifferent to our struggles; He is close and ready to help. When we place our trust in Him, we find that no trial is too big for His care.

If you're feeling overwhelmed by your circumstances, run to God as your refuge. Trust that He is your strength and that He will help you through every trial.

Call to Action: Reflect on what it means for God to be your refuge. Spend time in prayer, asking Him to help you trust in His strength and protection during difficult times.

Prayer: Lord, thank You for being my refuge and strength. When I face trouble, help me to run to You for protection and peace. Let me trust in Your care, knowing that You are always with me, providing the strength I need. Amen.

October 4
God Will Never Leave You

Verse: *"Be strong and courageous. Do not be afraid or terrified because of them, for the Lord your God goes with you; He will never leave you nor forsake you."*

(Deuteronomy 31:6, NIV)

Message: One of the greatest promises in Scripture is that God will never leave us or forsake us. Deuteronomy 31:6 encourages us to be strong and courageous, knowing that the Lord goes with us through every trial. We don't have to face our struggles alone—God is with us, walking beside us and fighting our battles. This truth gives us the strength and courage to face difficult situations with confidence, trusting that God is always present and faithful.

Moses spoke these words to the Israelites as they were about to enter the Promised Land, a place filled with challenges and unknown dangers. Yet they were reassured that God would be with them, just as He had been throughout their journey in the wilderness. In the same way, God goes with us through every season of life, including the trials we face. His promise to never leave us gives us the courage to move forward, knowing that we are never abandoned or forgotten.

If you're feeling afraid or alone in your trials, remember that God is with you. He will never leave you, and you can trust Him to guide you through whatever you're facing.

Call to Action: Reflect on any fears or anxieties you may be facing. Spend time in prayer, asking God to remind you of His presence and to give you the courage to face your trials with strength.

Prayer: Father, thank You for Your promise to never leave me or forsake me. Help me to trust in Your presence and to find strength in knowing that You are with me. Give me the courage to face my trials, knowing that I am never alone. Amen.

October 5
Peace in the Storm

Verse: *"Peace I leave with you; my peace I give you. I do not give to you as the world gives. Do not let your hearts be troubled and do not be afraid."*

(John 14:27, NIV)

Message: In the midst of life's storms, Jesus offers us a peace that the world cannot give. John 14:27 reminds us that His peace is different from the temporary and fleeting peace the world offers. Jesus' peace is deep, lasting, and available to us even in the midst of trials. When we are going through difficult seasons, we can rest in the peace that comes from knowing that Jesus is in control and that He is with us. This peace allows us to face our struggles with calm hearts, trusting that God is working on our behalf.

When Jesus calmed the storm in Mark 4, He demonstrated His authority over even the most chaotic situations. The disciples were terrified as the storm raged around them, but Jesus simply spoke, and the wind and waves obeyed. In the same way, Jesus speaks peace into the storms of our lives. No matter what we are facing, His peace is available to calm our hearts and remind us that He is in control.

If your heart is troubled or afraid, turn to Jesus and ask for His peace. Trust that He can calm the storms in your life and bring you the peace that only He can give.

Call to Action: Reflect on any areas of your life where you need the peace of Jesus. Spend time in prayer, asking Him to calm your heart and fill you with His perfect peace.

Prayer: Lord, thank You for the peace that only You can give. Help me to trust in Your control, even in the midst of life's storms. Calm my heart and fill me with Your peace, so that I can face my trials with confidence and trust in You. Amen.

October 6
God is Our Strong Tower

Verse: "The name of the Lord is a fortified tower; the righteous run to it and are safe."

(Proverbs 18:10, NIV)

Message: In times of trouble, we have a place of refuge—the Lord, our strong tower. Proverbs 18:10 paints a vivid picture of God as a fortified tower that the righteous can run to for safety. When life's storms rage and trials overwhelm us, we don't have to rely on our own strength. Instead, we can run to God, knowing that He is our protector and stronghold. His name alone carries power, and when we trust in Him, we are shielded from the fear and uncertainty that trials bring.

Throughout Scripture, we see God acting as a place of refuge for His people. David often referred to God as his fortress and deliverer during times of persecution and danger. Just as David found safety in God, we too can find protection and peace when we place our trust in Him. Trials may come, but God's presence offers us a place of security, where we are safe from the attacks of the enemy and the anxieties of life.

If you're feeling vulnerable or afraid, run to God, your strong tower. Trust in His protection and find safety in His presence.

Call to Action: Reflect on any situations in your life where you need to run to God for refuge. Spend time in prayer, asking Him to be your strong tower and to protect you in the midst of your trials.

Prayer: Lord, thank You for being my strong tower and refuge. Help me to run to You in times of trouble, trusting that You are my protector. Let me find safety and peace in Your presence, knowing that You are with me in every trial. Amen.

October 7
God Works All Things for Good

Verse: *"And we know that in all things God works for the good of those who love Him, who have been called according to His purpose."*

(Romans 8:28, NIV)

Message: Romans 8:28 is one of the most comforting promises in Scripture—it reminds us that no matter what trials we face, God is working all things for our good. This doesn't mean that everything we go through will be easy or pleasant, but it does mean that God is sovereign over every situation. He can take even the most difficult and painful circumstances and use them for a greater purpose in our lives. When we trust in His goodness, we can find hope, even in the midst of trials.

Joseph's life is a powerful example of this truth. Despite being sold into slavery by his brothers, falsely accused, and imprisoned, Joseph remained faithful to God. In the end, God used those trials to position Joseph to save many lives during a time of famine. What others meant for harm, God used for good (Genesis 50:20). In the same way, God can take the hardships we face and turn them into opportunities for growth, blessing, and His glory.

If you're struggling to see how God is working in your situation, ask Him to help you trust that He is working for your good, even when you can't yet see the outcome.

Call to Action: Reflect on any trials in your life where you need to trust that God is working for your good. Spend time in prayer, asking Him to help you believe in His purpose and plan for your life.

Prayer: Father, thank You for the promise that You work all things for good. Help me to trust in Your sovereignty, even when I don't understand what's happening in my life. Give me faith to believe that You are working for my good and for Your glory in every situation. Amen.

October 8
God's Grace is Sufficient

Verse: "But He said to me, 'My grace is sufficient for you, for my power is made perfect in weakness.'"

(2 Corinthians 12:9, NIV)

Message: In our trials, it's easy to feel weak and inadequate, but God's grace is more than enough to sustain us. In 2 Corinthians 12:9, God reminds us that His power is made perfect in our weakness. We don't have to be strong in our own abilities because God's grace fills in the gaps. When we rely on His strength, we experience the fullness of His power working in us and through us. Our trials become opportunities for God's grace to shine brightly, as He carries us through what we cannot handle on our own.

Paul's experience of God's grace in his weakness is a powerful example of how we can trust God in the midst of our struggles. Despite pleading with God to remove a "thorn" from his life, Paul learned to embrace his weakness because it allowed God's strength to be displayed in greater measure. Like Paul, we can find comfort in knowing that God's grace is sufficient for every trial we face. He doesn't always remove the difficulties, but He gives us the strength to endure them with grace and peace.

If you're feeling weak or overwhelmed by your trials, ask God to remind you of His grace and to help you lean on His strength, not your own.

Call to Action: Reflect on areas of your life where you need to rely more on God's grace. Spend time in prayer, asking Him to show you how His power can be made perfect in your weakness.

Prayer: Lord, thank You for Your grace, which is sufficient for every trial I face. Help me to lean on Your strength, not my own, and to trust that Your power is made perfect in my weakness. Fill me with Your grace and help me to endure with faith and peace. Amen.

October 9
God is Faithful in Every Season

Verse: *"The Lord is faithful, and He will strengthen you and protect you from the evil one."*

(2 Thessalonians 3:3, NIV)

Message: One of the greatest assurances we have as believers is that God is faithful, no matter what season of life we are in. 2 Thessalonians 3:3 reminds us that the Lord will strengthen us and protect us from the evil one. His faithfulness doesn't depend on our circumstances; it is unchanging and unwavering. When we face trials, we can trust in God's faithfulness to guide us, protect us, and give us the strength we need to persevere.

Throughout the Bible, we see countless examples of God's faithfulness. From providing manna in the wilderness to delivering His people from captivity, God has always been faithful to His promises. He never abandons His people, and He won't abandon us in our trials. Even when we can't see how things will work out, we can trust that God is at work, fulfilling His promises and strengthening us to endure. His faithfulness is a rock we can stand on, even when everything else feels uncertain.

If you're going through a difficult season, remind yourself of God's faithfulness. He will never fail you, and He will give you the strength to endure.

Call to Action: Reflect on God's faithfulness in your life. Spend time in prayer, thanking Him for His constant presence and asking Him to give you strength and protection in your current trials.

Prayer: Father, thank You for Your faithfulness in every season of my life. Help me to trust in Your strength and protection, knowing that You will never leave me. Strengthen me in my trials, and let me rest in the assurance of Your faithful love. Amen.

October 10
God's Peace Guards Your Heart

Verse: *"And the peace of God, which transcends all understanding, will guard your hearts and your minds in Christ Jesus."*

(Philippians 4:7, NIV)

Message: In the midst of trials, God offers us a peace that surpasses all understanding. Philippians 4:7 promises that this peace will guard our hearts and minds in Christ Jesus. It's a peace that goes beyond human comprehension—a peace that remains even when our circumstances don't change. This peace comes from knowing that God is in control and that we can trust Him with every aspect of our lives. It acts as a shield, protecting us from the anxiety and fear that trials often bring.

When Jesus calmed the storm in Mark 4, He asked His disciples why they were afraid. His presence with them should have been enough to bring peace, even in the midst of the storm. In the same way, God's presence with us brings peace that transcends our understanding. As we keep our focus on Him, His peace guards our hearts from fear and anxiety, allowing us to navigate trials with a calm and steady spirit.

If you're feeling anxious or overwhelmed by your trials, ask God to fill you with His peace that transcends understanding. Trust that He will guard your heart and mind, giving you the strength to endure.

Call to Action: Reflect on any areas of your life where you need God's peace. Spend time in prayer, asking Him to guard your heart and mind with His peace, trusting that He is in control.

Prayer: Lord, thank You for the peace that only You can give. Help me to rest in that peace, even when my circumstances are difficult. Guard my heart and mind in Christ Jesus, and help me to trust in Your care and provision. Amen.

October 11
God Hears Your Cry

Verse: "*I waited patiently for the Lord; He turned to me and heard my cry.*"

(Psalm 40:1, NIV)

Message: In the midst of trials, it's easy to feel as though God is distant or silent, but Psalm 40:1 reassures us that God hears our cry. When we wait on Him, He turns to us, listens to our prayers, and responds in His perfect timing. Our cries for help do not go unnoticed by the Lord. He is attentive to our needs, and even when the answers seem delayed, we can trust that He is working on our behalf. Our patience in trials is an act of faith, trusting that God hears us and will act according to His wisdom and love.

David, who wrote this psalm, often found himself in desperate situations, fleeing from enemies and facing hardship. Yet, time and again, he cried out to God, and God delivered him. In the same way, God hears us when we call out to Him. Our prayers do not fall on deaf ears. Though the waiting may be difficult, it's in those moments that our faith is strengthened, and we learn to trust in God's perfect plan.

If you're in a season of waiting, be encouraged that God hears your cry. He is not far off but is close, listening and ready to respond in His perfect timing.

Call to Action: Reflect on any prayers that you've been waiting for God to answer. Spend time in prayer, asking Him to give you patience and faith as you wait, trusting that He hears your cry.

Prayer: Lord, thank You for hearing my prayers. Help me to wait patiently on You, trusting that You hear my cry and will answer in Your perfect timing. Strengthen my faith as I wait, and remind me that You are always near. Amen.

October 12
God's Comfort in Sorrow

Verse: "*Praise be to the God and Father of our Lord Jesus Christ, the Father of compassion and the God of all comfort, who comforts us in all our troubles.*"

(2 Corinthians 1:3-4, NIV)

Message: When we face sorrow or grief, God is the source of all comfort. 2 Corinthians 1:3-4 reminds us that God is the "Father of compassion" and the "God of all comfort." In our darkest moments, when we feel overwhelmed by sadness or loss, God's comfort is there to carry us through. He doesn't leave us to endure our pain alone. Instead, He draws near, wrapping us in His loving arms and offering us peace and consolation. His comfort is a reminder that He sees our pain and walks with us through it.

The Bible is filled with examples of God comforting His people. When Hagar was weeping in the wilderness, God heard her cry and provided for her (Genesis 21:17). When Jesus wept at the death of His friend Lazarus, He shared in the sorrow of those mourning (John 11:35). God understands our sorrow, and He offers us comfort in the midst of it. His presence is enough to soothe our hearts and remind us that we are never alone in our suffering.

If you are experiencing sorrow, lean into God's comfort. Allow Him to be your source of peace and healing, trusting that He is with you in your pain.

Call to Action: Reflect on any areas of grief or sorrow in your life. Spend time in prayer, asking God to comfort you in your troubles and to fill you with His peace.

Prayer: Father, thank You for being the God of all comfort. In my sorrow, help me to lean on You and find peace in Your presence. Comfort me in my troubles, and remind me that You are always near, carrying me through every trial. Amen.

October 13
God's Light in Darkness

Verse: *"The light shines in the darkness, and the darkness has not overcome it."*

(John 1:5, NIV)

Message: In the darkest moments of life, God's light shines brightly. John 1:5 reminds us that the light of Christ shines in the darkness, and the darkness cannot overcome it. No matter how overwhelming our trials may seem, they cannot extinguish the light of God's presence in our lives. His light brings hope, clarity, and guidance, even when everything around us feels uncertain. As we walk through trials, God's light illuminates our path and reminds us that we are never walking in darkness alone.

Throughout Scripture, light represents God's presence and truth. When the Israelites were wandering in the wilderness, God led them with a pillar of fire by night, guiding them through the darkness (Exodus 13:21). In the same way, God's light guides us through the dark seasons of life. His Word is a "lamp to our feet and a light to our path" (Psalm 119:105), helping us navigate the difficulties we face with hope and assurance. No matter how dark our circumstances, the light of God's love and presence is always shining, leading us toward His peace and comfort.

If you're feeling lost or overwhelmed in your trials, remember that God's light is shining in the darkness. Trust that He is guiding you and that the darkness will not overcome you.

Call to Action: Reflect on areas of your life where you feel surrounded by darkness or uncertainty. Spend time in prayer, asking God to shine His light into those areas and to guide you through them.

Prayer: Lord, thank You for being the light that shines in the darkness. Help me to trust in Your guidance and presence, even when my path feels unclear. Let Your light shine brightly in my life, leading me toward hope, peace, and clarity. Amen.

October 14
God is Your Shield

Verse: *"You are my refuge and my shield;*
I have put my hope in Your word."

(Psalm 119:114, NIV)

Message: When we face trials and attacks from the enemy, God is our shield and refuge. Psalm 119:114 declares that God is our protector, and we can put our hope in His Word. He is our shield, defending us from the spiritual attacks and fears that try to overwhelm us. In the midst of life's battles, we can trust in His protection and find refuge in His presence. His Word offers us hope and security, reminding us that we are not defenseless, but are covered by His mighty hand.

David often described God as his shield and refuge, relying on God's protection during times of danger and fear. Just as a physical shield defends against attacks, God is our spiritual shield, guarding us from harm. His Word is full of promises that we can cling to when we feel threatened or afraid. When we place our hope in His Word, we find the strength and courage to stand firm in the face of trials, knowing that God is fighting for us.

If you feel under attack or overwhelmed by trials, ask God to be your shield. Trust in His protection, and let His Word be your source of hope and strength.

Call to Action: Reflect on any areas of your life where you need God's protection. Spend time in prayer, asking God to be your shield and to help you place your hope in His Word.

Prayer: Father, thank You for being my shield and refuge. Help me to trust in Your protection and to place my hope in Your Word. Guard me from fear and attacks, and remind me that You are always with me, defending and protecting me in every trial. Amen.

October 15
God Restores the Broken

Verse: *"He heals the brokenhearted and binds up their wounds."*

(Psalm 147:3, NIV)

Message: God is in the business of healing and restoring. Psalm 147:3 reminds us that He heals the brokenhearted and binds up their wounds. When we face trials that leave us feeling wounded or broken, God is there to bring healing and restoration. He doesn't leave us in our pain but comes close to mend our hearts and give us hope. His healing may not always be immediate, but it is always thorough, working in the deepest parts of our souls to bring peace and wholeness.

The Bible is full of stories of God's restorative power. Whether it was Jesus healing the sick and restoring sight to the blind, or God bringing the Israelites out of captivity, His desire is always to restore what has been broken. No matter how deep our wounds or how severe our trials, God's healing touch is powerful enough to make us whole again. He is the Great Physician, and His love for us is greater than any trial we face.

If you're feeling broken or wounded by life's trials, turn to God for healing. Trust that He can restore your heart and bind up your wounds with His love and grace.

Call to Action: Reflect on any areas of brokenness in your life where you need God's healing. Spend time in prayer, asking Him to heal your heart and restore what has been broken.

Prayer: Lord, thank You for being my healer. When I am brokenhearted, help me to turn to You for healing and restoration. Bind up my wounds and make me whole again, filling me with Your peace and love. Amen.

October 16
God's Strength in Your Weakness

Verse: *"The Lord gives strength to His people; the Lord blesses His people with peace."*

(Psalm 29:11, NIV)

Message: When we are feeling weak and worn down by trials, Psalm 29:11 promises that the Lord gives strength to His people. God doesn't expect us to go through difficult seasons on our own. He provides the strength we need to endure, even when we feel like we have nothing left to give. Along with His strength, He blesses us with peace, allowing us to face trials with a calm assurance that comes from knowing He is in control.

Throughout Scripture, God consistently provided strength to those who trusted Him. Whether it was Gideon leading a small army against a much larger force or David standing against Goliath, God's strength empowered His people to overcome impossible odds. He still does this today. When we admit our weaknesses and turn to Him for help, He fills us with His strength and equips us to face whatever challenges lie ahead.

If you are feeling weak or overwhelmed by trials, turn to God for strength. He will supply you with what you need to keep moving forward and will give you peace as you trust in His power.

Call to Action: Reflect on areas of your life where you feel weak or powerless. Spend time in prayer, asking God to give you His strength and to bless you with peace in the midst of your trials.

Prayer: Lord, thank You for being my source of strength. When I am weak, help me to rely on Your power. Fill me with the strength I need to face my trials, and bless me with peace as I trust in Your care. Amen.

October 17
God Knows Your Struggles

Verse: *"You have kept count of my tossings; put my tears in Your bottle. Are they not in Your book?"*

(Psalm 56:8, NIV)

Message: God knows every tear we shed and every sleepless night we endure. Psalm 56:8 beautifully illustrates that God is intimately aware of our struggles—He keeps count of our tossings and collects our tears in His bottle. This image shows us that God is not indifferent to our pain. He sees, He knows, and He cares deeply. In the midst of trials, it's comforting to know that we are never forgotten by God. He is fully aware of every hardship we face, and He is with us through it all.

David wrote this psalm during a time when he was being pursued by his enemies. Even in the midst of his fear and uncertainty, David found comfort in knowing that God was keeping track of his struggles. Just as God saw David's distress, He sees yours. Every tear, every moment of anxiety, and every fear is known by God, and He promises to be with you through it all. His care for you is deep and personal.

If you're feeling unseen in your trials, remember that God sees every tear and every struggle. You are not alone, and He is walking with you through every moment.

Call to Action: Reflect on any struggles or hardships you've been carrying alone. Spend time in prayer, thanking God for seeing and caring about every detail of your life, and asking Him to give you peace in His presence.

Prayer: Father, thank You for seeing every tear and knowing every struggle I face. Help me to find comfort in knowing that You care deeply for me. Remind me that I am never alone, and that You are with me through every trial. Amen.

October 18
God Gives You Courage

Verse: *"Have I not commanded you? Be strong and courageous. Do not be afraid; do not be discouraged, for the Lord your God will be with you wherever you go."*

(Joshua 1:9, NIV)

Message: God calls us to be strong and courageous, especially in times of trial. Joshua 1:9 is a powerful reminder that we don't have to be afraid or discouraged because the Lord is with us wherever we go. This promise was given to Joshua as he prepared to lead the Israelites into the Promised Land, a daunting task that required great courage and faith. Just as God was with Joshua, He is with us today, giving us the courage to face our own challenges.

Throughout the Bible, God repeatedly told His people to "fear not" because He was with them. Whether it was Moses confronting Pharaoh or Peter stepping out of the boat to walk on water, God's presence brought courage in the face of fear. When we remember that God is with us, we can face our trials with confidence, knowing that He will guide us and provide the strength we need to overcome.

If you're feeling afraid or discouraged by your circumstances, ask God to give you courage. Trust that He is with you wherever you go and that He will lead you through your trials.

Call to Action: Reflect on any fears or discouragements you're facing. Spend time in prayer, asking God to fill you with His courage and strength as you trust in His presence.

Prayer: Lord, thank You for Your constant presence in my life. Help me to be strong and courageous, trusting that You are with me wherever I go. Take away my fear and discouragement, and fill me with the confidence that comes from knowing You are by my side. Amen.

October 19
God's Word Brings Hope

Verse: *"My soul is weary with sorrow;*
strengthen me according to Your word."

(Psalm 119:28, NIV)

Message: In times of sorrow and trial, God's Word is a source of strength and hope. Psalm 119:28 reminds us that when our souls are weary, God's Word can renew and strengthen us. The Bible is full of promises that bring comfort and hope to those who are struggling. When we turn to Scripture in our darkest moments, we find the encouragement and peace we need to keep going. God's Word is a lamp to our feet, guiding us through difficult seasons and reminding us of His faithfulness.

The psalmist who wrote these words was no stranger to hardship, but he found comfort in God's promises. Throughout Psalm 119, we see a deep reliance on God's Word as a source of life, strength, and guidance. When we immerse ourselves in Scripture, we are reminded of God's goodness, even when our circumstances are hard. His promises give us hope that He is at work in our lives and that He will see us through every trial.

If your soul is weary, turn to God's Word for strength. Let His promises renew your spirit and fill you with hope for the future.

Call to Action: Reflect on any areas of your life where you need the strength and hope that comes from God's Word. Spend time reading Scripture, and ask God to strengthen you according to His promises.

Prayer: Father, thank You for the strength and hope that Your Word provides. When I am weary, help me to turn to Your promises for comfort and renewal. Strengthen my soul according to Your Word, and remind me of Your faithfulness in every situation. Amen.

October 20
God Will Restore Your Joy

Verse: *"Restore to me the joy of Your salvation and grant me a willing spirit, to sustain me."*

(Psalm 51:12, NIV)

Message: Trials often rob us of our joy, but God promises to restore it. Psalm 51:12 is a heartfelt prayer asking God to restore the joy of His salvation. When we go through difficult seasons, it's easy to lose sight of the joy that comes from knowing we are saved and loved by God. But God is in the business of restoration. He not only restores our joy but also gives us the strength and willingness to continue walking in faith, even when the path is hard.

David, who wrote this psalm, had experienced deep sorrow and regret, but he knew that God could restore his joy. In the same way, when we turn to God in the midst of our trials, He can renew our hearts and fill us with His joy once again. This joy doesn't depend on our circumstances—it comes from the deep assurance that we belong to God and that He is working all things for our good.

If you've lost your joy during a difficult season, ask God to restore it. Trust that He can renew your heart and fill you with the joy that comes from knowing Him.

Call to Action: Reflect on any areas of your life where you've lost your joy. Spend time in prayer, asking God to restore the joy of His salvation and to renew your spirit with hope and peace.

Prayer: Lord, thank You for the joy of Your salvation. When life's trials steal my joy, help me to turn to You for restoration. Restore my joy, and grant me a willing spirit to sustain me through every challenge I face. Amen.

October 21
God is Faithful to Rescue You

Verse: *"The righteous person may have many troubles, but the Lord delivers him from them all."*

(Psalm 34:19, NIV)

Message: Life is full of challenges, and even those who walk closely with God will face troubles. However, Psalm 34:19 gives us the comforting promise that the Lord delivers His people from all of their troubles. This doesn't mean that we won't experience hardship, but it does mean that God is faithful to rescue us in His perfect timing. No matter what you're going through, you can trust that God will see you through it, providing the help and deliverance you need.

David, who wrote this psalm, experienced many hardships, including being pursued by King Saul, fleeing from enemies, and enduring personal failures. Yet he constantly turned to God for rescue and found that God was faithful. We may not always be delivered immediately, but God promises that He is working behind the scenes for our ultimate good. Our trials are temporary, but God's faithfulness endures forever.

If you're facing troubles today, remind yourself that God will deliver you. Trust in His faithfulness and timing, knowing that He is working for your good.

Call to Action: Reflect on the troubles you are currently facing and spend time in prayer, asking God to deliver you and give you the strength to endure while trusting in His perfect timing.

Prayer: Lord, thank You for Your promise to deliver me from all my troubles. Help me to trust in Your timing and to remember that You are faithful. Strengthen me as I wait for Your deliverance, and remind me that You are always working for my good. Amen.

October 22
God Walks with You Through the Fire

Verse: *"When you pass through the waters, I will be with you; and when you pass through the rivers, they will not sweep over you. When you walk through the fire, you will not be burned; the flames will not set you ablaze."*

(Isaiah 43:2, NIV)

Message: Isaiah 43:2 offers one of the most powerful promises in Scripture: God is with us through every trial, no matter how difficult. Whether we face overwhelming waters or fiery trials, God promises to walk with us and protect us. This doesn't mean we won't face challenges, but it does mean that those challenges will not destroy us. God is sovereign over all circumstances, and He holds us in the palm of His hand, ensuring that we are never alone in our trials.

The story of Shadrach, Meshach, and Abednego in Daniel 3 illustrates this truth. When they were thrown into the fiery furnace for refusing to worship an idol, they were not consumed by the flames. Instead, God walked with them in the fire, and they came out unharmed. Just as God was with them, He is with you in your trials, walking beside you and protecting you from being overwhelmed.

If you're walking through a difficult season, remember that God is with you in the fire. Trust in His protection and presence, knowing that He will bring you through safely.

Call to Action: Reflect on any "fiery" trials you are currently facing. Spend time in prayer, asking God to walk with you through these trials and to protect you as you trust in His presence.

Prayer: Father, thank You for walking with me through every trial. When I feel overwhelmed by life's challenges, help me to trust in Your protection and presence. Remind me that You are with me through the fire, and that You will bring me through safely. Amen.

October 23
God Restores What is Broken

Verse: *"I will repay you for the years the locusts have eaten."*

(Joel 2:25, NIV)

Message: Trials often leave us feeling as though we've lost precious time, opportunities, or relationships. But Joel 2:25 reminds us that God is a God of restoration. He promises to restore the years that were lost or damaged by the trials we face. Whether it's emotional pain, missed opportunities, or broken relationships, God has the power to restore and redeem what has been broken. His restoration is complete, healing the deepest wounds and restoring what seemed irreparably lost.

The Israelites experienced this kind of restoration after enduring seasons of devastation and hardship. God not only brought them back from exile but also restored their land and their relationship with Him. In the same way, God can restore the broken areas of our lives. His timing and methods may be different from what we expect, but He is faithful to redeem the years that were marked by suffering. When we trust Him, we can look forward to the ways He will bring beauty out of ashes.

If you're feeling the weight of what has been lost in your life, turn to God and ask Him for restoration. Trust that He can redeem the broken areas of your life and bring healing and wholeness.

Call to Action: Reflect on areas of your life that feel broken or lost. Spend time in prayer, asking God to restore what has been damaged and to bring healing and redemption to those areas.

Prayer: Lord, thank You for being a God of restoration. When I feel the weight of what has been lost in my life, help me to trust in Your power to restore and redeem. Heal the broken areas of my life, and bring beauty from the ashes of my trials. Amen.

October 24
God's Grace is Sufficient for You

***Verse**: "Let us then approach God's throne of grace with confidence, so that we may receive mercy and find grace to help us in our time of need."*

(Hebrews 4:16, NIV)

Message: In our times of trial, we are invited to approach God's throne of grace with confidence, knowing that we will find the help we need. Hebrews 4:16 reminds us that God's grace is always available to us, and we can come boldly before Him to receive His mercy and grace. His grace is sufficient for every trial we face, providing the strength, wisdom, and comfort we need to persevere. No matter how overwhelming our circumstances may seem, God's grace is more than enough to carry us through.

The apostle Paul experienced this firsthand when he faced a persistent trial that he referred to as a "thorn in the flesh" (2 Corinthians 12:7). Despite pleading with God to remove it, Paul learned that God's grace was sufficient for him. Rather than removing the trial, God gave Paul the strength to endure it with grace. In the same way, God's grace is available to you in your time of need, providing you with the help and strength to face whatever challenges come your way.

If you're feeling overwhelmed by your trials, approach God's throne of grace with confidence. Trust that He will give you the grace and mercy you need to endure and overcome.

Call to Action: Reflect on any areas of your life where you need God's grace. Spend time in prayer, asking Him to fill you with His grace and to help you approach His throne with confidence.

Prayer: Father, thank You for the grace that is always available to me. When I am overwhelmed by my trials, help me to approach Your throne of grace with confidence, trusting that You will give me the help and strength I need. Amen.

October 25
God Will Bring You Through

Verse: *"Even though I walk through the darkest valley, I will fear no evil, for You are with me; Your rod and Your staff, they comfort me."*

(Psalm 23:4, NIV)

Message: Psalm 23:4 reminds us that even when we walk through the darkest valleys in life, we have no need to fear because God is with us. His presence brings comfort, protection, and guidance. The image of God's rod and staff symbolizes His care and leadership, guiding us through difficult times and ensuring our safety. No matter how dark the valley may seem, God's presence is a constant source of comfort and hope. He will not leave us in the valley—He will bring us through it.

David, the author of this psalm, had faced many dark valleys in his life, including battles, betrayal, and loss. Yet, he found comfort in knowing that God was with him every step of the way. In the same way, when we walk through seasons of fear, uncertainty, or pain, we can trust that God is walking beside us. His presence assures us that we are never alone, and His guidance leads us toward the hope and peace that only He can provide.

If you're walking through a dark valley, hold on to the promise that God is with you. Trust that He will guide you and bring you through to the other side.

Call to Action: Reflect on any dark valleys you may be walking through right now. Spend time in prayer, asking God to guide you and comfort you as you trust in His presence and protection.

Prayer: Lord, thank You for walking with me through every dark valley. Help me to trust in Your presence and to find comfort in knowing that You are with me. Lead me through this valley, and guide me toward the peace and hope that only You can provide. Amen.

October 26
God's Peace in the Midst of Chaos

Verse: *"You will keep in perfect peace those whose minds are steadfast, because they trust in You."*

(Isaiah 26:3, NIV)

Message: In the chaos of life, God offers us perfect peace. Isaiah 26:3 reminds us that God will keep in perfect peace those who trust in Him and remain steadfast in their faith. When trials threaten to overwhelm us, we can anchor our hearts in God's promises, knowing that He is sovereign and in control. This peace is not dependent on our circumstances but on our trust in God's faithfulness and love.

When Jesus calmed the storm on the Sea of Galilee, He demonstrated that no situation is too chaotic for His peace to reign. The disciples were terrified by the storm, but Jesus was at peace because He knew His Father's power and plan. When we focus on God rather than the chaos around us, we experience the peace that surpasses understanding. No matter the intensity of the storm, God's peace can guard our hearts and minds when we trust in Him.

If you're feeling overwhelmed by the chaos in your life, turn your focus to God and trust in His ability to bring peace in the midst of the storm.

Call to Action: Reflect on any areas of your life where you are feeling overwhelmed. Spend time in prayer, asking God to fill you with His perfect peace as you trust in Him.

Prayer: Lord, thank You for offering me perfect peace in the midst of chaos. Help me to keep my mind steadfast and focused on You, trusting that You are in control. Fill my heart with Your peace, even when life feels overwhelming. Amen.

October 27
God's Promises Never Fail

Verse: *"Not one of all the Lord's good promises to Israel failed; every one was fulfilled."*

(Joshua 21:45, NIV)

Message: One of the most comforting truths in Scripture is that God's promises never fail. Joshua 21:45 reminds us that every single promise God made to Israel was fulfilled. God is faithful to His Word, and we can trust that He will keep His promises to us as well. In the midst of trials, it can be easy to doubt whether God will come through, but His track record shows us that He always does. He is faithful to complete what He has started in our lives.

When Abraham waited years for the fulfillment of God's promise of a son, or when the Israelites wandered in the desert before reaching the Promised Land, God was faithful to His Word. Delays or difficult circumstances never alter God's promises. In the same way, whatever promise God has made to you, He will fulfill. We may not see it immediately, but we can be confident that His Word will come to pass in our lives.

If you're doubting whether God's promises will be fulfilled in your life, remember His faithfulness throughout Scripture and trust that He will fulfill His Word in your situation.

Call to Action: Reflect on the promises God has made to you through His Word. Spend time in prayer, thanking Him for His faithfulness and asking Him to help you trust in His promises.

Prayer: Father, thank You for Your faithfulness and for the promises You've made. Help me to trust that every promise You have made will be fulfilled in my life. Strengthen my faith as I wait on You, and remind me that Your promises never fail. Amen.

October 28

God Gives You Rest in Your Trials

Verse: *"Come to me, all you who are weary and burdened, and I will give you rest."*

(Matthew 11:28, NIV)

Message: When we are weary and burdened by life's trials, Jesus invites us to come to Him and find rest. Matthew 11:28 offers a beautiful promise of rest for our souls. We don't have to carry the weight of our struggles on our own. Jesus calls us to bring our burdens to Him, and in exchange, He gives us rest and peace. This rest is not just physical but spiritual and emotional, providing relief from the heaviness of life's challenges.

In the Gospels, we see Jesus taking time to withdraw and rest, even in the midst of His busy ministry. He modeled the importance of finding rest in the presence of God. When we come to Jesus with our burdens, we find the refreshment and renewal we need to keep going. He offers us rest for our souls, restoring our strength and giving us the peace we need to face each day.

If you're feeling weary and overwhelmed, accept Jesus' invitation to come to Him and find rest. Let Him carry your burdens and renew your strength.

Call to Action: Reflect on any burdens you've been carrying alone. Spend time in prayer, giving those burdens to Jesus and asking Him to give you rest and peace.

Prayer: Lord, thank You for inviting me to come to You when I am weary. Help me to bring my burdens to You and trust that You will give me rest. Restore my strength and give me the peace I need to face each day. Amen.

October 29
God's Plans Are for Your Good

Verse: *"'For I know the plans I have for you,' declares the Lord, 'plans to prosper you and not to harm you, plans to give you hope and a future.'"*

(Jeremiah 29:11, NIV)

Message: In the midst of trials, it can be difficult to see how God's plans are working for our good. Yet Jeremiah 29:11 assures us that God's plans are always for our good, to give us hope and a future. Even when life feels uncertain or painful, we can trust that God has a plan, and that plan is to prosper us and not to harm us. He sees the bigger picture and is guiding us toward a future filled with hope and purpose.

The Israelites received this promise while they were in exile, facing a season of great difficulty and uncertainty. Despite their circumstances, God's plan for them remained one of hope and restoration. In the same way, even when we are in seasons of trial, God's plans for us remain good. He is working behind the scenes, orchestrating everything for our good and His glory.

If you're struggling to understand God's plan for your life, trust that His plans are for your good. He is leading you toward a future filled with hope.

Call to Action: Reflect on the areas of your life where you need to trust God's plan. Spend time in prayer, asking Him to help you trust that His plans for you are good, even when you can't see the full picture.

Prayer: Father, thank You for the promise that Your plans for me are good. Help me to trust in Your plan, even when life feels uncertain. Give me hope and remind me that You are leading me toward a future filled with Your purpose and love. Amen.

October 30
God is Your Everlasting Rock

Verse: *"Trust in the Lord forever, for the Lord, the Lord Himself, is the Rock eternal."*

(Isaiah 26:4, NIV)

Message: In the face of trials, we need a firm foundation to stand on. Isaiah 26:4 reminds us that the Lord is our eternal Rock, the unshakable foundation we can trust forever. No matter what storms come our way, God remains steadfast and unmovable. When we place our trust in Him, we are building our lives on a solid foundation that cannot be shaken by the trials of life.

Throughout Scripture, God is referred to as a Rock—a symbol of strength, stability, and protection. David often described God as his Rock, a refuge in times of trouble. Just as a rock provides shelter and safety, God provides security and stability in our lives. He is the same yesterday, today, and forever, and we can trust Him to be our foundation in every season of life.

If you're feeling shaken by your trials, anchor yourself in God, your eternal Rock. Trust in His steadfast love and unshakable strength.

Call to Action: Reflect on the areas of your life where you need to trust God as your Rock. Spend time in prayer, asking Him to be your firm foundation and to give you strength and stability in the midst of trials.

Prayer: Lord, thank You for being my everlasting Rock. Help me to trust in You as my firm foundation, even when life feels uncertain. Give me the strength and stability I need to face my trials, and remind me that You are always with me. Amen.

October 31
God Will Never Forsake You

Verse: *"The Lord Himself goes before you and will be with you; He will never leave you nor forsake you. Do not be afraid; do not be discouraged."*

(Deuteronomy 31:8, NIV)

Message: As we close this month focused on God being with us in our trials, we are reminded in Deuteronomy 31:8 that God will never leave us or forsake us. He goes before us, preparing the way, and walks beside us, ensuring that we are never alone. This promise is a source of great comfort, especially during difficult times. We don't have to face our struggles in fear or discouragement because God is always with us. His presence is constant, and His love is unchanging.

Moses spoke these words to Joshua as he prepared to lead the Israelites into the Promised Land—a daunting task filled with uncertainty and challenges. Yet, the assurance of God's presence gave Joshua the courage to move forward in faith. In the same way, God's presence in our lives gives us the courage to face our trials with confidence, knowing that He will never abandon us.

If you're feeling discouraged or afraid, hold on to the promise that God will never leave you. Trust that He is with you and will guide you through every trial.

Call to Action: Reflect on any fears or discouragements you may be carrying. Spend time in prayer, asking God to remind you of His constant presence and to give you the courage to move forward in faith.

Prayer: Father, thank You for the promise that You will never leave me or forsake me. Help me to trust in Your constant presence, even when I feel afraid or discouraged. Give me the courage.

November

Living with Gratitude and Grace

November 1
A Heart of Gratitude

Verse: *"Give thanks to the Lord, for He is good; His love endures forever."*

(Psalm 107:1, NIV)

Message: Gratitude is at the heart of a life lived in God's grace. Psalm 107:1 calls us to give thanks to the Lord, not just for what He does, but for who He is—good, loving, and eternal. When we cultivate a heart of gratitude, we begin to see God's hand at work in every aspect of our lives. Whether in times of joy or trial, there is always something to be thankful for because God's love endures forever. His goodness is not dependent on our circumstances, and His love never fails.

The Israelites often experienced seasons of hardship, but time and again, they were reminded to give thanks to God for His enduring love. When they wandered in the wilderness, when they faced enemies, or when they rejoiced in victories, God's love remained constant. In the same way, we are called to give thanks in every season. A grateful heart changes our perspective, helping us to focus on God's unchanging character rather than the challenges we face.

If you've been struggling to find reasons to be thankful, take a moment to reflect on God's goodness and His steadfast love. Gratitude will shift your focus from what is lacking to the abundance of God's grace.

Call to Action: Reflect on areas of your life where you can express gratitude to God. Spend time in prayer, giving thanks for His enduring love and goodness.

Prayer: Lord, thank You for Your goodness and love that endures forever. Help me to cultivate a heart of gratitude, even in difficult seasons. Let my life be a reflection of thankfulness for all that You are and all that You've done. Amen.

November 2
Gratitude in All Circumstances

Verse: *"Give thanks in all circumstances; for this is God's will for you in Christ Jesus."*

(1 Thessalonians 5:18, NIV)

Message: Gratitude isn't just reserved for the good times—it's a posture of the heart that we are called to maintain in all circumstances. 1 Thessalonians 5:18 tells us that it is God's will for us to give thanks in every situation. This doesn't mean we are thankful for the trials themselves, but we are grateful for God's presence and work in the midst of them. When we thank God in all circumstances, we acknowledge His sovereignty and trust that He is using everything for our good.

Job's story in the Bible illustrates the power of gratitude in difficult circumstances. Even after losing his wealth, family, and health, Job continued to bless the name of the Lord. He didn't understand why he was suffering, but he trusted that God was still good and worthy of praise. Gratitude in all circumstances strengthens our faith, reminding us that God is with us in both the valleys and the mountaintops.

If you're facing challenges, take a moment to thank God for His presence in your life. Trust that He is working behind the scenes, even in difficult times.

Call to Action: Reflect on your current circumstances and spend time in prayer, thanking God for His presence and faithfulness, even in the challenges you face.

Prayer: Father, thank You for Your presence in every situation. Help me to give thanks in all circumstances, trusting that You are with me and that You are working for my good. Strengthen my heart with gratitude, no matter what I'm facing. Amen.

November 3
Grace Upon Grace

Verse: *"Out of His fullness we have all received grace in place of grace already given."*

(John 1:16, NIV)

Message: God's grace is abundant and overflowing. John 1:16 tells us that we have received grace upon grace from the fullness of God. His grace doesn't run out, nor is it dependent on our worthiness. Instead, it is given freely, over and over again, as we live in relationship with Him. Whether we are just beginning our walk with Christ or have been following Him for years, we continually receive His grace in every moment of our lives.

The apostle Paul experienced this grace in his own life. Despite his past as a persecutor of Christians, Paul encountered the grace of God on the road to Damascus, and his life was forever changed. He became one of the greatest evangelists of the Gospel, proclaiming the message of grace to the world. Like Paul, we are recipients of God's amazing grace—grace that covers our sins, strengthens us in our weaknesses, and empowers us to live for Him.

If you've been feeling unworthy of God's grace, remember that His grace is given freely, not based on what we've done but on His love for us. Receive the grace He offers today.

Call to Action: Reflect on the ways you've experienced God's grace in your life. Spend time in prayer, thanking Him for the grace He continually pours out on you.

Prayer: Lord, thank You for the grace that You give so abundantly. Help me to receive Your grace with an open heart, knowing that it is not earned but given freely out of Your love. Let Your grace transform my life and lead me closer to You. Amen.

November 4
Grateful for God's Provision

Verse: *"And my God will meet all your needs according to the riches of His glory in Christ Jesus."*

(Philippians 4:19, NIV)

Message: God is our provider, and Philippians 4:19 assures us that He will meet all of our needs according to the riches of His glory in Christ Jesus. Whether our needs are physical, emotional, or spiritual, God's provision is abundant and more than enough. When we live with an attitude of gratitude, we acknowledge that everything we have comes from Him. Gratitude opens our hearts to see the ways God is providing for us, even in unexpected ways.

The Israelites learned to trust in God's provision during their time in the wilderness. Each day, God provided manna from heaven, meeting their physical needs and teaching them to rely on Him. Just as He provided for them, He provides for us today. Sometimes His provision may not come in the way we expect, but it is always exactly what we need. When we trust in His provision, we can live with peace and gratitude, knowing that our needs are in His hands.

If you're struggling with worry or lack, take a moment to thank God for His provision. Trust that He will meet all your needs according to His glorious riches.

Call to Action: Reflect on how God has provided for you, and spend time in prayer, thanking Him for meeting your needs. Ask Him to help you trust in His provision for the future.

Prayer: Father, thank You for being my provider. Help me to trust in Your provision and to live with a heart of gratitude for all that You have given me. Remind me that You are always faithful to meet my needs according to Your riches in Christ Jesus. Amen.

November 5
Grace to Forgive

Verse: *"Be kind and compassionate to one another, forgiving each other, just as in Christ God forgave you."*

(Ephesians 4:32, NIV)

Message: One of the greatest expressions of grace we can offer is forgiveness. Ephesians 4:32 calls us to be kind and compassionate, forgiving others just as Christ forgave us. God's grace has covered our sins, and we are called to extend that same grace to others. Forgiveness is not always easy, especially when we've been hurt deeply, but when we choose to forgive, we release the burden of resentment and allow God's grace to bring healing.

Jesus demonstrated the ultimate act of forgiveness on the cross, praying for those who crucified Him, saying, "Father, forgive them, for they do not know what they are doing" (Luke 23:34). His example shows us that forgiveness is not about the worthiness of the other person but about our willingness to reflect God's grace. When we forgive, we free ourselves from the chains of bitterness and open the door to healing and restoration.

If you're holding onto unforgiveness, ask God for the grace to forgive. Trust that His grace is sufficient to help you release the hurt and extend forgiveness to others.

Call to Action: Reflect on any areas of your life where you may be holding onto unforgiveness. Spend time in prayer, asking God to give you the grace to forgive and to experience the freedom that comes with forgiveness.

Prayer: Lord, thank You for the grace and forgiveness You've given me. Help me to extend that same grace to others, even when it's difficult. Give me the strength to forgive, and let Your grace bring healing and restoration to my heart. Amen.

November 6
Gratitude for God's Faithfulness

Verse: *"Because of the Lord's great love we are not consumed, for His compassions never fail. They are new every morning; great is Your faithfulness."*

(Lamentations 3:22-23, NIV)

Message: God's faithfulness is something we can always be thankful for, no matter the season of life we are in. Lamentations 3:22-23 reminds us that His compassions never fail and His faithfulness is renewed every morning. Even when we face trials, God's steadfast love remains. His faithfulness is a constant in our lives, providing hope and encouragement when things seem uncertain. Living with gratitude for God's faithfulness changes our perspective, helping us to focus on His unchanging character rather than our fluctuating circumstances.

Jeremiah, who wrote Lamentations, was in the midst of deep sorrow and hardship when he penned these words. Yet, even in the darkest times, he was able to recognize God's enduring faithfulness. This teaches us that gratitude for God's faithfulness isn't dependent on life being easy; it's rooted in the understanding that God is always with us, sustaining us with His love. When we embrace this truth, we can face each day with gratitude, knowing that God's mercies are new every morning.

If you're feeling overwhelmed or discouraged, take a moment to thank God for His faithfulness. He is with you, and His mercies are fresh every day.

Call to Action: Reflect on God's faithfulness in your life, especially in times of difficulty. Spend time in prayer, thanking Him for His steadfast love and for the new mercies He provides each day.

Prayer: Father, thank You for Your great faithfulness. Help me to remember that Your compassions never fail and that Your mercies are new every morning. Let my heart overflow with gratitude for Your constant love and care. Amen.

November 7
Grace in Your Weakness

Verse: "But He said to me, 'My grace is sufficient for you, for My power is made perfect in weakness.'"

(2 Corinthians 12:9, NIV)

Message: God's grace is most evident in our moments of weakness. In 2 Corinthians 12:9, Paul recounts how God told him, "My grace is sufficient for you, for My power is made perfect in weakness." This is a powerful reminder that we don't have to rely on our own strength. Instead, we can rest in God's grace, knowing that His power shines through our weakest moments. Grace allows us to acknowledge our limitations and rely fully on God's strength to carry us through.

Paul's "thorn in the flesh" was a persistent struggle, yet he learned to rejoice in his weakness because it allowed God's grace to work in greater measure. Like Paul, we often find that it's in our weakest moments that we experience God's grace most fully. Rather than trying to be self-sufficient, we can embrace our need for God and trust that His grace will sustain us. His grace fills the gaps where our strength fails, and His power is made perfect in our weakness.

If you're feeling weak or inadequate, ask God to fill you with His grace. Trust that His power is sufficient to carry you through any challenge.

Call to Action: Reflect on areas of your life where you feel weak or overwhelmed. Spend time in prayer, asking God to show His strength through your weakness and to fill you with His grace.

Prayer: Lord, thank You for Your grace, which is sufficient for me. In my weakness, help me to trust in Your power. Fill me with Your grace and remind me that Your strength is made perfect when I depend on You. Amen.

November 8
Gratitude for the Gift of Salvation

Verse: *"For it is by grace you have been saved, through faith—and this is not from yourselves, it is the gift of God."*

(Ephesians 2:8, NIV)

Message: The greatest reason for gratitude is the gift of salvation. Ephesians 2:8 reminds us that we are saved by grace through faith—it is not something we earn or achieve but a gift from God. This free gift of salvation is a demonstration of God's incredible love and grace toward us. We were once separated from God, but through Jesus Christ, we have been brought near and reconciled to Him. Living with gratitude for our salvation shifts our focus to the eternal, reminding us of the incredible grace that has been poured out on us.

When we reflect on the price Jesus paid for our salvation, gratitude naturally overflows. He took on the punishment we deserved so that we could be forgiven and have eternal life. This grace is not something we can repay but something we can live out with thankfulness and humility. Salvation is the foundation of our relationship with God, and each day, we have the opportunity to thank Him for this incredible gift of grace.

If you've been taking your salvation for granted, take time today to reflect on the grace that has been given to you. Let your heart be filled with gratitude for the gift of eternal life.

Call to Action: Reflect on the gift of salvation in your life and spend time in prayer, thanking God for the grace that saved you. Let this gratitude inspire you to live each day for Him.

Prayer: Father, thank You for the gift of salvation. I am grateful for the grace You've shown me, saving me through faith in Jesus Christ. Help me to live with a heart full of gratitude for the incredible gift of eternal life. Amen.

November 9
Extending Grace to Others

Verse: *"Bear with each other and forgive one another if any of you has a grievance against someone. Forgive as the Lord forgave you."*

(Colossians 3:13, NIV)

Message: Just as we have received grace from God, we are called to extend that same grace to others. Colossians 3:13 encourages us to bear with one another and forgive, just as the Lord forgave us. This means showing grace to those who may have wronged us, offering forgiveness and understanding even when it's difficult. Living with grace toward others reflects the heart of God and strengthens our relationships.

Jesus taught about forgiveness throughout His ministry, emphasizing the importance of showing grace to others. In the parable of the unforgiving servant (Matthew 18:21-35), He highlighted the need to forgive others as we have been forgiven. When we extend grace, we free ourselves from bitterness and allow God's love to work through us. It's not always easy, but living with a heart of grace brings peace and restoration to our relationships and reflects the love of Christ to those around us.

If you've been holding onto unforgiveness, ask God to help you extend grace to those who have wronged you. Trust that His grace is enough to heal and restore.

Call to Action: Reflect on any relationships in your life where you need to extend grace and forgiveness. Spend time in prayer, asking God to give you the strength to forgive and to show grace to others.

Prayer: Lord, thank You for the grace You've shown me. Help me to extend that same grace to others, even when it's difficult. Teach me to forgive as You have forgiven me, and let my life be a reflection of Your love and grace. Amen.

November 10
Living with Thankfulness

***Verse**: "Let the peace of Christ rule in your hearts, since as members of one body you were called to peace. And be thankful."*

(Colossians 3:15, NIV)

Message: Thankfulness is a key part of living in peace and grace. Colossians 3:15 calls us to let the peace of Christ rule in our hearts and to live with thankfulness. When we focus on the blessings in our lives and the peace that comes from Christ, we naturally cultivate a heart of gratitude. Thankfulness shifts our mindset from what we lack to what we have been given, reminding us of God's faithfulness and provision.

In the busyness of life, it's easy to overlook the many blessings God has poured into our lives. But when we intentionally choose to be thankful, we experience the peace of Christ in a deeper way. This thankfulness isn't just for the big things—it's for the small, everyday blessings as well. Living with thankfulness keeps our hearts aligned with God's grace, helping us to see His goodness in every situation.

If you've been struggling with a lack of peace or contentment, take time to focus on what you are thankful for. Let gratitude fill your heart and lead you into a deeper experience of Christ's peace.

Call to Action: Reflect on the blessings in your life, both big and small. Spend time in prayer, thanking God for His faithfulness and asking Him to help you live with a heart of gratitude.

Prayer: Father, thank You for the many blessings You've given me. Help me to live with a heart of thankfulness, always focusing on Your goodness and grace. Let Your peace rule in my heart as I choose gratitude each day. Amen.

November 11
Gratitude for God's Unfailing Love

Verse: "But I trust in Your unfailing love; my heart rejoices in Your salvation."

(Psalm 13:5, NIV)

Message: One of the greatest gifts we can be thankful for is God's unfailing love. Psalm 13:5 reminds us that, even when life is hard, we can trust in God's constant love. His love is never dependent on our actions or circumstances—it is steadfast, unfailing, and unconditional. Living with gratitude for God's unfailing love helps us keep our hearts centered on Him, especially during difficult times. His love provides hope, even when everything else feels uncertain.

David, the author of this psalm, faced many trials, yet he chose to trust in God's love and rejoice in His salvation. In the same way, we are invited to rejoice in God's love and grace, knowing that His love for us never wavers. When we live with gratitude for His love, we experience a deeper sense of peace, joy, and trust in His plan for our lives. His love is the anchor that holds us firm in every storm.

If you're feeling distant or uncertain, take a moment to reflect on God's unfailing love for you. Thank Him for His constant presence and care in your life.

Call to Action: Reflect on how God's unfailing love has carried you through different seasons of life. Spend time in prayer, thanking Him for His steadfast love and rejoicing in His salvation.

Prayer: Father, thank You for Your unfailing love. No matter what I face, help me to trust in Your love and rejoice in the salvation You've given me. Let my heart overflow with gratitude for Your constant care and presence in my life. Amen.

November 12
Grace for Today

Verse: *"The Lord has done it this very day; let us rejoice today and be glad."*

(Psalm 118:24, NIV)

Message: Every day is a gift of grace from God, and Psalm 118:24 reminds us to rejoice in the present moment. God's grace is sufficient for today, and we are called to live in the present, embracing the grace He provides. Sometimes, we can become consumed by worries about tomorrow or regrets about the past, but God invites us to focus on today and to trust Him for what we need right now.

Jesus taught His disciples to trust God daily when He said, "Give us this day our daily bread" (Matthew 6:11). This daily dependence on God keeps us anchored in His grace, allowing us to experience His provision and joy in the present moment. When we learn to live with gratitude for the grace God gives us today, we find peace and contentment, knowing that He is in control of both our present and our future.

If you've been anxious about the future or weighed down by the past, focus on God's grace for today. Rejoice in the gift of this day and trust Him to provide what you need.

Call to Action: Reflect on the grace God has given you today. Spend time in prayer, asking Him to help you live in the present moment and to trust in His provision for each day.

Prayer: Lord, thank You for the grace You provide for today. Help me to rejoice in the present moment, trusting that You will meet my needs and carry me through each day. Teach me to live with gratitude for Your daily grace. Amen.

November 13
Gratitude in Worship

Verse: "Come, let us bow down in worship, let us kneel before the Lord our Maker."

(Psalm 95:6, NIV)

Message: Worship is one of the greatest expressions of gratitude we can offer to God. Psalm 95:6 invites us to come before the Lord in worship, bowing down in humility and thanksgiving. When we worship God, we acknowledge His greatness, His goodness, and His grace in our lives. True worship flows from a heart that is filled with gratitude for who God is and all He has done.

Throughout the Bible, we see examples of people expressing their gratitude through worship. Whether it was the Israelites offering sacrifices of thanksgiving or the psalmists singing songs of praise, worship was always a response to God's goodness and grace. When we come before God in worship with a heart of gratitude, we enter into a deeper relationship with Him, experiencing His presence in a powerful way.

If your worship has felt dry or routine, take time today to reflect on God's goodness and come before Him with a heart of gratitude. Let your worship be an outpouring of thankfulness for who He is.

Call to Action: Reflect on your personal worship life and how you can deepen your sense of gratitude in worship. Spend time in prayer, thanking God for who He is and for all He has done.

Prayer: Father, thank You for the privilege of worshiping You. Help me to come before You with a heart full of gratitude, recognizing Your greatness and goodness in my life. Let my worship be an offering of thankfulness for all You are and all You have done. Amen.

November 14
Grace in Difficult Relationships

Verse: *"If it is possible, as far as it depends on you, live at peace with everyone."*

(Romans 12:18, NIV)

Message: Living with grace extends to our relationships, even the difficult ones. Romans 12:18 encourages us to live at peace with everyone, as far as it depends on us. This means that we are called to extend grace and forgiveness, even when relationships are challenging. Grace allows us to be peacemakers, seeking reconciliation and harmony rather than holding onto grudges or bitterness.

Jesus exemplified this kind of grace in His interactions with others. Whether it was forgiving those who crucified Him or showing compassion to those who rejected Him, Jesus always chose grace. In the same way, we are called to extend grace in our relationships, even when it's difficult. By doing so, we reflect the love of Christ and create opportunities for healing and restoration.

If you're struggling with a difficult relationship, ask God to give you the grace to live at peace with others. Trust that His grace is enough to bring reconciliation and healing.

Call to Action: Reflect on any difficult relationships in your life. Spend time in prayer, asking God to give you the grace to live at peace with others and to be a source of reconciliation.

Prayer: Lord, thank You for the grace You've shown me. Help me to extend that grace to others, especially in difficult relationships. Teach me to be a peacemaker, living in harmony and reflecting Your love in all my interactions. Amen.

November 15
Gratitude for God's Provision

Verse: *"The Lord is my shepherd, I lack nothing."*

(Psalm 23:1, NIV)

Message: Psalm 23:1 offers a powerful reminder that, with the Lord as our Shepherd, we lack nothing. God is our provider, and He meets all of our needs according to His perfect wisdom and timing. When we live with gratitude for God's provision, we learn to trust in His care and guidance. Rather than focusing on what we lack, we can rest in the assurance that God provides everything we need.

David, who wrote this psalm, experienced God's provision time and again, whether in times of abundance or in times of great need. He knew that, as long as the Lord was his Shepherd, he would be cared for. In the same way, we can trust in God's provision for every area of our lives. Whether we need physical sustenance, emotional support, or spiritual guidance, God is faithful to provide for us. Living with gratitude for His provision brings peace and contentment, even in seasons of uncertainty.

If you're feeling anxious about your needs, take a moment to thank God for His provision. Trust that He will continue to guide and care for you as your Shepherd.

Call to Action: Reflect on how God has provided for you in the past and present. Spend time in prayer, thanking Him for His care and provision, and trusting Him to meet your needs in the future.

Prayer: Father, thank You for being my Shepherd and provider. Help me to live with gratitude for Your provision and to trust that You will continue to meet my needs. Let my heart be at peace, knowing that I lack nothing in You. Amen.

November 16
Gratitude for God's Strength

Verse: *"The Lord is my strength and my shield; my heart trusts in Him, and He helps me."*

(Psalm 28:7, NIV)

Message: In moments of weakness, it's comforting to know that the Lord is our strength. Psalm 28:7 reminds us that God is not only our protector but also the source of the strength we need to face life's challenges. When we trust in Him, He becomes our shield, guarding us from discouragement and fear. Living with gratitude for God's strength enables us to face trials with confidence, knowing that we are not relying on our own power but on His.

David, who often faced physical and emotional battles, declared that God was his strength. Whether he was running from enemies or dealing with personal failure, he found that God's power was always sufficient to carry him through. In the same way, God is ready to strengthen us in our moments of need. When we place our trust in Him, He provides the courage and stamina to continue forward, no matter how difficult the path may seem.

If you've been feeling drained or discouraged, turn to God for strength. Thank Him for being your source of power and ask Him to help you lean on His strength each day.

Call to Action: Reflect on areas in your life where you need God's strength. Spend time in prayer, thanking Him for His power and asking Him to be your strength in every challenge you face.

Prayer: Father, thank You for being my strength and my shield. Help me to trust in You completely, relying on Your strength to carry me through every trial. Let my heart be filled with gratitude for the power You give me each day. Amen.

NOVEMBER 17
GRACE TO TRUST IN GOD'S TIMING

> ***Verse***: *"The Lord is good to those whose hope is in Him, to the one who seeks Him; it is good to wait quietly for the salvation of the Lord."*
>
> ***(Lamentations 3:25-26, NIV)***

Message: Trusting God's timing can be one of the most challenging aspects of faith. Lamentations 3:25-26 encourages us to hope in the Lord and wait quietly for His salvation. God's timing is perfect, even when it doesn't align with our own expectations. Living with grace means trusting that God knows what is best for us and that He will act at the right time. Patience in waiting is a reflection of our faith in His plans.

Throughout Scripture, we see examples of people who had to wait on God. Abraham waited for the promised son, Joseph waited for deliverance from prison, and the Israelites waited for the fulfillment of God's promises. In every case, God's timing proved to be perfect, and His plans were fulfilled in ways that brought about the greatest good. Trusting in God's timing allows us to live with peace and patience, knowing that He is working all things together for our good.

If you've been struggling with waiting, ask God for the grace to trust in His timing. Thank Him for the good He is working in your life, even when you can't yet see it.

Call to Action: Reflect on areas of your life where you are waiting for God to act. Spend time in prayer, asking Him to give you patience and grace to trust in His perfect timing.

Prayer: Lord, thank You for Your perfect timing. Help me to trust in Your plans and to wait patiently for Your will to be done. Fill me with grace as I wait, and remind me that You are always working for my good. Amen.

November 18
Gratitude for God's Guidance

Verse: *"Whether you turn to the right or to the left, your ears will hear a voice behind you, saying, 'This is the way; walk in it.'"*

(Isaiah 30:21, NIV)

Message: God's guidance is a precious gift, and Isaiah 30:21 reminds us that He is always directing our steps. Whether we are facing major life decisions or simply navigating the day-to-day, God promises to guide us. When we listen for His voice and seek His will, we can trust that He will lead us down the right path. Gratitude for God's guidance keeps us humble, reminding us that we are not walking alone.

In the Old Testament, the Israelites were led by God through the wilderness by a pillar of cloud by day and a pillar of fire by night. Today, we may not see physical signs of God's guidance, but His Spirit is with us, leading us in the way we should go. When we take time to listen to His voice and follow His direction, we experience His peace and confidence, knowing that we are on the path He has set before us.

If you're seeking guidance or clarity, thank God for His promise to lead you. Trust that He is guiding you, even when the way forward seems unclear.

Call to Action: Reflect on any decisions or situations where you need God's guidance. Spend time in prayer, asking Him to direct your steps and thanking Him for His faithfulness to lead you.

Prayer: Father, thank You for guiding me in every season of life. Help me to trust Your direction and to listen for Your voice as You lead me. Thank You for always being with me, showing me the way to walk. Amen.

November 19
Grace in Forgiving Yourself

Verse: *"There is now no condemnation for those who are in Christ Jesus."*

(Romans 8:1, NIV)

Message: One of the most difficult aspects of grace is learning to extend it to ourselves. Romans 8:1 reminds us that there is no condemnation for those who are in Christ Jesus. When we come to God in repentance, He forgives us completely. However, it can be hard to forgive ourselves and let go of guilt or shame. Living with grace means accepting the forgiveness that God has already extended and walking in the freedom that Christ has given us.

Peter's story illustrates this beautifully. After denying Jesus three times, Peter was devastated by his failure. Yet, after Jesus' resurrection, Peter was not only forgiven but also restored and commissioned to lead the early church. In the same way, God's grace covers our mistakes and restores us to wholeness. When we accept His forgiveness, we can release the burden of guilt and live in the freedom of His grace.

If you've been holding onto guilt or struggling to forgive yourself, ask God to help you accept His grace. Thank Him for the forgiveness He has already given you and for the freedom that comes with it.

Call to Action: Reflect on any areas of your life where you need to forgive yourself. Spend time in prayer, asking God to help you let go of guilt and to accept the freedom of His grace.

Prayer: Lord, thank You for the forgiveness and grace You've given me through Christ. Help me to accept that grace for myself and to let go of any guilt or shame. Let me walk in the freedom that comes from knowing I am forgiven and loved by You. Amen.

November 20
Gratitude for God's Faithfulness in Every Season

Verse: *"Let us hold unswervingly to the hope we profess, for He who promised is faithful."*

(Hebrews 10:23, NIV)

Message: God's faithfulness is constant, no matter the season of life we are in. Hebrews 10:23 encourages us to hold onto hope because God is faithful to keep His promises. Whether we are in a season of blessing or trial, we can trust that God is with us and that He is working for our good. Gratitude for God's faithfulness reminds us that we are never alone and that His promises are sure.

Throughout the Bible, God's faithfulness is evident. From the fulfillment of His promises to Abraham to His provision for the Israelites in the wilderness, God has always been faithful to His people. In our own lives, we can look back and see how God has been faithful in every season, providing for our needs, guiding us, and fulfilling His promises. When we live with gratitude for His faithfulness, our hearts are filled with hope, even in difficult times.

If you're going through a challenging season, take time to thank God for His faithfulness. Trust that He will continue to be faithful, guiding and providing for you in every season of life.

Call to Action: Reflect on how God has been faithful to you in the past and present. Spend time in prayer, thanking Him for His unchanging faithfulness and asking Him to help you hold onto hope.

Prayer: Father, thank You for Your faithfulness in every season of my life. Help me to hold onto hope, knowing that You are always with me and that You will fulfill Your promises. Let my heart be filled with gratitude for Your constant love and care. Amen.

November 21
Gratitude for God's Protection

Verse: *"The Lord will keep you from all harm*
—He will watch over your life."

(Psalm 121:7, NIV)

Message: One of the many things we can be grateful for is God's constant protection. Psalm 121:7 reminds us that the Lord watches over us and keeps us from harm. Whether we realize it or not, God's hand is always upon us, guiding us away from danger and keeping us safe in ways we may never see. Living with gratitude for God's protection helps us to trust in His care, even when life feels uncertain or dangerous.

The Israelites experienced God's protection throughout their journey from Egypt to the Promised Land. God shielded them from their enemies, provided for them in the wilderness, and led them safely to their destination. In the same way, God's protection surrounds us today. When we live with gratitude for His care, we become more aware of His presence and trust Him to lead us through any situation.

If you've been feeling anxious or fearful, thank God for His protection. Trust that He is watching over you and will keep you from harm, even when you cannot see the full picture.

Call to Action: Reflect on the ways God has protected you in your life. Spend time in prayer, thanking Him for His protection and asking Him to help you trust in His care.

Prayer: Lord, thank You for Your constant protection. Help me to trust that You are watching over me and keeping me safe in every situation. Let my heart be filled with gratitude for Your care and protection. Amen.

November 22
Grace to Let Go of Worry

Verse: *"Cast all your anxiety on Him because He cares for you."*
(1 Peter 5:7, NIV)

Message: God invites us to cast all of our worries and anxieties on Him because He cares for us. 1 Peter 5:7 is a reminder that we don't have to carry our burdens alone. God's grace is sufficient to handle all of our worries, and He desires for us to give them to Him. Living with grace means releasing control and trusting that God is in charge of every detail of our lives.

Jesus taught His disciples not to worry, reminding them that God cares for the birds of the air and the flowers of the field, and He will surely care for His children (Matthew 6:25-34). When we trust in God's care, we can let go of the worries that weigh us down and experience His peace. Grace allows us to release our anxieties and rest in the knowledge that God is in control and that He cares for us deeply.

If you've been holding onto worry, take a moment to give it to God. Trust that He cares for you and will provide for your needs.

Call to Action: Reflect on any worries or anxieties you've been holding onto. Spend time in prayer, casting those anxieties on God and trusting Him to care for you.

Prayer: Father, thank You for caring for me. Help me to cast all my worries on You and to trust that You are in control of every situation. Let Your grace fill my heart with peace as I release my anxieties to You. Amen.

November 23
Gratitude for God's Faithful Provision

> **Verse:** *"And God is able to bless you abundantly, so that in all things at all times, having all that you need, you will abound in every good work."*
>
> **(2 Corinthians 9:8, NIV)**

Message: God's provision is both abundant and faithful. 2 Corinthians 9:8 reminds us that God is able to bless us abundantly, providing everything we need so that we can abound in good works. Living with gratitude for God's provision opens our eyes to the ways He blesses us, even in the smallest details. When we trust in His provision, we are freed from worry and able to focus on how we can serve others.

In the Bible, we see God's provision in both miraculous and ordinary ways. From providing manna for the Israelites in the wilderness to multiplying the loaves and fishes to feed thousands, God has always provided for the needs of His people. When we live with gratitude for His provision, we acknowledge that everything we have comes from Him and that He will continue to meet our needs in the future.

If you've been worrying about your needs, take time to thank God for His faithful provision. Trust that He will continue to provide for you as you live in service to Him.

Call to Action: Reflect on how God has provided for your needs. Spend time in prayer, thanking Him for His abundant provision and asking Him to help you trust in His care.

Prayer: Lord, thank You for Your faithful provision. Help me to live with gratitude, recognizing that everything I have comes from You. Let me trust in Your care and use the blessings You've given me to serve others. Amen.

November 24
Grace to Extend Kindness

Verse: *"Be kind and compassionate to one another, forgiving each other, just as in Christ God forgave you."*

(Ephesians 4:32, NIV)

Message: Living with grace means extending kindness and compassion to others. Ephesians 4:32 calls us to be kind and forgiving, just as God has forgiven us. Grace enables us to see others through the eyes of Christ and respond with love, even when it's difficult. When we live with kindness and compassion, we reflect God's love to the world around us.

Jesus consistently showed kindness to those around Him, whether it was healing the sick, comforting the grieving, or extending grace to those who had fallen into sin. He calls us to do the same. When we choose to be kind, we participate in God's redemptive work, spreading His love and grace to those who need it most.

If you've been struggling to show kindness to someone, ask God to fill you with His grace. Let His love guide your interactions and help you extend compassion to others.

Call to Action: Reflect on someone in your life who needs kindness and compassion. Spend time in prayer, asking God to help you extend grace to them and show them His love.

Prayer: Father, thank You for the grace You've given me. Help me to extend that same kindness and compassion to others, even when it's difficult. Let my actions reflect Your love and bring healing to those around me. Amen.

November 25
Gratitude for God's Peace

Verse: "And the peace of God, which transcends all understanding, will guard your hearts and your minds in Christ Jesus."

(Philippians 4:7, NIV)

Message: God's peace is a gift that transcends all understanding. Philippians 4:7 assures us that God's peace will guard our hearts and minds in Christ Jesus. Living with gratitude for God's peace helps us navigate life's challenges with calm assurance, knowing that He is in control. His peace is not dependent on our circumstances but is rooted in His presence with us.

When Jesus calmed the storm for His disciples, He demonstrated that no situation is too chaotic for His peace to reign. In the same way, God's peace guards our hearts from anxiety, fear, and worry, providing us with a sense of security in His love. When we live with gratitude for His peace, we experience the freedom to trust Him fully, even in the midst of life's storms.

If you've been feeling anxious or unsettled, ask God to fill you with His peace. Thank Him for the gift of peace that transcends understanding and trust Him to guard your heart and mind.

Call to Action: Reflect on any areas of your life where you need God's peace. Spend time in prayer, thanking Him for the peace He provides and asking Him to fill your heart with His calming presence.

Prayer: Lord, thank You for Your peace that transcends all understanding. Help me to rest in that peace, trusting that You are in control of every situation. Let Your peace guard my heart and mind, filling me with calm assurance in Your love. Amen.

November 26
Grace to Live Humbly

Verse: *"Humble yourselves, therefore, under God's mighty hand, that He may lift you up in due time."*

(1 Peter 5:6, NIV)

Message: Living with grace involves humility. 1 Peter 5:6 calls us to humble ourselves under God's mighty hand, trusting that He will lift us up in His timing. Humility is a recognition of our dependence on God's grace and a willingness to submit to His will. When we live humbly, we acknowledge that everything we have and everything we accomplish is a result of God's grace, not our own efforts.

Jesus modeled humility throughout His life, from washing His disciples' feet to submitting to the will of the Father in the Garden of Gethsemane. He showed us that true greatness comes from serving others and living in humble obedience to God. When we embrace humility, we open ourselves up to receive more of God's grace and to be used by Him in powerful ways.

If you've been struggling with pride or self-reliance, ask God to give you the grace to live humbly. Trust that He will lift you up in His perfect timing.

Call to Action: Reflect on any areas of your life where you need to embrace humility. Spend time in prayer, asking God to help you live humbly and to trust in His timing for your life.

Prayer: Father, thank You for the example of humility that Jesus set. Help me to humble myself before You, recognizing that everything I have comes from Your grace. Teach me to live in humble submission to Your will, trusting that You will lift me up in due time. Amen.

November 27
Gratitude for God's Unchanging Character

Verse: *"Jesus Christ is the same yesterday and today and forever."*

(Hebrews 13:8, NIV)

Message: One of the most comforting truths we can be grateful for is that God's character never changes. Hebrews 13:8 reminds us that Jesus Christ is the same yesterday, today, and forever. In a world that is constantly shifting and changing, God's unchanging nature provides us with stability and security. We can trust that His love, grace, and faithfulness will never waver, no matter what circumstances we face.

Throughout history, God has proven Himself to be faithful, loving, and just. From the time of the patriarchs to the life of Jesus, His character has remained consistent. This unchanging nature gives us confidence that the same God who was faithful to His people in the past will be faithful to us today. Living with gratitude for God's unchanging character strengthens our faith and helps us to trust Him more fully.

If you're feeling uncertain about the future, thank God for His unchanging nature. Trust that He will continue to be faithful and loving in every season of your life.

Call to Action: Reflect on how God's unchanging character has provided stability in your life. Spend time in prayer, thanking Him for His consistency and faithfulness, and trusting Him for the future.

Prayer: Lord, thank You for being unchanging in Your love and faithfulness. Help me to trust in Your character, knowing that You are the same yesterday, today, and forever. Let my heart be filled with gratitude for Your constant presence in my life. Amen.

November 28
Grace to Live Generously

Verse: *"Each of you should give what you have decided in your heart to give, not reluctantly or under compulsion, for God loves a cheerful giver."*

(2 Corinthians 9:7, NIV)

Message: Grace leads us to live generously, giving freely from the abundance God has given us. 2 Corinthians 9:7 encourages us to give cheerfully, not out of obligation but from a heart that is grateful for God's blessings. Generosity is a reflection of God's grace in our lives. When we give freely and joyfully, we participate in God's work of blessing others and spreading His love.

Jesus demonstrated radical generosity throughout His ministry. He gave His time, compassion, and ultimately His life for the sake of others. As His followers, we are called to live with that same spirit of generosity. Whether it's giving our resources, time, or encouragement, living generously allows us to reflect God's grace and experience the joy of giving.

If you've been hesitant to give, ask God to fill your heart with grace and generosity. Trust that as you give, He will provide for your needs and bless others through you.

Call to Action: Reflect on how you can live more generously. Spend time in prayer, asking God to help you give cheerfully and to use your generosity to bless others.

Prayer: Father, thank You for the many blessings You've given me. Help me to live generously, giving freely and cheerfully from the abundance of Your grace. Let my generosity reflect Your love and bring blessings to others. Amen.

November 29
Gratitude for God's Nearness

Verse: *"The Lord is near to all who call on Him, to all who call on Him in truth."*

(Psalm 145:18, NIV)

Message: One of the greatest blessings we can be grateful for is God's nearness. Psalm 145:18 assures us that the Lord is near to all who call on Him. God is not distant or unreachable—He is close to us, ready to hear and respond when we seek Him. Living with gratitude for God's nearness reminds us that we are never alone. His presence is always with us, guiding, comforting, and strengthening us.

In the Bible, we see God drawing near to His people time and again. From walking with Adam and Eve in the garden to sending Jesus to live among us, God's desire has always been to be close to His people. Today, through the Holy Spirit, God's presence is with us in a very real and personal way. When we live with gratitude for His nearness, we find peace and comfort in knowing that He is always just a prayer away.

If you've been feeling distant from God, take a moment to call on Him. Thank Him for His nearness and trust that He is always with you.

Call to Action: Reflect on how God's nearness has brought you comfort and peace. Spend time in prayer, thanking Him for being close to you and asking Him to help you remain aware of His presence each day.

Prayer: Lord, thank You for being near to me. Help me to live with gratitude for Your constant presence in my life. Remind me that You are always close, ready to guide and comfort me in every situation. Amen.

November 30
Grace to Finish Well

Verse: *"Let us not become weary in doing good,
for at the proper time we will reap a harvest if we do not give up."*

(Galatians 6:9, NIV)

Message: As we come to the end of the month, Galatians 6:9 encourages us not to grow weary in doing good. Living with grace means persevering in the work God has called us to, even when it's difficult. God promises that, in due time, we will reap a harvest if we do not give up. Grace gives us the strength to continue doing good, trusting that our efforts will bear fruit in God's timing.

The apostle Paul faced many trials in his ministry, but he never gave up. He continued to preach the Gospel, serve others, and live for Christ, knowing that his labor was not in vain. In the same way, we are called to finish well, trusting that God sees our efforts and will reward our faithfulness. When we rely on His grace, we find the strength to persevere and finish the race set before us.

If you've been feeling weary, ask God to fill you with His grace and strength to keep going. Trust that He will bring a harvest from your faithful work in His perfect timing.

Call to Action: Reflect on any areas of your life where you've been growing weary. Spend time in prayer, asking God to give you the grace to finish well and to trust in His promise of a harvest.

Prayer: Father, thank You for the grace that sustains me. Help me to persevere in doing good, even when I feel weary. Give me the strength to finish well and to trust that You will bring a harvest in Your perfect time. Amen.

December

The Gift of Christ

December 1
The Promise of a Savior

Verse: *"Therefore the Lord Himself will give you a sign: The virgin will conceive and give birth to a son, and will call Him Immanuel."*

(Isaiah 7:14, NIV)

Message: Long before the birth of Christ, God gave His people the promise of a Savior. Isaiah 7:14 foretells the miraculous birth of Jesus, the one who would be called "Immanuel," meaning "God with us." This prophecy is a beautiful reminder that God's plan of salvation was set in motion long before we ever realized our need for it. The coming of Christ is the fulfillment of God's promise to rescue His people, showing His great love and faithfulness.

The birth of Jesus was the answer to centuries of waiting. For generations, the people of Israel clung to the hope of a promised Messiah who would deliver them. When Christ was born, He fulfilled that ancient promise in a way that exceeded all expectations. Not only did Jesus come to save the people from political oppression, but He also came to save humanity from sin and death. His arrival brought the ultimate gift—God Himself, living among us.

As we enter the Christmas season, take time to reflect on the significance of Christ's birth. Thank God for fulfilling His promise to send a Savior and for the gift of Jesus, who is "God with us."

Call to Action: Reflect on the significance of Jesus being called "Immanuel." Spend time in prayer, thanking God for His faithfulness in sending a Savior to be with us.

Prayer: Father, thank You for fulfilling Your promise to send a Savior. Thank You for the gift of Jesus, who is Immanuel, God with us. Help me to live with a heart of gratitude for the incredible gift of Christ and to remember that You are always with me. Amen.

December 2
The Light of the World

***Verse**: "When Jesus spoke again to the people, He said, 'I am the light of the world. Whoever follows Me will never walk in darkness, but will have the light of life.'"*

(John 8:12, NIV)

Message: Jesus came into a world filled with darkness to be the light that leads us to life. In John 8:12, Jesus declares that He is the light of the world and that those who follow Him will never walk in darkness. This is a powerful promise, reminding us that Jesus came not only to save us from sin but also to guide us in the way of truth and righteousness. His light illuminates the path before us, giving us hope and direction in a dark world.

Throughout the Bible, light is often used as a metaphor for God's presence and truth. When Jesus was born, a star shone brightly in the sky, leading the wise men to His birthplace. In the same way, Jesus' life and teachings guide us out of the darkness of sin and into the light of His grace. As we follow Him, we are transformed by His light, becoming bearers of His love and truth in the world around us.

If you're feeling lost or overwhelmed, remember that Jesus is the light that will guide you. Follow Him, and He will lead you into life and truth.

Call to Action: Reflect on areas of your life where you need Jesus' light to shine. Spend time in prayer, asking Him to guide you and illuminate the path before you.

Prayer: Lord, thank You for being the light of the world. Help me to follow You and walk in the light of Your truth. Shine Your light into the areas of my life where I need direction and hope, and guide me toward the life You have for me. Amen.

December 3
The Gift of Salvation

Verse: *"For the wages of sin is death, but the gift of God is eternal life in Christ Jesus our Lord."*

(Romans 6:23, NIV)

Message: The birth of Christ represents the greatest gift ever given—the gift of salvation. Romans 6:23 tells us that while the wages of sin is death, the gift of God is eternal life through Jesus Christ. This incredible gift is freely offered to all who believe in Jesus, providing us with forgiveness, redemption, and the promise of eternal life. Salvation is not something we can earn or achieve on our own; it is a gift of grace given by God through His Son.

Jesus' birth, life, death, and resurrection were all part of God's plan to offer salvation to the world. Through His sacrifice, Jesus paid the penalty for our sins and made a way for us to be reconciled to God. The gift of salvation is an invitation to enter into a relationship with God, one that is marked by grace, love, and eternal life. As we reflect on the gift of Christ this season, let us remember the significance of His coming and the hope He brings to our lives.

If you've received the gift of salvation, take time to thank God for it. If you haven't yet accepted this gift, open your heart to the incredible love and grace that Jesus offers.

Call to Action: Reflect on the gift of salvation and what it means to you. Spend time in prayer, thanking God for the gift of eternal life through Christ and asking Him to help you live in light of that gift.

Prayer: Father, thank You for the incredible gift of salvation. Thank You for sending Jesus to save me from my sins and to offer me eternal life. Help me to live each day in gratitude for this gift and to share the hope of salvation with others. Amen.

December 4
God's Love Made Visible

Verse*: "This is how God showed His love among us: He sent His one and only Son into the world that we might live through Him."*

(1 John 4:9, NIV)

Message: The birth of Jesus is the ultimate expression of God's love for humanity. 1 John 4:9 tells us that God showed His love by sending His one and only Son into the world so that we might live through Him. Jesus is the embodiment of God's love, and through His life, death, and resurrection, we are given the opportunity to experience that love in a personal and transformative way. The gift of Christ is God's love made visible, a love that is selfless, sacrificial, and eternal.

God's love is not distant or abstract—it is real, tangible, and accessible to us through Jesus. When we look at the life of Christ, we see the depth of God's love in action. Jesus healed the sick, comforted the brokenhearted, and ultimately gave His life so that we might live. This love is available to us today, offering us forgiveness, healing, and the promise of eternal life. As we celebrate the birth of Christ, let us remember that His coming is the greatest demonstration of God's love for us.

If you've been struggling to feel loved, remember that God's love is always available to you through Jesus. Embrace the gift of His love and let it transform your heart and life.

Call to Action: Reflect on the ways God has shown His love to you through Christ. Spend time in prayer, thanking Him for His love and asking Him to help you live in the light of that love each day.

Prayer: Lord, thank You for showing Your love by sending Jesus into the world. Help me to embrace the gift of Your love and to live each day in the knowledge that I am deeply loved by You. Let Your love guide my actions and my relationships with others. Amen.

December 5
The Humble King

Verse: "But you, Bethlehem Ephrathah, though you are small among the clans of Judah, out of you will come for Me one who will be ruler over Israel, whose origins are from of old, from ancient times."

(Micah 5:2, NIV)

Message: The birth of Jesus in Bethlehem fulfills the prophecy in Micah 5:2, highlighting the humble circumstances of His arrival. Though Bethlehem was small and seemingly insignificant, it was chosen as the birthplace of the King of Kings. Jesus, the long-awaited Messiah, did not come in the way people expected. Instead of arriving with power and glory, He came humbly, born in a stable, and laid in a manger. His humble beginnings reflect the heart of God's kingdom—a kingdom where humility, love, and service reign.

Throughout His life, Jesus continued to demonstrate humility. He washed His disciples' feet, associated with the outcasts of society, and ultimately laid down His life for the salvation of the world. His humility is an example for us to follow. As we celebrate the gift of Christ, we are reminded that true greatness is found not in power or prestige but in serving others with love and humility, just as Jesus did.

If you've been striving for recognition or success, take time to reflect on the humility of Christ. Ask God to help you follow Jesus' example and live a life marked by humility and service.

Call to Action: Reflect on areas of your life where you can practice humility. Spend time in prayer, asking God to help you follow the example of Christ and live with a heart of humility and service.

Prayer: Father, thank You for sending Jesus, the humble King. Help me to follow His example of humility and to serve others with love. Teach me to live a life that reflects the values of Your kingdom, where humility and service are honored. Amen.

December 6
The Prince of Peace

Verse: "For to us a child is born, to us a son is given, and the government will be on His shoulders. And He will be called Wonderful Counselor, Mighty God, Everlasting Father, Prince of Peace."

(Isaiah 9:6, NIV)

Message: One of the most comforting titles given to Jesus in Isaiah 9:6 is "Prince of Peace." As the Prince of Peace, Jesus came to bring reconciliation between God and humanity. His birth heralded a new era of peace—peace with God, peace within ourselves, and peace with others. This peace is not simply the absence of conflict but the deep, abiding presence of God's love and grace in our lives, which brings wholeness and healing.

Throughout His ministry, Jesus showed us how to live in peace. Whether He was calming storms, healing broken hearts, or forgiving sins, His actions were always marked by peace. When we receive the gift of Christ, we are invited into a relationship with the Prince of Peace. His peace guards our hearts and minds and gives us the strength to face life's challenges without fear. As we follow Him, we are called to be peacemakers, sharing His peace with those around us.

If you're feeling anxious or unsettled, remember that Jesus is the Prince of Peace. Turn to Him, and let His peace fill your heart and guide you in every situation.

Call to Action: Reflect on areas of your life where you need Christ's peace. Spend time in prayer, asking Him to fill you with His peace and to help you live as a peacemaker.

Prayer: Lord, thank You for being the Prince of Peace. Fill my heart with Your peace and help me to live in a way that reflects Your love and grace. Guide me to be a peacemaker in my relationships and to trust in Your peace in every situation. Amen.

December 7
The Word Became Flesh

Verse: "The Word became flesh and made His dwelling among us. We have seen His glory, the glory of the one and only Son, who came from the Father, full of grace and truth."

(John 1:14, NIV)

Message: The incarnation of Jesus is one of the most profound mysteries of the Christian faith—God Himself became flesh and lived among us. John 1:14 reminds us that the eternal Word, through whom all things were created, entered into His own creation as a human being. Jesus' coming was an expression of God's love and desire to dwell with His people. Through Him, we have seen the glory of God, full of grace and truth.

Jesus didn't come into the world as a distant, unreachable deity. Instead, He came as one of us, experiencing the joys and sorrows of human life. His presence among us shows that God is not far off but deeply involved in our lives. In Christ, we see the fullness of God's grace and truth—grace that brings forgiveness and truth that leads to freedom. The gift of Christ is the gift of God's presence with us, walking alongside us through every season of life.

If you've been feeling distant from God, remember that Jesus came to be with us. Embrace the gift of His presence and let Him walk with you through whatever you're facing.

Call to Action: Reflect on the significance of God becoming flesh in Jesus. Spend time in prayer, thanking Him for His willingness to come and dwell among us and asking Him to reveal more of His grace and truth in your life.

Prayer: Father, thank You for sending Jesus, the Word made flesh. Help me to understand the depth of Your love and grace in sending Him to dwell among us. Let me experience Your presence in a real and tangible way, and guide me in Your truth. Amen.

DECEMBER 8
THE LAMB OF GOD

Verse: "*The next day John saw Jesus coming toward him and said, 'Look, the Lamb of God, who takes away the sin of the world!'*"

(John 1:29, NIV)

Message: Jesus is the Lamb of God who came to take away the sin of the world. John the Baptist's declaration in John 1:29 points to Jesus' ultimate purpose—He came to offer Himself as the perfect sacrifice for our sins. In the Old Testament, lambs were sacrificed as a temporary atonement for sin, but Jesus' sacrifice on the cross was once and for all. His death and resurrection provided the way for us to be reconciled with God and freed from the power of sin.

The imagery of Jesus as the Lamb of God reminds us of the great cost of our salvation. Jesus, the sinless Son of God, willingly laid down His life for us. His sacrifice was motivated by love—a love so deep that He was willing to take our place and bear the punishment we deserved. Because of His sacrifice, we are no longer slaves to sin but have been given the gift of forgiveness, freedom, and eternal life.

If you've been carrying the weight of sin or guilt, remember that Jesus, the Lamb of God, has already taken it away. Trust in His sacrifice and receive the freedom He offers.

Call to Action: Reflect on the significance of Jesus being the Lamb of God. Spend time in prayer, thanking Him for His sacrifice and asking Him to help you live in the freedom and forgiveness He has provided.

Prayer: Lord Jesus, thank You for being the Lamb of God who takes away the sin of the world. Thank You for Your sacrifice on the cross and for the gift of forgiveness and freedom that You have given me. Help me to live in light of that freedom and to share the good news of Your love with others. Amen.

December 9
The Good Shepherd

Verse: *"I am the good shepherd. The good shepherd lays down His life for the sheep."*

(John 10:11, NIV)

Message: Jesus describes Himself as the Good Shepherd, one who cares deeply for His sheep and is willing to lay down His life for them. John 10:11 reveals the heart of Christ—His love for us is so great that He was willing to sacrifice everything to protect and save us. As our Good Shepherd, Jesus not only provides for our needs but also guides us, protects us, and leads us to eternal life.

Throughout Scripture, the image of a shepherd caring for his flock is used to illustrate God's relationship with His people. Just as a shepherd knows each sheep by name and guards them from danger, Jesus knows us intimately and watches over us with love and care. When we stray, He seeks us out and brings us back into the safety of His fold. The gift of Christ is the gift of a Shepherd who loves us unconditionally and gave His life so that we could live.

If you've been feeling lost or unsure of your direction, remember that Jesus, the Good Shepherd, is always with you, guiding and protecting you. Trust in His care and follow His lead.

Call to Action: Reflect on how Jesus, as the Good Shepherd, has guided and cared for you. Spend time in prayer, thanking Him for His love and protection and asking Him to help you follow His voice.

Prayer: Lord Jesus, thank You for being the Good Shepherd who lays down His life for the sheep. Thank You for guiding me, protecting me, and caring for me with Your love. Help me to trust in Your care and to follow wherever You lead me. Amen.

December 10
The Hope of Glory

Verse: "*To them God has chosen to make known among the Gentiles the glorious riches of this mystery, which is Christ in you, the hope of glory.*"

(Colossians 1:27, NIV)

Message: One of the greatest gifts we receive in Christ is the hope of glory. Colossians 1:27 speaks of the mystery revealed to us—that Christ lives in us, and He is the hope of glory. This hope is not just for the future but also for the present. Christ's presence in our lives gives us the strength and confidence to face whatever comes our way, knowing that we are never alone and that our future is secure in Him.

The hope of glory is the promise of eternal life with God, but it also transforms the way we live today. With Christ dwelling in us, we have access to His power, His wisdom, and His peace. This hope gives us the courage to endure trials, the strength to persevere, and the assurance that God is working all things for our good. The gift of Christ is the gift of hope—a hope that sustains us in this life and carries us into the life to come.

If you've been feeling hopeless or discouraged, remember that Christ in you is the hope of glory. Let His presence fill you with hope and strength for today and the future.

Call to Action: Reflect on the hope you have in Christ. Spend time in prayer, thanking Him for the hope of glory and asking Him to fill you with His strength and peace.

Prayer: Father, thank You for the hope of glory that I have in Christ. Thank You for the promise of eternal life and for the presence of Christ in my life today. Fill me with hope, strength, and peace as I trust in Your plan and Your purpose for my life. Amen.

December 11
The Bread of Life

Verse: *"Then Jesus declared, 'I am the bread of life. Whoever comes to Me will never go hungry, and whoever believes in Me will never be thirsty.'"*

(John 6:35, NIV)

Message: Jesus calls Himself the Bread of Life, meaning that He is the one who sustains and nourishes our souls. Just as bread satisfies our physical hunger, Jesus satisfies our deepest spiritual longings. He offers us eternal sustenance, the kind that can never be taken away or fade. When we come to Jesus, we find everything we need for life, both now and forever.

In the same way that God provided manna for the Israelites in the wilderness, Jesus offers us spiritual nourishment that never runs out. His words, His love, and His presence fill us in ways that nothing else can. When we seek satisfaction in the things of the world, we are left empty, but when we turn to Jesus, we find true fulfillment. The gift of Christ is the gift of spiritual sustenance, a source of life that never runs dry.

If you've been feeling empty or unfulfilled, come to Jesus, the Bread of Life. He will nourish your soul and fill you with His peace and love.

Call to Action: Reflect on areas of your life where you've been seeking satisfaction apart from Christ. Spend time in prayer, asking Jesus to fill you with His presence and nourish your soul.

Prayer: Lord, thank You for being the Bread of Life. Help me to come to You for the sustenance my soul needs. Fill me with Your love and peace, and teach me to rely on You for all my needs. Amen.

December 12
The Alpha and the Omega

Verse: *"I am the Alpha and the Omega, the First and the Last, the Beginning and the End."*

(Revelation 22:13, NIV)

Message: Jesus describes Himself as the Alpha and the Omega, the First and the Last, the Beginning and the End. This title reveals that Christ is eternal and sovereign over all things. He was present at creation, and He will be there at the end of time, ruling with authority over everything. The gift of Christ is the gift of a Savior who is eternal, unchanging, and all-powerful.

From the beginning of time, Jesus has been part of God's plan for salvation. His birth, life, death, and resurrection were not isolated events but part of the larger story of God's redemption of the world. Because Jesus is the Alpha and the Omega, we can trust that He holds all of history—and our lives—in His hands. No matter what we face, we can have confidence in His power and His plan for our future.

If you've been feeling uncertain about the future, remember that Jesus is the Alpha and the Omega. Trust in His eternal power and love to guide you through every season of life.

Call to Action: Reflect on the eternal nature of Christ and how that gives you hope for the future. Spend time in prayer, thanking Jesus for being the Alpha and the Omega, and asking Him to help you trust in His plan for your life.

Prayer: Father, thank You for sending Jesus, the Alpha and the Omega. Help me to trust in Your eternal plan and to remember that You are in control of all things. Give me peace as I rely on Your wisdom and power. Amen.

December 13
The Gift of Grace

Verse: *"For the grace of God has appeared that offers salvation to all people."*

(Titus 2:11, NIV)

Message: The birth of Christ is the ultimate demonstration of God's grace. Titus 2:11 tells us that the grace of God has appeared, offering salvation to all people. Grace is unearned, unmerited favor, and it is the foundation of our relationship with God. Through Christ, we receive the gift of salvation, forgiveness, and eternal life—gifts we could never earn on our own.

Jesus' entire life was a display of God's grace. He extended grace to sinners, the brokenhearted, and the outcasts, showing them that they were loved and accepted by God. His grace is still available to us today, inviting us to enter into a relationship with Him, not based on our own efforts, but on His love. The gift of Christ is the gift of grace, freely given to all who believe.

If you've been struggling to earn God's favor, remember that His grace is a gift. Rest in the knowledge that you are loved and accepted because of Jesus.

Call to Action: Reflect on how God's grace has been evident in your life. Spend time in prayer, thanking Him for the gift of grace and asking Him to help you live in the freedom of that grace each day.

Prayer: Lord, thank You for the incredible gift of Your grace. Help me to rest in Your love and to stop striving to earn Your favor. Let Your grace transform my heart and guide me to live in the freedom You have given me. Amen.

December 14
The Resurrection and the Life

Verse: "Jesus said to her, 'I am the resurrection and the life. The one who believes in Me will live, even though they die.'"

(John 11:25, NIV)

Message: In John 11:25, Jesus declares Himself as the resurrection and the life, offering us the hope of eternal life through Him. His resurrection from the dead is the foundation of our faith and the ultimate proof of His power over sin and death. Because of Jesus, we have the promise of life after death—a life spent in the presence of God for all eternity. The gift of Christ is the gift of resurrection and eternal life.

When Jesus raised Lazarus from the dead, He demonstrated His power to bring life where there was death. This miracle foreshadowed His own resurrection, which would secure eternal life for all who believe in Him. The gift of Christ means that death no longer has the final word. Through Him, we are given the hope of new life, both now and forever.

If you're struggling with fear of death or uncertainty about the future, remember that Jesus is the resurrection and the life. Trust in His promise of eternal life, and find peace in the hope He offers.

Call to Action: Reflect on the hope of resurrection and eternal life that Jesus offers. Spend time in prayer, thanking Him for the gift of life and asking Him to help you live with hope and confidence in His promise.

Prayer: Father, thank You for the gift of eternal life through Jesus. Help me to trust in Your promise and to live each day with hope, knowing that death has been defeated and that I will live with You forever. Amen.

December 15
The King of Kings

Verse: *"On His robe and on His thigh He has this name written: King of kings and Lord of lords."*

(Revelation 19:16, NIV)

Message: Jesus is not only the Savior of the world but also the King of Kings and Lord of Lords. Revelation 19:16 describes Jesus' return in glory, when He will establish His eternal kingdom and rule over all creation. As King of Kings, Jesus reigns with authority, power, and justice. The gift of Christ is the gift of a King who is sovereign over all things, yet who came in humility to serve and save.

Throughout His earthly ministry, Jesus spoke of the kingdom of God, inviting people to enter into a relationship with Him and to experience the blessings of His reign. His kingship is marked by love, righteousness, and peace, and one day He will return to fully establish His kingdom on earth. In the meantime, we are called to live as citizens of His kingdom, submitting to His rule and sharing His love with the world.

If you've been feeling powerless or overwhelmed, remember that Jesus is the King of Kings. Trust in His authority and reign, and find peace in knowing that He is in control of all things.

Call to Action: Reflect on the kingship of Christ and how that impacts your life. Spend time in prayer, thanking Jesus for being the King of Kings and asking Him to help you live in submission to His rule.

Prayer: Lord Jesus, thank You for being the King of Kings and Lord of Lords. Help me to submit to Your authority and to live as a faithful citizen of Your kingdom. Let Your rule bring peace, justice, and love to my life and to the world. Amen.

December 16
The Way, the Truth, and the Life

Verse: *"Jesus answered, 'I am the way and the truth and the life. No one comes to the Father except through Me.'"*

(John 14:6, NIV)

Message: Jesus makes a bold and exclusive claim in John 14:6: He is the way, the truth, and the life, and no one comes to the Father except through Him. This declaration emphasizes that Jesus is the only path to salvation and eternal life. Through His life, death, and resurrection, Jesus opened the way for us to be reconciled with God. The gift of Christ is the gift of access to the Father, truth for our lives, and eternal life in His presence.

When we follow Jesus, we are walking in the way that leads to life. His teachings provide us with truth, and His presence fills us with life. Jesus is not just one option among many—He is the only way to experience the fullness of God's love and grace. The gift of Christ is the gift of a relationship with the Father, made possible through Him.

If you've been searching for direction or meaning, remember that Jesus is the way, the truth, and the life. Follow Him, and He will lead you to the Father.

Call to Action: Reflect on the significance of Jesus being the way, the truth, and the life. Spend time in prayer, thanking Him for opening the way to the Father and asking Him to guide you in His truth each day.

Prayer: Lord Jesus, thank You for being the way, the truth, and the life. Help me to follow You faithfully and to trust in Your truth. Lead me to the Father, and let my life reflect the love and grace that You have shown me. Amen.

December 17
The Light Has Come

Verse: *"The true light that gives light to everyone was coming into the world."*

(John 1:9, NIV)

Message: The coming of Christ is described as the arrival of the true light. John 1:9 tells us that Jesus is the light that gives light to everyone. His birth marked the beginning of a new era—an era in which the darkness of sin and death would be overcome by the light of God's love and grace. The gift of Christ is the gift of light, a light that shines in the darkness and leads us to life.

In a world that often feels dark and uncertain, Jesus is the light that guides us. His teachings show us how to live, and His presence fills us with hope and peace. When we walk in the light of Christ, we experience the joy and freedom that come from knowing Him. The gift of Christ is the gift of a light that never fades and a hope that never fails.

If you've been feeling lost in the darkness, turn to Jesus, the true light. Let His light guide you and fill you with hope.

Call to Action: Reflect on areas of your life where you need the light of Christ to shine. Spend time in prayer, asking Jesus to fill you with His light and to lead you out of darkness and into His love.

Prayer: Father, thank You for sending Jesus, the true light that gives light to everyone. Help me to walk in His light and to trust in His guidance. Fill my heart with hope and peace as I follow the light of Christ. Amen.

December 18
The Son of God

Verse: *"And a voice from heaven said, 'This is My Son, whom I love; with Him I am well pleased.'"*

(Matthew 3:17, NIV)

Message: At Jesus' baptism, God the Father declared from heaven, "This is My Son, whom I love; with Him I am well pleased." This powerful statement confirms Jesus' identity as the Son of God. As the Son of God, Jesus has a unique and intimate relationship with the Father, and through Him, we are invited to become children of God as well. The gift of Christ is the gift of sonship, of being adopted into God's family and experiencing His love and approval.

Throughout His ministry, Jesus revealed the Father's heart to us. He showed us what it means to live in relationship with God and to trust in His love. As God's beloved Son, Jesus perfectly fulfilled His Father's will, and through His obedience, He made a way for us to be reconciled with God. The gift of Christ is the gift of knowing God as our Father and experiencing His love in a personal and transformative way.

If you've been struggling to feel loved or accepted, remember that through Christ, you are a beloved child of God. Embrace the gift of sonship and let God's love fill your heart.

Call to Action: Reflect on what it means to be a child of God. Spend time in prayer, thanking God for sending His Son and asking Him to help you live in the confidence of His love.

Prayer: Father, thank You for sending Jesus, Your beloved Son. Help me to embrace my identity as Your child and to live in the assurance of Your love and approval. Let my life reflect the love and grace that You have given me through Christ. Amen.

December 19
The Joy of the Lord

Verse: *"But the angel said to them, 'Do not be afraid. I bring you good news that will cause great joy for all the people.'"*

(Luke 2:10, NIV)

Message: The birth of Christ is described as good news that will cause great joy for all people. The angel's announcement to the shepherds in Luke 2:10 reminds us that the coming of Jesus is a reason for joy. His birth brings the hope of salvation, the promise of peace, and the assurance of God's love. The gift of Christ is the gift of joy—a joy that transcends circumstances and fills our hearts with gladness.

Joy is a central theme of the Christmas story. The shepherds rejoiced at the news of Jesus' birth, the wise men traveled far to worship Him, and Mary treasured the miracle of His arrival in her heart. This joy is not based on external circumstances but on the incredible reality that God has come to be with us. The gift of Christ brings joy because it reminds us that we are loved, we are saved, and we have hope in Him.

If you've been feeling weighed down by worries or sadness, turn to Jesus and remember the joy of His coming. Let His presence fill your heart with gladness and peace.

Call to Action: Reflect on the joy that Christ's coming brings to your life. Spend time in prayer, thanking God for the gift of Jesus and asking Him to fill your heart with His joy.

Prayer: Lord, thank You for the joy that comes from knowing You. Help me to embrace the joy of Your presence in my life and to share that joy with others. Let my heart be filled with gladness as I reflect on the good news of Your coming. Amen.

December 20
The Gift of Eternal Life

Verse: *"For God so loved the world that He gave His one and only Son, that whoever believes in Him shall not perish but have eternal life."*

(John 3:16, NIV)

Message: John 3:16 is one of the most well-known and cherished verses in the Bible, and it reminds us of the incredible gift of eternal life that comes through Christ. God's love for the world was so great that He gave His only Son to save us from sin and death. The gift of Christ is the gift of eternal life, a life that begins now and continues forever in the presence of God.

Eternal life is more than just a promise for the future—it's a present reality for those who believe in Jesus. Through Him, we experience the fullness of life, a life filled with purpose, hope, and the presence of God. The gift of eternal life is a gift of grace, freely given to all who believe. It's the assurance that no matter what happens in this life, we have the hope of eternity with God.

If you've been feeling unsure about the future, remember the promise of eternal life in Christ. Trust in His love and grace, and rest in the assurance that you are secure in Him.

Call to Action: Reflect on the gift of eternal life and what it means to you. Spend time in prayer, thanking God for the gift of His Son and the promise of eternal life, and ask Him to help you live in the light of that promise each day.

Prayer: Father, thank You for the gift of eternal life through Your Son, Jesus Christ. Help me to live each day with the hope and assurance of eternity with You. Let my heart be filled with gratitude for this incredible gift, and guide me to share the hope of eternal life with others. Amen.

December 21
The Righteous Judge

Verse: *"For He has set a day when He will judge the world with justice by the man He has appointed. He has given proof of this to everyone by raising Him from the dead."*

(Acts 17:31, NIV)

Message: Jesus is not only our Savior but also the righteous judge. Acts 17:31 tells us that God has set a day when Jesus will judge the world with justice. The fact that Jesus is our judge is good news because we know that He is both just and merciful. His judgment will be fair, and His love for humanity is evident in His willingness to die for our sins. The gift of Christ is the gift of a righteous judge who will one day set everything right.

Jesus' role as judge means that we can trust in His justice. In a world that is often unfair and broken, we have the hope that one day all wrongs will be made right. The gift of Christ is not only the gift of salvation but also the promise of a future where justice, righteousness, and peace will reign. We can live with confidence, knowing that our judge is also our Savior, full of grace and truth.

If you've been struggling with injustice or wrongs in the world, take comfort in the fact that Jesus is the righteous judge. Trust in His justice and His plan to make all things new.

Call to Action: Reflect on the justice of Christ and what it means for your life. Spend time in prayer, thanking Jesus for being the righteous judge and asking Him to help you live with hope in His justice and grace.

Prayer: Lord, thank You for being the righteous judge. Help me to trust in Your justice and to live with the hope that one day all wrongs will be made right. Let Your grace and truth guide my heart as I await the fulfillment of Your perfect plan. Amen.

December 22
The Gift of Hope

Verse: "May the God of hope fill you with all joy and peace as you trust in Him, so that you may overflow with hope by the power of the Holy Spirit."

(Romans 15:13, NIV)

Message: Jesus brings hope into our lives—hope that transcends our circumstances and gives us confidence in God's promises. Romans 15:13 speaks of God as the God of hope, who fills us with joy and peace as we trust in Him. Through Christ, we have a hope that is steadfast and sure, rooted in the faithfulness of God. The gift of Christ is the gift of hope, a hope that fills us with joy and peace even in the midst of life's challenges.

The hope that Jesus offers is not wishful thinking but a confident expectation in God's promises. His birth, life, death, and resurrection all point to the reality that God is faithful and will fulfill everything He has promised. This hope sustains us in difficult times, reminding us that our future is secure in Christ. The gift of hope is one of the greatest blessings we receive through Jesus, and it gives us the strength to persevere and trust in God's plan.

If you've been feeling hopeless, turn to the God of hope. Let Him fill you with joy and peace as you trust in Him and rely on His promises.

Call to Action: Reflect on the hope you have in Christ and how it has sustained you. Spend time in prayer, thanking God for the gift of hope and asking Him to fill you with joy and peace as you trust in Him.

Prayer: Father, thank You for being the God of hope. Fill me with joy and peace as I trust in You, and let my heart overflow with hope through the power of the Holy Spirit. Help me to live each day with confidence in Your promises. Amen.

December 23
The Good News of Great Joy

Verse: *"But the angel said to them, 'Do not be afraid. I bring you good news that will cause great joy for all the people.'"*

(Luke 2:10, NIV)

Message: The birth of Jesus is the ultimate good news. In Luke 2:10, the angel announced to the shepherds that Jesus' birth was good news of great joy for all people. This news is still just as powerful today. Jesus came to bring salvation, peace, and hope to the world, and His birth is the beginning of God's plan to redeem humanity. The gift of Christ is the gift of good news—a message of hope, joy, and salvation for all.

The shepherds' response to the angel's announcement was one of awe and joy. They immediately went to find Jesus and share the good news with others. In the same way, we are called to receive the good news of Christ with joy and to share it with those around us. The gift of Christ is not only a personal gift but also one that is meant to be shared, bringing hope and joy to the world.

If you've been feeling weighed down by the cares of life, remember the good news of Jesus' birth. Let His coming fill you with great joy, and share that joy with others.

Call to Action: Reflect on how the good news of Jesus has impacted your life. Spend time in prayer, thanking God for the gift of salvation and asking Him to help you share the good news with others.

Prayer: Lord, thank You for the good news of great joy that Jesus brings. Help me to receive that joy and to share it with others. Let my life be a reflection of the hope and salvation that You have given me through Christ. Amen.

December 24
The Savior is Born

Verse: *"Today in the town of David a Savior has been born to you; He is the Messiah, the Lord."*

(Luke 2:11, NIV)

Message: On that first Christmas night, the world received the greatest gift it would ever know—Jesus, the Savior, was born. Luke 2:11 announces the birth of the Messiah, the one who would save humanity from sin and death. Jesus' birth is the fulfillment of God's promise to send a Savior, and His arrival is the reason we celebrate Christmas. The gift of Christ is the gift of salvation, hope, and life for all who believe.

The shepherds, who were the first to hear the news of Jesus' birth, responded with wonder and joy. They went to see the newborn King and then spread the word about what they had seen. This is the natural response to the gift of Christ—when we encounter Jesus, we are filled with awe and compelled to share the good news with others. The Savior's birth is the greatest story ever told, and it continues to bring hope and joy to the world.

As you celebrate Christmas, take time to reflect on the true meaning of the season—the birth of our Savior. Let the joy of His coming fill your heart and inspire you to share His love with others.

Call to Action: Reflect on the significance of Jesus' birth in your life. Spend time in prayer, thanking God for sending the Savior and asking Him to help you live in the joy and hope of Christ's coming.

Prayer: Father, thank You for the gift of Jesus, our Savior. Help me to remember the true meaning of Christmas and to celebrate the birth of Christ with joy and gratitude. Let His coming fill my heart with hope, and guide me to share His love with those around me. Amen.

December 25
Emmanuel – God With Us

Verse: "The virgin will conceive and give birth to a son, and they will call Him Immanuel" (which means 'God with us').

(Matthew 1:23, NIV)

Message: On Christmas Day, we celebrate the birth of Jesus, who is called "Immanuel," meaning "God with us." This name is a powerful reminder of the true meaning of Christmas—that God Himself came to dwell among us through His Son, Jesus Christ. The gift of Christ is the gift of God's presence, showing us that we are never alone. Jesus came to bring us into relationship with God, offering us His love, grace, and companionship.

From the moment Jesus was born, He was "God with us," walking alongside humanity, sharing in our joys and sorrows, and ultimately giving His life for our salvation. His presence changes everything, giving us hope, peace, and assurance that we are deeply loved by God. As we celebrate the birth of Christ, we remember that through Him, God is always with us—guiding, comforting, and strengthening us in every season of life.

If you've been feeling distant from God, remember that through Christ, He is always with you. Embrace the gift of His presence and let it bring you peace and joy this Christmas.

Call to Action: Reflect on the significance of Jesus being called "Immanuel" in your life. Spend time in prayer, thanking God for His presence with you and asking Him to help you live in the assurance of His love and guidance.

Prayer: Lord, thank You for sending Jesus, Immanuel, to be with us. Help me to live each day in the knowledge that You are always with me, guiding and comforting me. Let the joy of Your presence fill my heart this Christmas and throughout the year. Amen.

December 26
The Word of Life

Verse: *"The Word became flesh and made His dwelling among us. We have seen His glory, the glory of the one and only Son, who came from the Father, full of grace and truth."*

(John 1:14, NIV)

Message: The incarnation of Jesus—God becoming flesh—is one of the greatest mysteries and gifts of the Christian faith. John 1:14 reminds us that the Word, who was with God from the beginning, took on human form and dwelled among us. Through Jesus, we see the glory of God, full of grace and truth. The gift of Christ is the gift of life itself, for in Him we find the fullness of God's love, grace, and truth.

Jesus didn't come to live apart from humanity; He came to walk with us, experience life as we do, and ultimately give His life for our salvation. His presence among us reveals the heart of God, and through Him, we are invited into a relationship with the Father. The Word of Life came to bring us life, both now and for eternity. The gift of Christ is the gift of divine presence, guiding us into all truth and filling us with grace.

If you've been searching for truth or meaning, remember that Jesus is the Word of Life. Turn to Him, and let His grace and truth guide you.

Call to Action: Reflect on the significance of the Word becoming flesh in your life. Spend time in prayer, thanking Jesus for coming to dwell among us and asking Him to help you live in the truth of His Word.

Prayer: Father, thank You for sending Jesus, the Word of Life, to dwell among us. Help me to understand the depth of Your love and grace in sending Him, and guide me to live in the truth of Your Word each day. Amen.

December 27
The True Vine

Verse: *"I am the vine; you are the branches. If you remain in Me and I in you, you will bear much fruit; apart from Me you can do nothing."*

(John 15:5, NIV)

Message: Jesus describes Himself as the True Vine, and we are the branches that draw life and strength from Him. In John 15:5, Jesus explains that if we remain in Him, we will bear much fruit, but apart from Him, we can do nothing. The gift of Christ is the gift of connection to the source of all life and fruitfulness. When we abide in Him, our lives are transformed, and we are empowered to live out His purposes.

Just as a branch depends on the vine for nourishment, we depend on Jesus for spiritual life and growth. When we remain connected to Him through prayer, His Word, and obedience, we experience the fruit of the Spirit—love, joy, peace, patience, kindness, goodness, faithfulness, gentleness, and self-control. The gift of Christ is the gift of abundant life, and through Him, we bear fruit that reflects His character and love.

If you've been feeling spiritually dry or disconnected, turn to Jesus, the True Vine. Abide in Him, and He will give you the strength and nourishment you need to bear fruit.

Call to Action: Reflect on your connection to Christ, the True Vine. Spend time in prayer, asking Him to help you remain in Him and to produce fruit that reflects His love and grace.

Prayer: Lord Jesus, thank You for being the True Vine. Help me to remain in You and to draw strength and life from Your presence. Let my life bear fruit that reflects Your character and brings glory to God. Amen.

December 28
The Door to Eternal Life

Verse: *"I am the gate; whoever enters through Me will be saved. They will come in and go out, and find pasture."*

(John 10:9, NIV)

Message: Jesus refers to Himself as the gate or door, the way through which we enter into eternal life. In John 10:9, Jesus promises that those who enter through Him will be saved and will find pasture. The image of the gate speaks to the protection, security, and provision that Jesus offers. He is the only way to salvation, and through Him, we find the safety and sustenance our souls long for.

Just as a shepherd watches over the gate to protect his sheep, Jesus watches over us, ensuring that we are safe and provided for. When we enter through Him, we experience the fullness of life that God desires for us. The gift of Christ is the gift of eternal life, a life that begins now and continues forever in His presence. Through Jesus, we find the peace and rest that our souls crave.

If you've been searching for peace or security, remember that Jesus is the gate to eternal life. Enter through Him, and He will provide for your every need.

Call to Action: Reflect on what it means to enter through Christ, the gate to eternal life. Spend time in prayer, thanking Him for being the way to salvation and asking Him to help you trust in His protection and provision.

Prayer: Lord, thank You for being the gate through which I enter into eternal life. Help me to trust in Your protection and provision, and guide me into the fullness of life that You have promised. Amen.

December 29
The Shepherd of Our Souls

Verse: *"For you were like sheep going astray, but now you have returned to the Shepherd and Overseer of your souls."*

(1 Peter 2:25, NIV)

Message: Jesus is not only the Good Shepherd but also the Shepherd and Overseer of our souls. 1 Peter 2:25 reminds us that, like sheep, we have all gone astray, but through Christ, we have returned to the care and guidance of the One who watches over our souls. The gift of Christ is the gift of a Shepherd who knows us intimately and cares for us deeply.

As the Shepherd of our souls, Jesus guides us, protects us, and provides for us. He knows our needs and leads us to places of peace and rest. When we stray, He gently brings us back into His care, offering forgiveness and grace. The gift of Christ is the gift of a relationship with the One who watches over us with love and compassion, ensuring that we are safe and cared for.

If you've been feeling lost or disconnected, return to Jesus, the Shepherd of your soul. Trust in His care, and let Him lead you to places of peace and restoration.

Call to Action: Reflect on how Jesus, as the Shepherd of your soul, has guided and cared for you. Spend time in prayer, thanking Him for His love and asking Him to continue leading you in His grace and truth.

Prayer: Father, thank You for sending Jesus, the Shepherd of my soul. Help me to trust in His care and to follow wherever He leads. Let my heart rest in the knowledge that I am loved and cared for by the Good Shepherd. Amen.

December 30
The Beginning of New Life

Verse: *"Therefore, if anyone is in Christ, the new creation has come: The old has gone, the new is here!"*

(2 Corinthians 5:17, NIV)

Message: One of the most beautiful gifts we receive through Christ is the gift of new life. 2 Corinthians 5:17 tells us that if anyone is in Christ, they are a new creation. The old life of sin and brokenness is gone, and the new life of grace, forgiveness, and transformation has begun. The gift of Christ is the gift of a fresh start, a new beginning filled with hope and promise.

Through Jesus, we are not just improved versions of our old selves—we are made entirely new. His grace transforms us from the inside out, renewing our hearts and minds and giving us the power to live in a way that honors God. The gift of Christ is the gift of redemption, a new beginning that is available to all who believe in Him. As we prepare to enter a new year, we can do so with the confidence that Christ has made us new, and His grace will carry us forward.

If you've been feeling stuck in the past, embrace the new life that Christ offers. Let go of the old and step into the new creation that God has made you to be.

Call to Action: Reflect on the new life you have in Christ. Spend time in prayer, thanking God for the gift of new beginnings and asking Him to help you live in the freedom and grace of your new identity in Him.

Prayer: Lord, thank You for making me a new creation in Christ. Help me to let go of the past and to embrace the new life You have given me. Let my heart be filled with gratitude for Your grace, and guide me to live in the freedom and hope of this new beginning. Amen.

December 31
The Gift that Transforms Us

Verse: *"Thanks be to God for His indescribable gift!"*

(2 Corinthians 9:15, NIV)

Message: As we reach the final day of the year, it is a time to reflect on the many blessings we have received, but most importantly, we thank God for the greatest gift of all—the gift of Christ. 2 Corinthians 9:15 calls this gift "indescribable," for there are no words that can fully capture the depth of God's love and grace in sending Jesus to us. Through Him, we have experienced forgiveness, redemption, and the promise of eternal life.

The gift of Christ is not just a one-time event; it transforms us every day. As we journey through life, we are constantly being renewed by His love, His grace, and His presence. He gives us the strength to overcome challenges, the wisdom to make decisions, and the peace that sustains us through every circumstance. As we reflect on this past year, we see how Christ's presence has shaped our hearts, our relationships, and our lives. His gift is truly beyond description, and it continues to work in us, making us more like Him.

As you prepare to step into a new year, take time to meditate on the transformation Christ has brought to your life. Let His love continue to guide you as you move forward with hope, joy, and gratitude for the incredible gift of knowing Him.

Call to Action: Reflect on how Christ has transformed your life throughout the year. Spend time in prayer, thanking God for the gift of His Son and asking Him to continue shaping your heart and life in the year ahead.

Prayer: Father, thank You for the indescribable gift of Jesus. As I reflect on this past year, I see how Your love and grace have transformed me. Help me to walk into the new year with gratitude, hope, and a heart open to Your continued work in my life. Amen.

Final Word

I am so thankful for you! You did it—you finished the year with success. Take this moment right now to think about it: What has God done in your life this year? How has He changed you? Do you feel closer to Jesus today than you did a year ago? I really hope so! My prayer is that this is just the start of God's presence and power showing up in your life every day."

Your journey through *With Jesus Daily* has brought you closer to God, but it doesn't end here. Like the disciples who walked daily with Jesus and went on to change the world, you are now called to take what you've learned and bring it to others. The transformation you've experienced isn't just for you—it's meant to overflow and impact those around you.

Jesus' final words to His followers were a call to action: "Go and make disciples of all nations" (Matthew 28:19, NIV). This wasn't a suggestion; it was a command. You have the same invitation today. As you continue walking *With Jesus Daily*, you are empowered to take His love and truth into a world that desperately needs it. Whether through conversations with friends, service in your community, or sharing the Gospel across the globe, your life is a testimony of His grace and power.

Look at the people who walked with God and did incredible things. Moses led an entire nation to freedom because he trusted in God's presence. Peter, once unsure and afraid, became a bold preacher of the Gospel after spending time with Jesus. And the Apostle Paul, once a persecutor of Christians, transformed the world by planting churches and spreading the message of Christ.

Now it's your turn. As you continue to walk *With Jesus Daily*, know that He goes with you—leading, guiding, and empowering you to share His message. Just as He promised His disciples, He promises you: "And surely I am with you always, to the very end of the age" (Matthew 28:20, NIV).

Go boldly! You are never alone. With Jesus by your side, you have the power to reach people in ways beyond what you could imagine. Near or far, your life can carry the hope and love of Jesus to those who need it most. The world is waiting. So go, and let your life shine His light in the darkness of this world.

Go in God's grace,

Jordan Nassie

About the Author

Jordan Nassie, based in the USA, began his journey to faith with a powerful, life-changing dream. One night, he saw himself facing eternity without Jesus, heading toward a life apart from God in Hell. Waking from that dream, he decided to follow Jesus as his personal Savior. Since then, Jordan has devoted his life to sharing the hope of Christ with the world. As the Global Pastor and Founder of Daily Churches, he has planted 168 churches across 23 nations and helped lead over 1.3 million people into a personal relationship with Jesus. His mission is clear: to inspire others to know God and make Him known, one life at a time.

Made in the USA
Monee, IL
30 July 2025